CELTIC
FORTIFICATIONS

CELTIC
FORTIFICATIONS

IAN RALSTON

TEMPUS

First published 2006

Tempus Publishing Limited
The Mill, Brimscombe Port,
Stroud, Gloucestershire, GL5 2QG
www.tempus-publishing.com

British Library Cataloguing in Publication Data.
A catalogue record for this book is available from the British Library.

ISBN 0 7524 2500 5

Typesetting and origination by Tempus Publishing Limited
Printed in Great Britain

CONTENTS

PREFACE

The theme of this book was proposed by Peter Kemmis Betty. As Peter knows, it has been a considerable time in the writing, as a number of vicissitudes, too tedious to discuss without a glass of malt to hand, intervened: it had to be set aside more than once. I am very grateful to him for his repeated forbearance.

A book like this, however, results from a whole range of experiences and collaborations, some formal, some informal, some fleeting, some long-lasting. It is not possible to list all those who have assisted me in my dealings with hill-forts and their ramparts in Britain, France and elsewhere. I hope that these remarks help to identify all those who have come to my aid during what is now an interest extending over – say it softly – some 30 years.

The idea that I might interest myself in Continental hill-forts came from my late friend Graham Ritchie, who wisely suggested in 1971 that an undergraduate dissertation on roundhouses in the French Iron Age was a high-risk strategy. The hill-forts of Berry were substituted. My first excavation experience there was co-excavating the *murus gallicus* and massive bank at Levroux with Olivier Buchsenschutz. Having subsequently excavated with Jean-Paul Guillaumet at Mont Beuvray in Burgundy, 30 years on we are still digging around Iron Age hill-forts (now at Bourges), although mercifully no longer working single-mindedly on their ramparts. A survey of sites in Limousin for my PhD was made feasible by several colleagues, but especially Guy Lintz. Taking part in the early years of the Beuvray project not only let me dig at the great Porte du Rebout, but also allowed me to see hill-forts in other countries whose archaeologists were involved in that undertaking. I am grateful for opportunities to visit Hungary (Miklos Szabo), Spain (Martin Almagro-Gorbea), Belgium (Pierre-Paul Bonenfant), Germany (Franz Schubert and Suzanne Sievers) Italy (Daniele Vitali) and Switzerland (Auguste Kaenel and Daniel Paunier). Successive directors of what is now the Centre archéologique européen du Mont Beuvray – Jean-Paul Guillaumet, Jean-Loup Flouest, Vincent Guichard – have also been very supportive. Amongst British and American colleagues, Carole Crumley, Colin Haselgrove and especially John Collis have been great sources of advice and information over many years.

In Scotland I have worked at sites principally in the north-east of the country. The opportunity to burn a timber-laced wall on Aberdeen City's landfill was provided by Simon Welfare, then directing *Arthur C. Clarke's Mysterious World* for Yorkshire Television. I hope to have grasped some of the science of vitrfication that David Sanderson and Janick Vernioles have so patiently taught me.

Leslie Alcock, Derek Alexander, Ian Armit, Jonathan Dempsey, Colvin and Moira Greig, Strat Halliday and his colleagues in the Scottish Royal Commission, Dennis Harding, Ian Keillar, the late Kirsty Sabine and John Smith, Ian Shepherd, Geoff Waters, Willie Watt and Shelly Werner, and my colleagues in the Centre for Field Archaeology and now CFA Archaeology Ltd, have all helped in various ways. Excursions south of the border have often been in the pleasant company of Gary Lock and the band in the Hill-Fort Studies Group.

Andy Dunwell at CFA kindly read a draft of the whole text, excising repetitions, my larger lunacies, and some of my more idiosyncratic phrasing, but bears no responsibility for remaining errors, which are entirely my responsibility. Illustrators and sources of illustrations are credited in individual captions. Those not acknowledged are my own.

Production of this book was efficiently managed by Tom Sunley and Laura Perehinec at Tempus. I am grateful to them for expeditiously seeing what follows through the press. I was able to undertake final tasks while a Brown Fellow at the University of the South, Tennessee.

My shortcomings with information technology have been alleviated by Ian Morrison and my son Tom. He, who climbed Caherconree at a shockingly young age, his sister, and his long-suffering mother, who saw hill-forts, admittedly in Provencc, by way of a honeymoon, have had to endure the writing of this book. I hope they like it.

Ian Ralston, Kinross, December 2005

1
FINDING AND DEFINING HILL-FORTS

For much of the later prehistory – the later Bronze and Iron Ages – of temperate Europe, the enclosures around defended sites form the most conspicuous surviving element of the archaeological record in the landscapes of today. They are now amongst the most visitable monuments of the period, and some of the famous examples – Maiden Castle in Dorset, or Danebury in neighbouring Hampshire, Mont Beuvray in Burgundy, Ullastret in Catalonia, or the Heuneburg in south-western Germany – attract large numbers of visitors. Since the pioneering days of field archaeology, thousands of such sites have been discovered, from southern Iberia to northern Scotland, and east to Anatolia and the lands north of the Black Sea. In Britain and Ireland, many examples are readily appreciable in upland pasture (*1*) or on moorland, and closer to the Mediterranean they may stand proud of *garrigue* or similar vegetation. In other areas of the Continent, however, many of the surviving examples are cloaked in more-or-less dense woodland. Across Europe, hill-forts are – unsurprisingly – much better represented in 'zones of likely survival', where subsequent human activity has been less inimical to their survival than elsewhere, but examples do occur in arable land (*colour plate 1*). Sites of this type also occur within built-up areas, some settled continuously since the Iron Age.

Many, although by no means all, hill-forts, date to the last millennium BC. Generally, the bulk of what is knowable about them has to be derived from archaeological approaches. In some areas, they were occupied by societies that came into direct, often military, contact with the literate civilisations of the Mediterranean basin. We therefore have a few contemporary descriptions of them in Classical literature, perhaps most famously in Julius Caesar's account of his conquest of Gaul and incursions into southern Britain in the first century BC. With varying degrees of certainty, depending on how securely the site may be identified, it is possible to take forward their study by attempting to meld the evidence from archaeological, place-name and historical (in the sense of documentary) sources, so that the mute data furnished by archaeology does not stand alone.

The expansion of the Roman Empire did not mean the end of the construction, use and refurbishment of this category of sites. In Britain and Ireland, southern

1 The multivallate hill-fort of Eggardon, Askerwell, is clearly marked against the Dorset skyline

Scandinavia and parts of central Europe, for example, hill-forts were also in use in the post-Roman centuries, and here, too, a few Early Historic documentary records make direct reference to particular examples. In some areas, too, sites were reoccupied during unsettled times in the later Roman Empire. Some such sites represent earlier forts, repaired or remodelled for renewed use; others were built entirely anew. But in many other cases, even for forts of the first millennium AD, it is their archaeological context that provides most of the information that can be discovered about them.

This account sets out, not to consider the evidence from hill-forts in general, still less the whole range of settlement sites that were constructed during the lengthy period from the later Bronze Age to the Early Historic. Rather, the aim is to introduce aspects of the archaeology of later prehistoric temperate Europe by focusing on a prominent element, both in the literal sense and metaphorically, of the archaeological record – the walls, banks and other features that served to define these promontory and hill-forts. Conventionally envisaged as 'defences' or 'fortifications', such features have long attracted archaeological attention. The treatment that follows will, of course, have to be very selective, and no pretence is made that an even, still less a complete, cover is achieved.

Since the nineteenth century, these structures have been studied in a wide variety of ways. They have been put forward as indicators of unsettled times; as witnesses of venture and resistance; and of invasion and migration. Others have envisaged them as tokens of the prestige and status of those who had them built. Given that they represent some of the most complex civil engineering tasks of their day of which we have direct archaeological evidence, they have also been assessed as the outcome of the mobilisation of substantial amounts of labour and, through the efforts entailed in their development, as major contributors to the structuring of people's ideas of community. Their existence has also allowed the separation of 'insiders' and 'outsiders'; and, importantly, as reflections of contemporary military strategies and assault techniques, they have figured largely in considerations of warfare during these centuries.

The shared architectural styles of fortification, or of particular technical devices, identified in these lines of enclosure may also be pointers to wider cultural linkages. As well as such concerns, it is clear that some, perhaps even many, such hill-forts were certainly not exclusively, indeed not necessarily primarily, defensive in intent; and a variety of symbolic roles has been suggested for some examples. The building of the works in which I am interested here effectively took locations which may previously have shown some relatively limited signs of human activity – a series of field boundaries, pathways and drove routes for animals, on occasion slighter monuments of earlier date – and 'remade the hill in a cultural form', as John Barrett (2000, 83) has succinctly phrased it in considering the evidence for the Somerset hill-fort of Cadbury Castle. Other fortification lines may have been the first constructions at the particular locations at which they were built.

Some later prehistoric fortifications, indeed, represent earthmoving on a grand scale, the results of which could not have failed to impress those who saw the outcome. In many cases, to the shock of the appearance of major new structures, it is fair to point out that their original appearance may have been much sharper, much less avoidable than they have subsequently become. In limestone or chalk areas, ramparts now grass-covered and relatively inconspicuous would have been white or pale yellow; elsewhere walls, presently cloaked in tumbled rubble, or overgrown with vegetation, would have cast much sharper shadows. But it would be wrong to think that the fortifications considered hereafter must originally all have been imposing structures: the existence of some apparently substandard defensive works points tentatively to other factors also having been instrumental in their construction.

In short, the sites described and discussed hereafter include many that were Celtic fortifications, in the sense that they were intended as defensive features, and were most probably built by speakers of a tongue within the group of languages that is so labelled. But others that are included in this study were constructed by Iron Age communities with different cultural and linguistic baggage, but which either shared architectural traits with, or may have influenced those of, the zone conventionally considered as 'Celtic Europe'. In numerous instances, it is far from possible to be categorical about the social and political affiliations of the builders of individual sites, or the language or languages they employed. The available evidence may be rather ambiguous, or indeed point to successive use of a single site by different groups. In many cases, sites may solely be known from accounts of surface fieldwork at them. Our 'Celtic fortifications' flag is thus to some extent one of convenience.

The vocabulary employed since the nineteenth century to describe and discuss these sites has been dominated by terms owing much to the military perspectives of their early students. One reason for this, at least initially important, was that many had attracted names redolent of such activity – for example, there are several examples of 'Danes' Camp' and 'Caesar's Camp' in England, as well as of 'Camp des Anglais' and 'Camp de César' in Francophone Europe. 'Heidengraben' (Heathens' Ditches) occur in the German speaking world. In Scotland, 'Bruce's Camp' appears. The celebrated name of 'Maiden Castle', again widely distributed in Britain, is rather more ambiguous: as Dr Hogg (1975) remarked, it may have been chosen for sites believed to be impregnable, but could have applied to ones containing girls who were not. But equally it is true that many of their early students, especially in the nineteenth century, would have had military experience, and the choice of seeing these sites in a defensive light and as indicators of troubled times readily fitted into their world view. The case of Emperor Napoleon III of France – little Napoleon – highlights this issue. He employed units of his army and some of his senior officers, such as Colonel Stoffel, in the examination of a wide range of sites in the field, destined to illuminate his didactic *History of Julius Caesar*. Some of this fieldwork will divert our attention in later chapters.

WHAT IS A HILL-FORT?

In this study, the term 'hill-fort' will be used in a broad and inclusive way, and without prejudice as to the assumed function or functions of these sites. The term is far from a wholly satisfactory one, but, as Hogg (1975, xi) remarked, '...all the alternatives which have been suggested are open to even more objections'. Alongside the presence of lines of enclosure, it is usually considered that the key common element of these sites is their landscape position, the general view being that the setting has to offer at least some – it may be slight – topographic advantage to the occupants by way of defensive possibilities. It has to be admitted that the topographic settings employed have to be considered very much in relation to the general characteristics of the landscapes in which the proposed hill-fort sits, perhaps nowhere more than in near-level areas like East Anglia. In such landscapes, the raised locations that were occupied may be only just appreciable.

Whilst the following paragraphs will attempt to produce some generalisations in terms of hill-fort forms and their topographic settings, it is tempting to adopt the 'rule of consistent irregularity' devised by R.W. Edwards to address one of the key characteristics of a very different set of fortifications, those of Armenia, whereby the plan of many a site appears almost 'as spontaneous as the ground on which it lies...' (Edwards 1987 12), for use in temperate Europe and the British Isles. To the generalisations that follow, then, there are numerous exceptions and variants.

The principal series of hill-forts crown individual hills: their enclosure lines are adapted to the configuration of the upper hill-slopes, so that they are known as 'contour forts'. The use of the term here, however, embraces enclosed sites in other locations, notably promontory forts, as well as those set on summits of whatever form (so that the resultant enclosure does not in any real sense conform closely to the contour form). In certain kinds of terrain, such as parts of the north European plain, or in eastern lowland Britain, the eminences on which hill-forts are set may be very slight indeed. In such landscapes, generally speaking those most likely to have been used for arable agriculture, even substantial fortifications may have been ploughed down sufficiently far for them to be unrecognisable on the ground. Here, some sites that qualify as hill-forts have been recognised solely as cropmarks: this is the case with the most extensively-excavated Scottish example, at Broxmouth (*colour plate 1*) for example, and also the lowest hill-fort in England, at Stonea in Cambridgeshire.

The key characteristic of the fort is the presence of at least a partial circuit of artificial enclosing works or defences and, depending on topographic requirements and human inclination, often considerably more than that. Descriptions of hill-forts sometimes explicitly include the idea that the topography of the site gave some military advantage to those sheltering within it; in many more instances such an idea is implicit, rather than more definitively stated. In some cases, sites are included in the category on the grounds of the scale of their defences, even if their landscape setting confers a negligible or indeed no recognisable defensive advantage in its own right. In broad terms, such forts are found from close to sea-level – at the *castro* of Baroña on the coast of Galicia for example – to altitudes well above those now routinely considered suitable for habitation, as at Mount Brandon or Caherconree in County Kerry, Eire (*colour plate 2*), or Tre'r Ceiri on the margins of Snowdonia (see Chapter 9). Whilst all hill-forts are at least partially enclosed by lines of earthworks, walls, or ditches, not all enclosed sites are considered to be forts, and, in English-language literature for example, the term 'enclosure' is often used as a catch-all for sites not considered sufficiently defensive in intent to be included. The boundary between these categories is undoubtedly a fuzzy one, partly to do with the surviving condition of their earthworks, but all the more so following the recognition that in some areas (as in south-central England) relatively lightly-defended hilltop enclosures occur, in this instance as a characteristic of the earliest part of the Iron Age. The problem is compounded when sites originally enclosed simply by stout wooden fences or palisades are considered: these have now entirely rotted away, leaving only earthfast traces, so that the present condition of such sites on the ground hardly gives any impression of how substantial some of these stockades may originally have been.

In many approaches to the definition of these sites, size matters. Many studies have thus tried to set a lower limit on the acreage encompassed by the enclosure to allow it to qualify as a hill-fort. A major problem that such an approach produces is that a figure that works reasonably for one region often seems inappropriate for another. Thus, within Britain, sites standardly classed as hill-forts in south-central England are generally substantially bigger than those that are found in the Anglo-Scottish

Border counties on either side of the Cheviot Hills. In France, contrastingly, scalar differences broadly suggest a reverse trend: many of the sites in the Mediterranean coastlands and their adjacent limestone uplands are distinctly smaller than their counterparts further north. As a rule of thumb, however, it would be relatively rare to find sites described as hill-forts in any of the archaeological traditions considered hereafter if the area taken in by their enveloping works did not extend to at least one quarter of a hectare (2500m²). Most are considerably bigger than that, extending from about one to several hectares in enclosed area.

At the other end of the scale, individual sites can cover hundreds, and occasionally thousands, of hectares. Sites of these dinosauric proportions are, however, very unusual, both in time and in space. A relatively high proportion of them belong to the final stages of the pre-Roman Iron Age, and these examples occur within a broad band that extends from Hungary through temperate Europe, west to Atlantic France and north into southern England. Many of these large examples are labelled '*oppida*', adopting a Latin term Julius Caesar employed to describe some of the settlements he encountered as he moved northwards into the heartland of France in the 50s BC. In conventional Iron Age terms, then, they are sites constructed and inhabited during the advanced stages of the La Tène culture, and are broadly attributable to the last two centuries BC, and the first decades AD, the latter period more especially in southern Britain. If the pattern just described suggests that more recent examples of hill-forts tend to be amongst the largest, we need to beware of imagining unilinear evolution everywhere towards the gigantic and the grand: there are a number of exceptions. In eastern Germany, the area of the former German Democratic Republic, for example, forts from the end of the Bronze Age and the earlier part of the Iron Age are as a general rule more extensive, if less densely inhabited, than those which succeeded them. Furthermore, some of the very largest protohistoric enclosed sites in Europe occur far to the east of the area traditionally attributed to the Celts, as at Belsk, in the Ukraine. In their case, we are far removed from the world of enclosed proto-towns that may be inferred from Caesar's descriptions of a few of the Gallic sites.

For southern Britain, the Ordnance Survey Iron Age map adopted two size limits which still usefully define the middle ranges of hill-fort sizes: in metric terms these fall at 1.2ha and 6ha (respectively about 3 and 20 acres). Further north in Britain, these thresholds would be difficult to operate; there are very few sites above 6ha in extent. The quarter hectare threshold proposed above, however, catches areas with some, and sometimes significant numbers, of small sites, such as the Scottish Borders, and is that used by A.H.A. Hogg in his later studies. The proportion of small enclosed sites probably reaches its zenith in Ireland, where sites classed as hill-forts remain relatively rare, but where numbers of small earthworks, generally known as raths and dominantly of the first millennium AD, occur in tens of thousands (Stout 1997). It is also important to bear in mind that individual sites may also vary in size through time. While some grow more extensive with the addition of extra lines of enclosure set downslope beyond their original circuits, the extent of others can shrink. Such

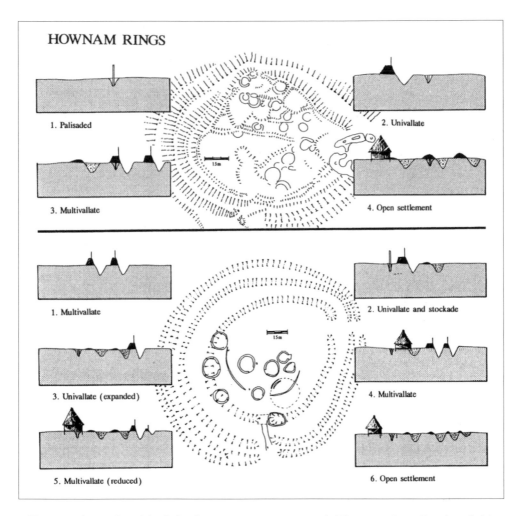

HOWNAM RINGS

1. Palisaded

2. Univallate

3. Multivallate

4. Open settlement

1. Multivallate

2. Univallate and stockade

3. Univallate (expanded)

4. Multivallate

5. Multivallate (reduced)

6. Open settlement

2 Two southern Scottish defensive sequences compared. Hownam Law, Roxburghshire, represents the classic model – palisade, wall, then banks – often used to put such sites in sequence, but Broxmouth does not conform to it. *Drawn by Gordon Thomas*

trends need not be unrelentingly unilinear either: some sites simply oscillate in size and in the apparent complexity of their enclosing works through time – Broxmouth, already mentioned, is a case in point (Hill 1982) (*2*). There has also been considered to be a need for a threshold to be set between the large forts and those altogether rare, if more massive in areal terms, examples. There is less absolute agreement about where this might fall: Hogg proposed 30ha for British sites; John Collis (1984) suggested 25ha as the minimal threshold for Continental *oppida* – not altogether the same thing, but again an indication that the grandest sites need consideration apart.

As has been mentioned, in some archaeological traditions an effort is made to distinguish between fortification and simple enclosure of the scale and configuration of the banks or other enveloping works. This is obviously a hazardous task, since natural erosion, along with the impacts of revegetation, ploughing and a host of other activities may have substantially altered the profile of the walls or banks and, where these exist, their accompanying ditches, over the many centuries since individual sites were abandoned. The potential variability of such impacts means that the dependence on the present-day surface characteristics of these fortifications can lead to faulty assessments. Some sites, as has been noted above, are now reduced to cropmarks, only visible from the air, whereas in others stone walls may still be imposing upstanding features. In many cases, it is simply not feasible to be categorical about the original scale of the defences from surface inspection of their current condition, although geophysical assays can help determine their characteristics without the need to resort to excavation.

In a number of areas, hilltop sites combining lines of enclosure of varying strength have been identified, thereby compounding the problem of distinguishing between forts and lesser enclosures. Classic examples include major hill-forts in south-west England such as Clovelly Dykes and Milber Down, both in Devon. In these, a heavily-defended inner enclosure is enveloped within a series of outer enclosures, generally, but not always, of smaller earthworks. Their landscape setting and the presence nearby of trackways suggest the suitability of their outer enclosures as livestock (cattle are usually suggested) kraals surrounding an inhabited space, and this kind of pattern can be replicated in other areas, in particular for present purposes where there is a subdivision of the space between inner and outer ramparts, sometimes accessible from a separate gate. The Ringses, on Doddington Moor in Northumberland, is a variant of this form. Such arrangements, mixing lines of enclosure of varying apparent strength, tend to emphasise how difficult it is tightly to define hill-forts as a distinctive class of sites.

How many sites might be considered as hill-forts in Europe? Dr A.H.A. Hogg estimated 2,000 or more in Great Britain and, deliberately excluding small, cognate and extremely numerous sites, notably the *raths* of Ireland, the present author's guesstimate for the total number of such sites at the European scale would fall in the 20,000-30,000 bracket. Nor are numbers of known sites finite. In many areas of Europe, archaeological fieldwork, professional and amateur, and that of mapping agencies, continues to identify new examples, albeit at a reduced rate. Capitalising on early survey programmes e.g. the Société préhistorique française's *Commission des enceintes préhistoriques et fortifications anhistoriques* and its English equivalent – the earthworks surveys compiled by the Earthworks Committee of the Congress of Archaeological Societies – of nearly a century ago, many sites have been identified for a considerable time, and hill-forts are often the archaeological monuments most likely to be depicted on standard 1:50,000 maps. Pioneer surveys at the national scale were compiled in the nineteenth century: in this regard, the 1898 publication by the Edinburgh lawyer, David Christison, *Early Fortifications of Scotland*, is worthy of note, since Christison is more usually remembered for his leadership in the following decade of the rather poor-quality excavation of a key hill-fort site, the assumed capital of the Scoti in the early centuries AD at Dunadd in Argyll.

Some of the newly-spotted sites are still upstanding features in the landscape that have simply escaped attention: the plan of one I recently visited in Argyll – Dun Daraich in Glen Finart in Cowal – although known from the 1960s to display signs of vitrified stonework, was only rendered comprehensible when the rhododendron thicket in which it was entangled was cleared, and the Glasgow Association of Certificated Field Archaeologists was able to survey and describe it. In Normandy, a massive enclosure at Quiévrecourt (Seine Maritime, France) seems to have escaped detection because of its low-lying position surrounded by the River Béthune (which flows into the Channel) and two of its tributaries, until it was affected a few years ago by a road-building scheme. Although some sectors of its bank did survive as an upstanding feature some 4m high, these were all in woodland, and this 63ha site had effectively not been recognised for what it is. Exploratory work demonstrated that this site had Late Bronze Age and then La Tène occupation; the bank is of *murus gallicus* construction, and was subsequently enveloped in the now-wooded massive earthen bank – a sequence of fortification styles that will be discussed below.

Although some major upstanding earthworks thus continue to be detected, the majority of recently identified examples are now in a distinctly reduced condition when they are first identified, often through aerial reconnaissance over the arable lands; still others are initially identified in rescue archaeological projects, sometimes within towns, as at Metz in northern France, or within Aylesbury in Buckinghamshire. A generation ago, Dr Hogg confidently estimated for Britain that fewer than 10 per cent of the original total of such sites remained unknown, but this is a figure that must now be treated with a considerable measure of caution. None the less, it remains likely that hill-forts are, in proportional terms, one of the most fully represented categories of prehistoric archaeological site in Europe, a combination of the fact that many are located in 'zones of likely survival', where subsequent activities are less likely entirely to have eliminated them, and because the very scale of the earthworks and ditches discussed in this book means that their wholesale elimination is harder to achieve than for lesser field monuments.

In Continental Europe, as here in Britain, the idea of enclosing sites with wooden palisades, walls or banks, accompanied or not by ditches, is a recurrent feature of the archaeological record from the Neolithic period onwards. In some areas, notably in central Europe, the presence of hill-forts in the Bronze Age is also well attested. To that extent, the search for a single origin for the more numerous traditions of later prehistoric hill-forts that are our primary subject here would be a fruitless exercise: they are likely to have emerged independently in a number of separate areas, whether through aggrandising earlier enclosing works, by building new enclosures at the junction of earlier boundaries in the landscape, or by other means. Once invented, and seen to confer safety, prestige or other advantage, they are likely to have been emulated. Such a perspective is, however, not a reason to argue for social and political immobilism in the Iron Age, with people growing up, living and dying within their own regions. Movement of populations certainly occurred, although the extensive invasions so often preferred by earlier archaeologists to explain significant changes in the archaeological record, were probably rarer than once imagined. In the case of some of the comparable architectural and structural details noted in some hill-forts considerable distances apart, independent invention may be a satisfactory explanation. But in other instances such similarities are likely to indicate contacts, whether direct or indirect, between their builders. Over much of Europe, evidence for the ridden horse, for vehicles equipped with lighter, spoked wheels, and for riverine craft and sea-going vessels, is much more extensive in the first millennium BC than in previous centuries: such developments clearly had the potential to facilitate contacts between communities.

Individual sites in parts of Britain broadly conform to these chronological patterns. Neolithic hill-forts are recorded at places like Carn Brae in Cornwall, a craggy summit with lengths of stone bank and considerable evidence (including arrowheads) for occupation. And, amongst the Neolithic activity at the great Gloucestershire site of Crickley Hill, there are clear signs of an attack by archers on the gate of its Neolithic enclosure. Evidence for hostility at gates will also characterise subsequent periods.

There were clearly Bronze Age enclosures and forts in Britain and Ireland too, although how common they were is made problematical by issues to do with the absolute dating systems – radiocarbon, to a lesser extent thermoluminescence – generally employed to date them. Rams's Hill, Berkshire, a site now ploughed out in arable land, is perhaps the classic southern instance; here the innermost enclosure belongs firmly to the Later, rather than the Middle, Bronze Age, but the outer enclosure is less securely dated. Now invisible in ground perspective view, this stood nearly 2m high when investigated by the Piggotts in the 1930s. Other forts such as Ivinghoe Beacon (Buckinghamshire) and Dinorben in north Wales have good claims for initial occupation considerably before the middle of the first millennium BC; at Ivinghoe, for example, there is metalwork to support the early date suggested by radiocarbon evidence. The Scottish vitrified forts, particularly as dated by thermo-luminescence, pose particular problems as regards their dating but, in light of the similarity of their shapes in plan, are unlikely to have been constructed over a period in excess of 2000 years, as seems to be implied from available determinations (see Chapter 7). Radiocarbon measurements and remanent magnetism suggest distinctly different date ranges for them. In other northern cases, continuing discoveries of Late Bronze Age metalwork suggest initial fortification at this time, even if it has so far been quite difficult to demonstrate enclosure of the summit at this time. This is the case, for example, at Traprain Law in East Lothian, a site – along with the other locally-substantial fort at Eildon Hill North in the Scottish Borders – usually put forward in support of the hypothesis that, as in eastern Germany, forts that are big in local-scale terms are early in the Scottish sequence. Older records also throw up some puzzles: at Drumcoltran in Dumfries and Galloway, for example, Middle Bronze Age rapiers are recorded as being recovered from a hill-fort ditch, implying that that enclosure is potentially older. In the meantime, probably the most coherent series of later Bronze Age earthworks are the eastern English lowland circular ditched enclosures of the type found at Springfield Lyons in Essex. In sum, as the British evidence stands at present, it appears likely that numbers of forts were clearly established within the Late Bronze Age, and a few examples were in use at earlier times.

What did hill-fort enclosures contain? Although this is not a central concern, I cannot avoid the question entirely, since it would be reasonable to postulate a link between the form of the enclosure and the nature of the internal evidence. In many instances, without archaeological excavation, it is of course impossible to be sure. Surface collection, on occasion aided by the judicious use of metal-detectors where the appropriate licence is granted, can be of assistance in some cases; and some remarkable results have been obtained through geophysics, notably in the mapping of a range of sites in southern England, clearly demonstrating that the interiors of some hill-forts are much 'busier' than others, in terms of the density of anomalies encountered. Aerial photography of cropmarks may suggest intensive use, with evidence of post-holes and narrow trenches indicating the former presence of buildings, or rather more substantial splodges that may indicate either batteries of storage pits or houses where floor-level deposits may be better preserved. At the other end of the scale, where subsequent destruction has been less severe, or where exceptional conditions of survival occur, upstanding structural evidence may still be found. In this regard, amongst the most remarkable evidence from anywhere in Europe occurs in the Cheviot Hills of the Anglo-Scottish border and in neighbouring uplands. Here, the combination of remarkably thin soils and the dentition of substantial numbers of *Ovis aries* produces a sheepscape in which very minor earthfast components of Iron Age buildings – notably circular grooves and ditches – are still displayed on the surface within some hill-forts, as at Wether Hill in Northumberland (see Chapter 9) or White Meldon in Peeblesshire. Remarkably, this key to the nature of their former occupation is still readable on the surface, although the timberwork has long since disappeared. In other areas, the footings of stone buildings survive within such sites, again providing a first indication of the nature of their use. Exceptionally, the wooden substructures of timber buildings, log-built with horizontal timbers like Davy Crockett's cabin in the *Blockbau* tradition of parts of the European Continent, may be revealed in excavation, as famously at the lake-margin fort of Biskupin in Poland. A host of other examples have produced a variety of other evidence for domestic occupation through excavation.

It is thus clear that some hill-fort sites were significant, permanent, places of settlement, but in other instances the available evidence points in a diametrically opposite way. Some hill-forts may have been only temporarily occupied, for example seasonally at times of markets, fairs or perhaps religious festivals. The 'afterlife' of some hill-forts can also include activities of this kind: there were fairs and markets on the summit of Mont Beuvray in Burgundy through the nineteenth century, for instance; local farmers complained that the trenches left open by the first excavator of the site, J.-G. Bulliot, were a hazard to their visiting livestock. White Horse Hill in Berkshire was also the site of a seasonal fair, especially at times when the neighbouring equine sculpture carved into the Down required to be scoured out (see Chapter 9). In other cases, the rhythms of site occupation seem to have been entirely different, not being related to annual or less frequent cycles of predictable activity, but rather to external threats or other intermittent and unpredictable reasons for insecurity or alarm. The hill-fort as refuge in times of trouble is thus a widely-used concept, which tends to be deployed in particular for forts in locations difficult of access, with few exploitable resources in their vicinities, or with little discernable sign of permanent occupation. Another feature that may be significant in this regard is the absence of a gateway in some forts, like a north-east Scottish series discussed subsequently.

It is thus impossible satisfactorily to generalise about the nature of occupation across the thousands of hill-fort sites that survive in Europe. Whilst there is no reason to advocate that the occupation of sites was consistent across time or space, a contributory problem in discussing this issue arises from the fact that in many cases archaeologists are forced to rely on excavation evidence derived from areas that are very small relative to the total areas enclosed. Although the use of 360 degree mechanical excavators and other earthmoving machinery has greatly simplified the labour requirements of stripping areas within sites (as it has too the excavation of some of the ramparts that surround them), in reality only a tiny proportion of the total number of sites known has been the subject of extensive excavation. This fundamentally conditions what can be said about them.

The smallness of the sample that has been excavated also remains true of the fortifications which are the key concern here. As I have noted previously, descriptions of their architecture are almost always derived from 'rampart cuttings which represent the slightest of incisions relative to the overall length of enceintes', coupled with an often-unstated and sometimes unjustifiable assumption that the remainder of the circuits under consideration were constructed in like manner to the portion examined.

Other functions are also evidenced in the record of hill-fort interiors. Storage of agricultural produce, for example, is sometimes readily apparent in the form of numbers of substantial storage pits, through the presence of appropriate buildings, such as small four-post structures that could have served as granaries, or in other ways – close to the Mediterranean, for example, by the inclusion of substantial numbers of large storage jars or *pithoi*. In Scotland, the below-ground storage features called souterrains usually seem to be secondary to hill-forts, as indicated by the example constructed within the ditch of the fort excavated by Gordon Childe at Castle Law, Midlothian, but this chronological sequence does not seem to hold true for Brittany. Elsewhere, a few Continental forts, generally datable towards the end of the first millennium BC, include evidence for either dry-stone or timber-built cellars, in some instances accessible down staircases, as at Mont Beuvray in Burgundy or Villeneuve-Saint-Germain near Soissons in Picardy. On occasion, as at Chateaumeillant in Berry, central France, such cellarage may be uncovered still packed with wine amphorae. Fully rock-cut features, perhaps more ambiguously interpreted as cellars, occur elsewhere including within the completely-excavated fort of the Altburg-bei-Bundenbach, near Trier in western Germany (Schindler 1977).

The recovery of animal bone within numerous sites suggests that livestock were certainly butchered and processed in them, and it is very likely that animals were sheltered, even stalled, within forts. In some instances, the buildings within hill-forts look no different from those found on contemporary farms, and this acts as a salutary reminder that the primary food-producing sector of the economy was central to all temperate European Iron Age societies. In other cases, the fact that the hill-fort enclosure is substantially larger than the settlement evidence it surrounds allows for there having been grazing for livestock within the fort itself.

A related issue is the provision of a water supply within these sites, of major significance if livestock and especially cattle are likely to have been kept within them for any length of time. Wells are known in some instances, and some others include cisterns that could be used to collect surface run-off, even if they had not been dug out sufficiently to reach the water-table. In other cases, rampart circuits seem to have been designed to include either springs, ponds or parts of watercourses. Maintaining access to water, or interrupting it, was a central issue in some of the recorded conflict at hill-forts (see Chapter 5). There are, however, many hill-fort sites where the arrangements for water provision are not apparent, and whilst there are means (e.g. barrels) for collecting rainwater that are likely to leave the archaeologist no discernable trace on dryland sites, it would be wrong to suggest that the fortifications with which we are concerned invariably included provision for a water supply.

Evidence of industry is encountered in a variety of forms. Peter Crew has examined hill-forts sited within Snowdonia in north-west Wales, which show good evidence for smelting and smithing iron, both in the form of relevant structural debris and processing wastes. In numbers of other cases, the extraction and working of iron seem to have been significant in the selection of particular locations for hill-forts: Stična in Slovenia and Kelheim in Bavaria, Germany, are examples, very different in date, which suggest that the proximity of exploitable iron ores was important in the economy of these sites. At Mont Beuvray, my colleague Jean-Paul Guillaumet has spotted that, under the mask of the present-day vegetation, the interior of that site was marked by gullying and cuttings produced by large-scale opencast mining, and this seemingly older than most of the Late Iron Age occupation evidence. In today's jargon, then, it is arguably the case that this major settlement of the most pro-Roman group in Gaul – the Aedui – was built on what was already a 'brownfield site' in the second century BC.

In numbers of other sites, broken clay moulds, unfinished objects discarded during production, pottery wasters and the like provide the kinds of artefactual evidence indicative of on-site craftsmanship. In some instances, very specialised types of objects seem to have been made in particular sites. At the end of the Hallstatt Iron Age of west-central Europe for instance, from the sixth and into the fifth century BC, there emerged a series of generally small hill-forts with readily-apparent signs of elite occupation, the so-called 'princely seats' or *Fürstensitze*, of which the Heuneburg adjacent to the upper Danube in Baden-Wurttemburg, and Mont Lassois, near the headwaters of the Seine (*colour plate 3*), are the most celebrated. A characteristic of such sites is the making of very elaborate brooches, the kind of prestige item required to hold fine, high-quality garments in place; several variants of these have distributions very much focused on such single sites. In the larger and more elaborate forts, there is sometimes evidence of particular craft industries being grouped in particular sectors within the site. To some extent, this kind of patterning is detectable from the mapped distributions of finds within sites like Biskupin in Poland, or the later *oppidum* at Manching in Bavaria. Broadly contemporary with the latter, the evidence, initially recognised in the nineteenth century, for workshops dedicated to a single industry is still best represented at Mont Beuvray where the Iron Age visitor, having accessed the 135ha inner enclosure of the site through one of its major gates, the Porte du Rebout, would have encountered a 'quarter' of enamel-workers' workshops on his or her left along the access road. To the right would have been metal-workers, in particular blacksmiths. Such concentrations recall the craft arrangements inside medieval urban places, and still detectable in sites like Palma de Mallorca. There is thus no doubt that people were processing raw materials and manufacturing objects within some hill-forts, but inevitably this was not universally the case and, in so far as the archaeological evidence takes us, the scale of artisanal activity represented in hill-forts could also be very variable.

Commerce and exchange are other activities detectable from evidence recovered within at least some sites. On later Iron Age enclosed settlements, in southern Britain as in many areas of the Continent, the most readily appreciable sign is the appearance of low value fiat currency, in the form of cast copper alloy tokens (often called 'potins'), comparable to the kind of small change required in market economies. Some types of these have very localised distributions, such that they may have only been acceptable as currency to pay for transactions within the area defined by the fortifications of a particular hill-fort. Other indications of trade include excavation evidence for goods emanating from afar: in temperate Europe, the most obvious products are those from the Mediterranean world. Represented on relatively few sites, in relatively modest quantities albeit of very high quality, in the Hallstatt period, more particularly in the later sixth and fifth centuries BC, such goods can in other instances suggest much more regular exchange of commodities on a greater scale. It does not, of course, follow conclusively that the exchange itself necessarily took place within the forts, but the proportion of the available evidence from them (and in some instances deposited in graves clustered in their surroundings) suggested that some of their inhabitants were key players in this activity.

The classic examples of long-distance commerce are furnished by the occurrences of sherds of late Republican Italian wine amphorae, recovered in very varying quantities on substantial numbers of sites from Bavaria west to the Atlantic fringe of Continental Europe and north into parts of southern Britain. In some cases, this evidence is present in quantities and archaeological contexts suggestive of substantial consumption at single events: i.e. feasting. Amongst the most spectacular evidence for such events is that presently being excavated from within the great fort at Corent in the Auvergne by Matthieu Poux. But not all consumption was of this kind, and on other sites the pattern of the arrival of amphorae may have been more spasmodic, and certainly less daunting in volumetric terms. Such long-distance exchanges as the wine amphorae betoken are complemented by other, more local-scale ones. A few commodities indicate northern sources, perhaps the most readily apparent in the record being amber, recovered naturally principally along the southern margin of the Baltic Sea and distributed from there. As in other domains, incontrovertible evidence for the significance of commerce on individual hill-fort sites can be very variable. And some important goods are all but archaeologically invisible: not the least of these is the human traffic in slaves.

Alongside these relatively mundane activities of living, processing and storing resources, manufacturing and trading, there are many indications that hill-forts were also arenas for other activities of a more symbolic or ritual kind. Such evidence is very varied in character, but the most straightforward subdivision that can be proposed is between those sites where evidence of such activities is in effect mixed in with other remains, and those where particular, spatially-defined, components of the site seem to reflect activities of these kinds. As a general rule, such spatial segregation seems to be a trait of later Iron Age sites, as at the Titelberg in Luxembourg, where a segment of the site is isolated by a substantial internal ditch; in some cases a sanctuary may have provided the original focus around which other activities that went into the making of the hill-fort coalesced. But there are exceptions, notably in southern areas such as Provence, where features such as temples may emerge rather earlier. These matters are considered in more detail in a later chapter. For the moment, without wishing to suggest that all hill-forts were 'central places' in any narrow economic or political sense, it is certainly possible to suggest that the resources and facilities they contained might have made them preferred targets for attack.

The enclosing banks and ditches considered here thus surrounded communities which were engaged in a wide range of tasks from the mundane to others much more specialist in character. It is as reasonable to ask how many people lived on these sites and for how long as it is hard to give a definitive answer. Classical authors provide us with a few figures, albeit only for major late sites, but these are prone to all the factors that suggest such estimates are an unreliable basis from which to calculate normal numbers. The 40,000 suggested to have been inside *Avaricum*, the promontory now central to present-day Bourges in Berry, central France, when Caesar laid siege to the site in 52 BC, even if true, included untold numbers displaced from other neighbouring sites as a product of the scorched-earth defence strategy then being practised. It would be unreasonable to envisage this as the usual peace-time population; in medieval times approximately the same physical space seems to have held 2,000–3,000 people. Equally the 57,000 cited in a north French *oppidum* reflects wartime conditions. Some comparative work on urban places elsewhere suggests that even late *oppida* sites may not have been very densely inhabited. But that some sites were indeed well used is otherwise perhaps best indicated by the degree of erosion – from foot and vehicle traffic, and very probably from livestock as well as people – in and on the approaches to their entrances. Alternatively, in some instances it is possible to count the numbers of internal buildings and multiply this by a 'guesstimated family size', making the sadly-unwarranted assumption that all structures were dwellings in contemporary use. It would certainly be possible to suggest that larger sites may have had a population of several thousand, but most hill-forts probably included human groups to be counted in tens or, at most, hundreds.

This focus on fortifications in portions of temperate Europe should, however, not blind us to the fact that the European story of these fortifications neither suggests they were unique to, nor especially precocious in, this continent. In the Near East, for example, effective fortifications were already being constructed in the Neolithic, with the elaborate 550ha settlement at Uruk being enclosed by a wall 9.5km long, with 900 towers, by the Early Dynastic period. Egyptian depictions of the third millennium BC make it plain that by then, warfare against fortified places was both a serious business – with crowbars for example being used to force open gates – and increasingly, in some of its aspects, a mechanised one. There are, for instance, contemporary illustrations of wheeled siege ladders. By the first millennium BC and Biblical times there, siege warfare was a highly sophisticated undertaking, which had provoked numerous changes – e.g. from casement-built to solid walls – in east Mediterranean defensive architecture. Only relatively tardily, with the expansion of the late Roman Republican army first into Iberia and subsequently Gaul, did similar factors begin significantly to impact on the sites considered here.

Equally, structures broadly similar to hill-forts have been recognised in many other areas of the globe, from the Eastern woodlands of North America to the Maori *pa*, like Maungakiekie on the Auckland isthmus of North Island, New Zealand. Very similar vocabularies are used to describe the structural features of some of these sites. At a time, too, when southern British hill-forts were explained very largely in terms of the invasionist model of the venture of new arrivals from outwith these islands, of cycles of invasion and the responses of resistance impinging on hill-fort construction and preferred defensive styles, it was salutary to consider the case of the development and evolution of Maori enclosures, where no such external push factor could easily have been anticipated. It is thus undeniable that the fortifications considered here are a small subset of an altogether larger and longer-lasting phenomenon.

2

THE SETTINGS AND
LANDSCAPES OF HILL-FORTS

One of the key characteristics that separates hill-forts from other categories of fortified sites found in Europe is that the form their enclosures take is often moulded to the local topography. In many areas, the classic examples are termed 'contour forts', reflecting the fact that their shape is closely related to the form of the eminence on which they are set, with individual lines of enclosure sweeping round the summit and generally staying close to a particular altitude, such that the plan of the enclosure offers a close match to the shape of the hill that accommodates them. A reasonable analogy for such circuits would be figure-hugging clothes, equally closely fitted to the three-dimensional bodies that wear them. Students of fashion will appreciate that at other times and in other places, the relationship between clothes and their wearers may be very different, with the shapes and materials of garments almost disguising the figures they drape. And in the case of some hill-fort plans too, the relationship between topographic form and plan outline may be much less direct. Before pursuing this comparison, it will be useful to outline the main settings in which hill-forts occur.

In many areas, contour forts surrounding individual – or occasionally multiple – summits form the dominant series numerically (*3, colour plate 4*). Whilst many of these are also set on hills that are prominent within their local landscapes, this is not invariably the case. In some instances, the topographic advantage offered by the site's location may be minimal, as occurs in East Anglia or parts of the Paris Basin, where site interiors may stand very little proud of the surrounding countryside. Generally, however, whether in Galicia or Baden-Wurttemburg, the locations selected for such sites confer much more significant topographic advantages to those resident within them. The equivalent term in German is *Ringwall,* but French makes do with *enceinte de contour*.

The absence of much, indeed in some cases any, height advantage may be compensated for by adjacent marshland or land otherwise difficult to cross, or simply by increasing the scale of the enclosing works. The Early Iron Age Lausitz culture site at Biskupin, Poland, shares with some of its neighbours a wetland location at a lake margin, whilst the highly atypical *oppidum* of Manching in southern Bavaria, was

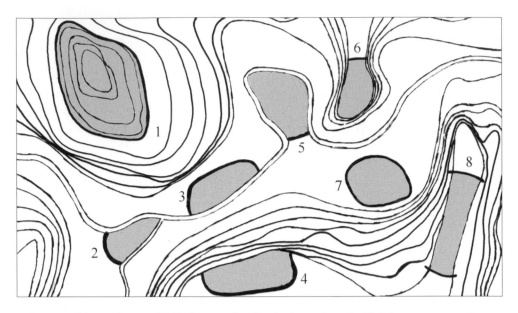

3 Topographic settings of hill-forts and related sites, after S. Fichtl. 1: contour fort 2: promontory at river confluence 3: backing onto river terrace 4: plateau edge 5: meander 6: promontory 7: slight eminence in plain 8: ridge. *Drawn by Jem Heinemeier*

formed by enveloping an earlier unenclosed village settlement within a substantial circular enclosure formed by 7km of timber-laced wall, around which a number of small streams had been diverted. Other instances of forts supplementing their man-made defences by recourse to neighbouring marsh include the fen-edge Stonea Camp in Cambridgeshire, whereas at the *oppidum* of *Vesontio* at Besançon in eastern France, the timber-laced defensive wall surrounding it is lapped by the River Doubs, which at one point becomes a harbour facility. River meanders are thus among the locations selected for sites, but such arrangements are unusual in proportional terms, and the majority of hill-fort defensive lines occur around positions that are variants of the contour fort tradition.

At the European scale, probably the second most numerous topographic locations employed by hill-forts, after settings on individual summits, are promontories. In some types of landscape, for example on limestone geologies, suitable promontories may be relatively common, but elsewhere they are much more infrequent. Koch and Schindler (1994) propose the German term *Spornburg* for such sites, which are normally referred to as *éperons barrés* in French. The great advantage of promontories is that, assuming they are relatively steep-sided, the line or lines of fortification may be focused on the direction of easiest approach, in general where the promontory is attached to a neighbouring block of upland. This principal defence can be accompanied by enclosing works on a lesser scale around the remainder of the circuit, where access is more difficult; or indeed obvious signs of fortification may be wholly absent here.

Perhaps the classic location for promontory forts is on the coastline. Amongst these sites, too, there is very considerable variability. Some coastal-edge sites are located on relatively low-lying promontories, which can be flanked by estuaries, inlets, gently shelving shorelines or similar features that would assist in encouraging seaborne access: cases would include Hengistbury Head on the Dorset coast near Christchurch, Drumanagh, near Loughshinny, County Dublin (Ireland), or the rather later, probably entirely Pictish, promontory fort at Burghead on the Moray Firth coast of north-east Scotland (see Chapter 9). At the other extreme are narrow promontories edged by sea-girt steep cliffs, where the line or lines of defence on the landward side may be very short in proportion to the entire perimeter of the site, but where shelving shorelines to beach boats or peaceful anchorages are lacking. In such cases, ready access to or from the sea was clearly not a factor in site selection. This would appear to be the case with some of the sites around the Breton and Cornish coasts, both classic 'cliff castle' areas (*4*), but also far to the north, as at St John's Point on Caithness, overlooking a group of skerries set in the hazardous Pentland Firth.

Whilst many of these promontory sites can be very small, in other instances it is possible to enclose substantial areas very economically in this manner: Scotland's largest, albeit undated, promontory fort at the Mull of Galloway, the extreme south-western point of the mainland, with its splendid view south over the Irish Sea to the Isle of Man, falls into this category. Here, the narrowest point across the headland is traversed by two lines of bank-and-ditch, still undated, which isolate some 40ha. An even more

4 The Rumps, Pentire Head, St Minver, Cornwall: the view landward from a rocky boss inside the site over the three banks (the outermost with a modern wall) drawn across the neck of this coastal promontory

spectacular example of massive area for slight enclosure wall is represented by the cliff-edged promontory of Dun Mingulay, projecting into the brooding Atlantic ocean from the western seaboard of that now-uninhabited island in the Western Isles.

Promontory forts occur in many areas edged by hard rock coastlines, along the Atlantic and North Sea coasts, as well as in some instances on the Mediterranean, and include celebrated examples such as Cap-Sizun in Finistère, Brittany, the 'cliff castles' of the Cornish coast such as The Rumps, and other examples extending north as far as the coastlines of Scotland's Northern Isles. Examples also occur on the Mediterranean coastline, as at Tamaris on the Côte Bleue near Marseilles (Bouches-du-Rhône, France). In at least some of these cases, the lack of suitable bays on the adjacent coastline means that ready access to boats and the sea would have been much less straightforward for their occupants than at sites such as Hengistbury. If, elsewhere, hill-fort defences may nowadays be under threat from rabbits, here the equivalent risk comes from other burrowing creatures, notably puffins: damage caused by the burrows dug by these birds was one of the reasons for Professor John Hunter's excavations on the Landberg promontory fort, Fair Isle.

Two other general points may be put forward in regard to coastal promontory forts. Such sites naturally cap more resistant rock strata, although of course even these may have been subject to considerable erosion since the promontory was inhabited. The configuration of weaker strata in their vicinity may not only determine the form of the seaward edges of the promontory, but can also contribute to their landward defences. Thus, most spectacularly, the ditches of the Caithness promontory fort of Holborn Head are formed by subsidiary geos exploited by the sea; these are complemented by relatively small man-made banks. With the waters of the Pentland Firth lapping at the bottom, these must qualify as the deepest hill-fort ditches anywhere (5)! It is also worth remarking that, whilst the inhabitants of coastal promontory forts in particular must have been at risk of being blown over the edge during the gales that at least intermittently prevail, particularly at higher latitudes, very few coastal promontory forts show any signs of their landward barriers being matched by subsidiary works around the remainder of their perimeters to prevent children, the frail or the elderly being toppled over the side by the force of the wind. The exceptions, such as the elaborate 'courts' within the fort at Burghead in Moray, are so rare that it is not possible simply to argue that their general absence is entirely the result of continuing coastal erosion since the sites were in use.

Elsewhere, promontory forts occur inland. They are very common in the limestone countryside of France, for example, where the earliest *éperons barrés* seem to have been erected during the Neolithic. Early occupation is also a characteristic of some promontory locations in the British Isles which were also in use during the Iron Age. Crickley Hill in Gloucestershire is a classic example. In Northern Ireland, the inland promontory forts of County Antrim form some of the most substantial enclosures of that country as on the basalt uplands at Knockdhu and multivallate Lurigethan.

Variants on the promontory as a topographic setting are offered by sites occupying interfluves between rivers, and set in meanders. A classic instance of a fort set within

5 Amongst the most impressive defences anywhere are the natural ditches formed by the sea's erosion of softer rock to form geos at the promontory fort of Holborn Head, Caithness

a meander occurs on the lowland site of Villeneuve-Saint-Germain, near Soissons on the Aisne river of northern France. Here a substantial spur of land extending to some 50ha set within a tight bend in the river is isolated by a pair of ditches and ramparts running parallel across the full width of the apex of the meander. On the Swiss-German frontier, two meanders – one in each country and thus separated by the River Rhine - form the *oppidum* of Altenburg-Rheinau. Other interfluve locations provide the settings for some of the biggest sites on the Continent. These include the 330ha *oppidum* of Villejoubert at Saint-Denis-des-Murs in Limousin (*colour plate 5*), a narrow, 4km-long promontory edged by the river Vienne and one of its affluents above their confluence, and the massive lowland promontory of the Fossé Saint Philibert at Yainville and Jumièges (Seine Maritime), which occupies most of one of the big meanders of the Seine to the west of Rouen in Normandy. This univallate fort, attributable to the end of the Bronze Age and reused in the La Tène Iron Age, encloses almost 2,000ha, assuming the Seine meander has not altered significantly in form or position since Iron Age times. Now partially set in woodland, it is one of the few later prehistoric sites on which I have seen copious signs of the activities of wild boar. Other interfluve sites can be diminutive, as in the case with forts set on narrow spurs of land between former meltwater channels in Scotland, the margins of the Massif central of France, and elsewhere.

Forts, too, can occupy islands, sometimes effectively being coterminous with them, although this seems to be relatively rare. The *oppidum* of *Lutetia* of the *Parisi* occupied the Ile de la Cité in mid-Seine at Paris; on a very much smaller scale, much of Eilean Buidhe, one of the Burnt Isles in the arm of sea that is the Kyles of Bute, between that island and Cowal, Argyll, is occupied by the remains of a heavily overgrown and vitrified small fort or dun.

The presence of cliffs as a significant feature in complementing artificial headlands has already been noted in the case of promontory forts, but there are a range of other circumstances in which advantage is taken of their presence. In some cases, this may simply be achieved by backing a length or rampart against a cliff. Amongst the most spectacular and photogenic of such enclosures is that defined by the crescentic stone wall delimiting Dun Aengus at the top of the high cliffs bounding the western side of the Aran Islands, some 50km off the Galway coast of the west of Ireland, above the crashing waves of the Atlantic Ocean. Also falling into this category is the large coastal fort of the Cité des Limes, at Bracquemont beside Dieppe at the mouth of the Seine. In plan, this is a large isosceles triangle, with one side defined by the high cliffs above the English Channel. A particularly well-preserved example of a dry-stone built wall sits atop the cliffs at the south end of the Mull of Kintyre in Argyll: Sròn Uamha enjoys wide views to the south over the North Channel to Northern Ireland (see Chapter 9). Such sites can be particularly prone to erosion, as the cliffs are undermined and slump: this process is clearly apparent, for example, at the coastal site of Dinas Dinlle, in north Wales (6).

The choice of such locations is not restricted to the coast, and inland cliffs can also have forts backed against them. A small but important example is the Camp du Château at Château-sur-Salins in the Jura of eastern France. This tiny, high-altitude fort has for long been known as another of the series of 'princely seats', the late Hallstatt set of sites marked out by the presence of significant Mediterranean imports and by high-quality local products. In nearby Lorraine, the Cité d'Affrique, considered below in relation to its calcined rampart (Chapter 7), equally edges a bluff above the River Moselle. Another, rectilinear example backs onto Salisbury Crags, a cliff overlooking Holyrood Palace and the new, expensive Scottish Parliament

6 Dinas Dinlle: erosion has provoked the collapse of much of the bivallate fort on this glacial hill on the Carnarfonshire coast

building in the royal park within the city of Edinburgh. Defences can also be backed onto steep river terraces (*3*, no.3), as at the Amalienfels, Kreis Sigmaringen (Biel 1987, no.33), in south-west Germany.

Hill-fort builders were also prepared to supplement the natural defences provided by cliff-edged, or otherwise steep-sided, blocks of upland to provide what is in effect an extreme variant of the contour fort. Such sites have been examined in particular in Germany, with a well-known example being the Goldberg in Baden-Wurttemburg, the site of an important excavation by Gerhard Bersu (later, as a refugee from German Fascism, the excavator of Little Woodbury). Most subsequent commentators on the Goldberg have focused on the plan of the internal structures, readily interpretable – as a result of the presence of rectilinear post-built buildings of different sizes and of palisades within it – to suggest the presence of social distinctions amongst its inhabitants, but these are all set within a level-topped, cliff-edged plateau overlooking agricultural land, with much of the perimeter not requiring any supplementary artificial defence. Such steep-edged upland plateaux providing good natural defence were amongst the favoured locations for early, later Bronze Age, defences in southern Germany, where the intermittent lengths of wall required to seal off individual points of easier access are referred to as *Abschnittswälle*. In these, detached lengths of walling are built solely where natural defence was considered insufficient. Sites broadly similar in the layout of their defences, however, occur elsewhere, where the topography allows: there are, for example, good instances around Mont Sainte Victoire in Provence, such as the 5ha hill-fort of Bayon, which is bordered almost entirely by natural cliffs.

This tradition of edging blocks of upland reaches its apogee in west-central Europe at gigantic sites such as the Heidengraben in south-west Germany. The surviving defences here take the form of both short, isolated lengths of wall, and other more extensive stretches, some punctuated with gates in recognisable Late La Tène style, the whole defining an area in excess of 1,000ha, making this site a strong claimant to be the largest Continental *oppidum* presently known. Of rather earlier date, apparently, is another 'grossraumige Naturfestung mit Abschnittsbefestigungen', translatable as the 'massive natural defensive position with isolated lengths of wall'. This site is attributable to the Hallstatt Iron Age and occupies the plateau around Ferschweiler (Kreis Bitburg-Prüm) in the Eifel of western Germany (*7*). Extending to some 2,575ha, this site dwarfs even the Heidengraben. Such locations can naturally provide particularly conspicuous landscape features: Ecce Homo, in Castile-La Mancha at Alcalá de Henares outside Madrid, is a good example. Where geology provided terrain with similarly suitable characteristics in Britain, these too were used: the biggest fort on the island of Arran in the Firth of Clyde for example, at Drumadoon, occupies a block of land edged by a fossil cliff of basaltic columns on the west of the island.

Cliffs were not the only geological features from which the builders of hill-forts were prepared to profit. Natural outcrops, such as tors, and massive erratics were also incorporated into defensive circuits, a trait far from unique to Europe; for example, if one considers the lengths of walling between rock outcrops at Great Zimbabwe

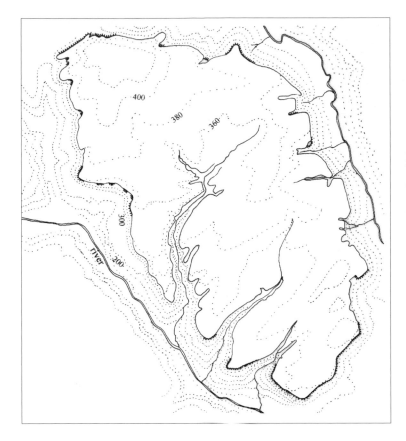

7 The Ferschweiler plateau, near Trier, Germany, is intermittently edged by a fortification, making it one of the most extensive enclosed sites in western Europe. It extends for approximately 8km north–south, and is on average about 4km broad. *Drawn by Samantha Dennis after Koch and Schindler 1994, plan 84*

and equivalent sites in southern Africa. In Scotland, craggy summits seem to have been particularly favoured during the first millennium AD, giving rise to a suite of complex enclosures normally termed either 'nucleated' or, slightly more sinisterly, 'nuclear forts'. It is sometimes suggested that such forts in their developed forms, characterised by a series of overlapping enclosures generally delimiting small, levellish patches of ground, splaying off downslope from a central 'citadel', provided a distinctive architectural mirror for the Early Historic period societies that originally created them. Even in Scotland, however, occupation of such locations was not confined to the first millennium AD. Dunadd, in Argyll, for example, long equated with the capital of the Scoti in the seventh and neighbouring centuries AD and a celebrated example of this class, also has unambiguous indications of pre-Roman Iron Age occupation (*colour plate 6*). Much of the interior of another Scottish site, the Mither Tap o' Bennachie in Aberdeenshire, is occupied by a bare granitic tor, with the main crescentic wall that defines this site backing onto subsidiary natural outcrops. Such tors occur within forts elsewhere, as at St Vaury in Creuse (Limousin), central France. Massive natural granite outcrops also framed the principal gateway at the Breton site of Huelgoat in Finistère, dug by Sir Mortimer Wheeler and apparently the principal *oppidum* of the *Osismi*.

Amongst other topographic locations selected for sites are ridges – where forts may sit on their summits, sometimes astride routeways running along these crests – and hill-slope positions. The latter seem to be particularly characteristic of south-west England, where they were the subject of a special study by the late Lady Aileen Fox.

Compared to all the sites considered above, where the lines of enclosure are generally well fitted to the terrain in which they are set, there are other hill-forts which are not so adapted, or at least much less clearly so. In the north of Britain, a classic series is offered by the oblong, gateless forts predominantly found in eastern Scotland, mostly north of the Tay estuary; many of these have stone-built walls which show extensive signs of vitrification, and they are considered further in a later chapter. For present purposes, however, the particular interest of these sites is the regularity of their plans (compounded by their absence of gateways). The rationale for the oblong shape may have been the use of straight lengths of timber laid horizontally in the internal timber framework contained within their lines of fortification, but the long, narrowish outline is retained even when a variant on it would have produced a much more readily defensible configuration. Thus at Finavon in Angus, a site first examined by Gordon Childe in the 1930s, one side of the enclosure is set back from the conglomerate cliff edging the site by several metres, whereas if the wall had been placed much closer to this feature the creation of a band of 'dead ground' (invisible to the site's inhabitants) at the foot of the cliff in the immediate vicinity would have been avoided.

Elsewhere, there are also concentrations of sites that are broadly of regular form, either rectilinear or curvilinear, seemingly regardless of the terrain on which they were set. Examples can be seen in particular in southern France, in bastioned single-walled enclosures like Le Fort at Taradeau, Var (*8*), set on the hill-edge some 20km

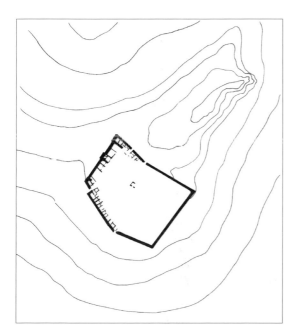

8 The geometric outline (with bastions) of the site of Le Fort at Taradeau, Var, is not closely adapted to the terrain on which it sits. *Drawn by Samantha Dennis after Brun et al. 1993*

inland from the Mediterranean coast at Saint Tropez. It will thus be abundantly clear to the reader that, whilst it is possible to sketch broad generalities in regard to the emplacement and form of sites in the landscape, local traditions and particular topographies are always likely to throw up variants on, or exceptions to, such schemes. A case is offered by the sites generally known as *castallaras* in the upland portion of the Alpes-Maritimes, where a wide range of dry-stone built enclosures, of very varying size and strength, but of which a high proportion are multivallate (perhaps here related to the Ligurian adoption of sling warfare) have survived in the pastoral landscapes especially at altitudes of 1,000m or above (Bretaudeau 1996).

Another noteworthy local series of sites, where the form of their enclosures relative to their settings seems to indicate a particular fashion that does not entirely conform to the configuration of the local topography, lies along the valley of the Viroin, a tributary of the Meuse set along the Franco-Belgian border, not far from the Grand Duchy of Luxembourg. Here, the river flows in a series of deeply-cut meanders, providing a series of steep-sided spurs suitable for fortification. Alongside a set of normal promontory forts, the Viroin also contains a series of enclosures termed *éperons tronqués* in French. In these, a line of rampart-and-ditch drawn, as is normal, across the easiest access from the neighbouring plateau, is matched towards the point of the promontory by a second line facing in the opposite direction, the effect in each case being to isolate a segment of some 2–3ha on the upper surface of the promontory, and calculatedly stopping short of the natural break-of-slope at its apex. The best-known example is the Plateau des Cinkes at Olloy-sur-Viroin (province of Namur, Belgium: *9*).

A further instance where the fit between the configuration of the topography and the position of the enclosure line sometimes departs from usual practice can be seen in some of the Late Iron Age *oppida* of west-central Europe. At Mont Beuvray, for example, much of the circuit of the inner, later, fortification conforms pretty closely to the various facets of the massif on which that line, over 5km long, is set. But this practice is not universally followed around the circuit, and at one point, adjacent to the gateway of the Porte du Rebout, the rampart suddenly plunges steeply downslope, apparently to include the headwaters of a stream within the circuit. On the more recently identified outer circuit at this site, which extends to some 10km in overall length, there are equally points where the wall-line runs at a sharp angle to the contour; building stable works in such settings must have posed particular problems. An even steeper section of wall, with all the problems of engineering stability that this would entail, is also apparent crashing across the contours on the Hungarian *oppidum* site at Velem Sankt Vid, on the western margin of that country (*10*). In this instance, the rationale for the decision over the route taken by the wall is not clear. The western German *oppidum* of Heidetränk-Talenge at Oberursel-Oberstedten (Hessen) in the Hoch-Taunus takes similar practices to an extreme. Here a reading of the site plan makes it plain that the key intention was to envelop twin hills (with summits at *c.*575m and 492m) on either side of the valley of a minor stream, and the need to achieve this meant giving precedence to that aim

9 Ridge-forts in southern Belgium: 1: Hanonet at Couvin 2: Camp Romain at Lompret 3: Les Cinkes at Olloy-sur-Viroin. *Drawn by Jem Heinemeier after Doyen and Warembol in Cahen-Delhaye* et al. *1984*

10 A section through the western defence, a timber-laced wall with stone-built wall-faces, of the *oppidum* at Velem Sankt Vid, near Sombathely, Hungary, demonstrating how this fortification and its accompanying ditch run steeply across the contours in a tradition that seems to be restricted to a few of the late, large *oppida* of continental Europe

over more routine defensive considerations. Much of this complex 130ha enclosure is thus bordered by lines of walling that drop across the contours towards the stream course from higher points on both sides.

Hill-forts can thus occupy very varied settings. In terms of altitude, these extend from slight rises within undulating low-lying landscapes, as in parts of the north European plain, to low promontories right on the coastal edge, as at the Castro de Baroña on the coast of Galicia in north-western Spain, to sites located at altitudes well above those at which settlement occurs at the present time. Such conspicuously high eminence sites in the British Isles extend from northern Scotland to County Kerry; and others occur on the Continent. These high eminence sites include examples certainly located at too high an altitude for routine habitation. A classic instance of this is Ben Griam Beg in Sutherland, on a mountain top near the junction of two significant valleys: the Strath of Kildonan and Strath Halladale. At an altitude of some 600m in northern Scotland, its outline is now, unsurprisingly, distorted by soil creep and other active periglacial processes (Chapter 9: *11*). The use of such austere locations, and the investigation of other sites which demonstrate little evidence for permanent settlement, has led to the suggestion that some of these sites were impermanent, and solely used as refuges as and when the need arose.

11 A vertical photograph of Ben Griam Beg, Sutherland, showing the distortion of the wall lines due to soil creep and similar processes. *Courtesy: the late Richard Feachem*

In many instances the site chosen for a hill-fort seems to represent a trade off between selecting a reasonably prominent and defensible location on the one hand, and choosing somewhere that could be effectively enclosed with relatively little effort on the other. And in some cases, the setting of particular hill-fort defences rather suggests that defence was far from being a primary consideration. In the case of late *oppida*, this often seems to be the case. At Mont Beuvray, for example, the combination of a number of factors very much suggests that a concern for defence was far from uppermost in the minds of those who commissioned the 15km or so of ramparts around the hill (see Chapter 9). As has been noted, sectors of the *murus gallicus*-style defence drop steeply across the contours of the hill, and this fact combined with the observation — as will be argued below — that the constructional style was already obsolescent militarily when it was built, are key indicators that pure defence was not the aim. Further, there are indications from the vicinity of the Porte du Rebout, the main excavated gate on the inner circuit, that parts of the wall were, if not jerry-built, certainly less than well constructed, perhaps too an indication that permanence and solidity were also not amongst the builders' priorities. At Beuvray, too, the character of the entranceway through the gate (discussed below) itself tends to emphasise a non-defensive agenda; it is nearly 20m wide. All these characteristics suggest that other considerations — prestige or sheer showiness, or simply a conspicuous boundary to delimit the jurisdiction of the local elite — may have been uppermost in the minds of those who commissioned such enclosures.

Similar issues of defensibility have been raised by the nature of the elaborate mid-sixth century BC mud-brick wall at the Heuneburg (Herbertingen-Hundersingen, Baden-Wurttemburg), although here in a less pressing form. It is frequently suggested that the materials and constructional details of these walls shows a less-than-complete assimilation of Mediterranean practices. In this instance, however, the evidence is somewhat ambiguous. Mud-brick, albeit a far from usual building material in temperate Europe, is perhaps not as rare as it appeared when the Heuneburg evidence was first identified. The packing together of projecting bastions — an unusual feature and designed to allow the defenders overlapping fields of fire — on the north side of the wall would not have rendered them inoperational, but would simply have required more defenders than had they been spaced further apart (see Chapter 9). Contrastingly, a famous Scottish case is slightly more contentious. This is the little multivallate fort at The Chesters, Drem, East Lothian, occupying a slight eminence above the neighbouring agricultural plain (*colour plate 7*), but dominated on its southern side by a more conspicuous ridge at least arguably within range for missile warfare. Here it may be argued that the advantages and limitations of a new-fangled defensive style had not been fully comprehended. But there are cases where the choice of site location — even allowing for subsequent erosion — gives rise to positions that are entirely overlooked and thus largely seem to escape any rational justification: on the western coastline of the Mull of Galloway in south-west Scotland, for example, are tiny promontory forts such as Dunorroch (*colour plate 8*), set well below the main cliff line that is almost immediately adjacent to them. These seem to make absolutely no sense as defensive locales.

SURROUNDING LANDSCAPES

Hill-forts have often been considered in relation to their neighbouring landscapes in terms of economic production, with the terrain surrounding them being assessed in terms of its potential, whether as arable land or as pasture, to produce foodstuffs or other resources for consumption by the population. This subject is not tackled here, since it is tangential to this enquiry. Other considerations related to past human perceptions of hill-fort sites, and especially regarding the positioning of their ramparts, can be formulated from a consideration of their surrounding landscapes, however, and a small selection of examples are rehearsed to illustrate something of the possibilities. The premise to be investigated is that the precise setting of the defences in the local topography may have messages to convey.

One major issue that has attracted attention in recent years is the extent to which the interiors of hill-forts were visible to people in the surrounding landscape. From a purely military perspective, it might be argued that it would be to the defending commandant's advantage if the deployment of the forces at his disposal could not be witnessed by those outside the fort. Had such considerations been uppermost when the defensive line was laid out, it would be reasonable to suppose that it might be placed as far upslope as feasible, consistent with other requirements, in order to restrict the field of vision within the fort as far as was possible to those located outside it. Contrastingly, in other instances, it is possible to argue that the enclosure line or lines are set further downslope than might otherwise be anticipated (e.g. placement at the military crest) and in this instance it can be hypothesised that the aim was precisely the contrary: that it was a deliberate intention that people outwith the fort but in its vicinity would be able to see activities going on within the hill-fort, even if they were not expected or perhaps permitted directly to participate in them (*12*). Mark Bowden and David McOmish (1989) have not only suggested that the visibility of the hill-fort interior from without decreases its defensiveness, but also that the placing of rampart-lines well downslope means that internal areas are out of sight of a defensive commander.

Sue Hamilton and John Manley, who have studied the hill-forts of south-east England from such a perspective, suggest that at certain periods within the Iron Age issues such of visibility are particularly relevant to the exact positioning of hill-forts and their defences. At some periods within the Iron Age, forts seem to have been located so as to be intervisible, as in the South Downs in the Early Iron Age. Middle Iron Age forts tend to have their usually univallate circuits placed sufficiently far downslope that the intention was to 'monumentalize rather than strategically obscure the hillfort interiors' (2001, 26). It can also be argued that certain activities going on within these sites were preferentially located so as to enable people outside to witness, albeit remotely, what was happening. In the case of the small South Downs hill-fort at the Caburn (near Lewes in Sussex) in the centuries around 300 BC, for example, they note that the internal area marked by the concentration of pits with the most ritually charged 'special deposits' are placed at the highest and most conspicuous locations within the site (*13*). Intervisibility between hill-forts seems to

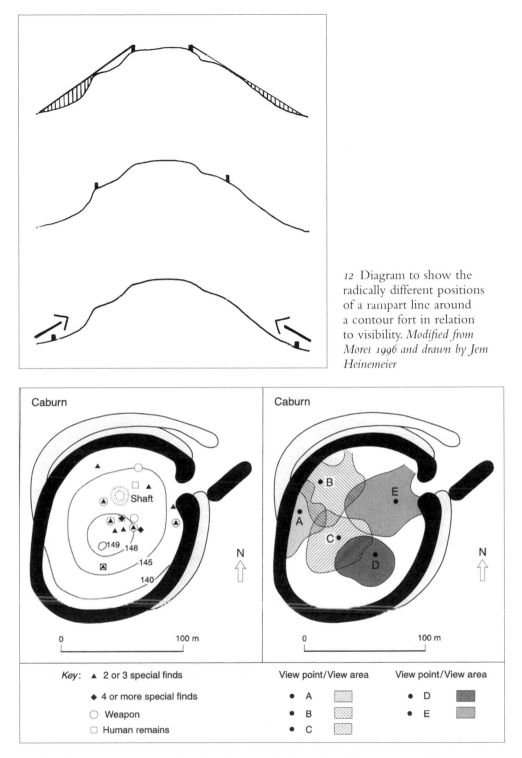

12 Diagram to show the radically different positions of a rampart line around a contour fort in relation to visibility. *Modified from Moret 1996 and drawn by Jem Heinemeier*

13 The Caburn, East Sussex: Sue Hamilton's definition of visibility zones within the site in relation to special finds. *By permission of Sue Hamilton after Hamilton and Manley 2001*

have been unimportant by this period, and by the final stages of the Iron Age the pattern of preferred locations in relation to visibility is again different. As with so many aspects of hill-forts, there is thus no single unchanging rule for such siting issues that can readily be transferred across space or through time. More work clearly needs to be done on such matters: it is noteworthy elsewhere, for instance in west-central Europe, that numbers of hoards have been identified in particular locations within certain enclosed sites, and it would be interesting to test the relevance of hypotheses of this kind in their case. The Bleibeskopf near Bad Nauheim in the Hoch-Taunus is a Late Bronze Age example, with several hoards notably deposited just within the wall-line (Buchsenschutz and Ralston, in press).

There is inevitably a speculative tinge to such broadly phenomenological viewpoints on the positioning of hill-fort defences. Other dimensions of relating hill-forts and the alignments of their fortifications around the hills on which they are set can be noted. For example, the three highest hill-forts in Scotland, Ben Griam Beg (Sutherland), Tap o' Noth (Aberdeenshire) and Mither Tap o' Bennachie (Aberdeenshire) are all on isolated hills of more-or-less the same form. Each is marked by a conspicuously long ridge, with a prominent summit at one end: all have enclosures placed solely around these summits. In the case of Mither Tap, the main entrance to the fort faces away from the ridge; in the case of the other two the original entrance positions are unclear. In all three instances it is possible to argue that the arrangement may have been a deliberate one: to spectators in the neighbouring lowlands people who had visibly processed along the neighbouring ridge would disappear from view once they accessed the hill-fort: certainly in the case of the oblong summit fort at Tap o' Noth, though not in the case of its outer enclosure; and also too in the case of the much less substantial dry-stone wall around the top of Ben Griam Beg. The huge granite tor that occupies much of the interior of the Mither Tap enclosure suggests a rather different arrangement, although here too figures immediately inside the wall-line of the massively built dry-stone enclosure would not have been apparent to anyone looking towards the summit from the low country round about.

Another way of relating hill-forts to their surrounding landscapes is to consider the orientation of their entrances. From a prosaic point of view, entrance positions might be placed to give readiest access to routeways, or to particular resources in the vicinity of the site. They might also be positioned with defensive considerations in mind. But, in some cases, notably in southern Britain, such prosaic, site-specific explanations seem unsatisfactory. In this region, it has been noted, particularly for the earlier centuries of the Iron Age, that entrances on forts seem fairly standardly to be positioned to the east and west, irrespective of the factors outlined above. In such cases, orientation relative to the sun may be important, and beyond that, wider issues of cosmology. In other cases, it is suggested that gates are positioned with regard to other significant features in the landscape. At Traprain Law, East Lothian, for example, it is argued that the main entrance on the north side of the inner defence is oriented directly on another neighbouring major fort, crowning the conspicuous

14 Kinpurney Hill, Angus. The inturned entrance to this large, unfinished fort in the Sidlaw Hills frames Schiehallion on the skyline

conical volcanic plug of North Berwick Law. Another comparable instance, which seems particularly telling to the present author, concerns an unfinished major fort on Kinpurney Hill in the Sidlaw Hills of Angus (*14*). Here, just about the only feature to be reasonably defined by earthworks, in a project seemingly abandoned at an early stage, is an entrance which frames the conspicuous mountain of Schiehallion – the name translating as 'the fairy hill of the *Caledonii*'.

3

THE ARCHITECTURE OF HILL-FORT DEFENCES

A number of markedly different styles of construction, using a variety of materials, can be recognised in hill-fort defences at the European scale. The basic, common feature inherent in this class of monument is the presence of one or more lines of rampart or wall, with or without a fronting ditch or ditches. The number of circuits of these works – whether enveloping much of a hilltop in the case of a contour fort, or simply drawn across the most straightforward access to a promontory – is one of the key elements, along with the size of the contained area, used in classification systems of them. For some – ones now set in pasture or found within woodland, and lacking any obvious above-ground evidence for internal structures – they may be the only information readily to be had without excavation. In English usage, a basic distinction is drawn between univallate, bivallate or multivallate enclosures, delimited respectively by single, double or multiple lines of enclosure. There are, however, complications in the operation of what seems a very straightforward system.

A key problem confronting the inquisitive visitor and the archaeological surveyor alike is that what is now apparent on the surface of any given site may never have functioned as a unitary system. The pattern of enclosure now apparent may represent accretion over time. There is plentiful evidence that individual hill-forts have complicated biographies, and were in some cases constructed, used and modified over several centuries. This period could extend from pre-Roman through to, in some areas at least, late Roman or post-Roman times. There are thus instances where enclosed sites might be reused after extended intervening periods during which they were left without serviceable defences, or when they were entirely abandoned. The recently published southern English site of South Cadbury (Somerset: Barrett *et al.* 2000) provides good indications of the potentially long sequences that may be involved including, in the case of this example, major episodes of fortification from early in the Iron Age, and further significant construction of defences marking the middle and later first millennium AD (Alcock 1995). It is thus clear that the lines of enclosure around a fort such as South Cadbury, which surface fieldwork might suggest as a unitary multivallate work marked by several contemporary lines of banks and ditches, may actually be the result of the accretion of several building episodes, none of which individually saw more than (say) a couple of defensive lines in commission.

Faced with trying to interpret an unexcavated fort with complex earthworks, the wise field-working archaeologist most probably starts from the premise that what is visible on the surface now is the product of several constructional periods, rather than adopting as the default that all that can be presently seen originally functioned contemporarily as a single unit. That said, there are, as ever, exceptions. Multivallate fortifications may thus have been erected to a single concept, over a short period of time (and it is sometimes suggested that their construction was directly linked to new attack technologies discussed elsewhere in this book); but in other cases they can be the outcome of a number of building episodes.

Simply from surface inspection, for instance, it is possible to envisage that there are major differences in the forms (for this purpose the scale of the enclosing works is irrelevant) of multivallation apparent on different sites. Two contrasting British examples, Maiden Castle in Dorset (*colour plate 9*), and the Brown Caterthun in Angus, highlight such differences. In the former, the crests of all the rampart lines generally run parallel with each other for much of the circuit, and the entrance gaps offer a coherent means of crossing the entire system, as well as opportunities for misleading or trapping the unwary incomer because of the elaboration of their overall plan. Contrastingly, the plan of the Brown Caterthun, equally multivallate since it is surrounded by even more lines of enclosure than is Maiden Castle, suggests that not all the systems of ramparts around this hill formed part of a single scheme. This is apparent because they vary in character from the single line faintly marked close to the summit to the outermost, incomplete and arguably unfinished, line. That there are multiple building episodes in this case is also readily apparent from the numerous entranceways – surprisingly many for a hill-fort – leading towards the interior of the site. Not all of these are aligned; not all run through all the circuits. Excavations directed by Andrew Dunwell confirm that the relatively slight defences surrounding this hilltop enclosure are the end result of several distinct phases of activity extending over a substantial part of the Iron Age. A useful rule of thumb, since surface appearances can also be deceptive, is thus to believe that all systems of hill-fort defences are likely to be complex until and unless they are proved simple, a process normally only possible by excavation.

Amongst the distinguished professors who developed the study of the British Iron Age in the generation after the Second World War, Christopher Hawkes was arguably the most significant in regard to the development of hill-fort studies, and in particular the architecture of hill-fort defences. Leaving to one side his own important fieldwork at St Catherine's Hill near Winchester and elsewhere, the Oxford professor made a number of important contributions to the understanding of such sites. A good case can be constructed that his 1931 paper in the journal *Antiquity* marks the baseline from which modern studies of this site type have developed: although heavily conditioned by the perceived importance of external links then in vogue as a way of explaining the architectural changes he noted, this article provided a new critical overview of the southern British evidence at least.

In terms of the architecture of hill-fort defences, however, his key paper was that written for the Festschrift for Sir Mortimer Wheeler in 1970. By now he was writing on a bigger canvas, and considering Continental as well as British examples. The first three words of its title – 'Fence, wall, dump…' encompass the fundamental variables in the architecture of Iron Age defences. Or, at least, the fundamental variables that are archaeologically recoverable – since, for example, thorn hedges, whether planted or laid, would generally be extremely hard to detect archaeologically. If the latter seem an unlikely component of the Iron Age record, it is perhaps worth recalling that in nineteenth-century India the British erected and then on a number of occasions realigned a great thorn hedge (Moxham 2001) ultimately well over 1000 miles in length: originally this may have been cut and laid, but subsequently considerably lengths of it were apparently planted. Abandoned in mid-Victorian times, little of it is apparently now detectable, and this folly probably represented the longest example of a tradition of the use of hedges in the control of access and defence that was also present in early medieval times (Nicholson 2004). In general hedges, such a significant element of boundaries in more recent Britain, are little considered in discussions (e.g. Collis 1996) of the significance of enclosure in later prehistory. Examples have, however, been postulated, notably in the case of the later Iron Age enclosed, probably sanctuary, site at Fison Way, Thetford, Norfolk, where eight are proposed (Gregory 1992).

A general theme in the literature has been to try to relate changes in architectural styles to developments in attack technologies, suggesting for hill-forts, as with the *enceintes* of ancient Near Eastern cities, Crusader castles, or indeed the now-redundant defences from the Cold War, that study of the defences constructed allows the nature of the threat to be gauged. In the case of Iron Age hill-forts, the use of fire, sling warfare, javelins and other projectiles, battering rams, and the Roman employment of artillery, have all been invoked, as will be discussed below. It would be premature to discount such factors in impacting on the form of defences; it would, however, be equally unrealistic to see such a consideration as being utterly dominant in conditioning their form. Such factors of course would help account for apparently sudden changes, since innovations in styles of attack may quickly impact on the technologies of defence, but frequently the evidence is not clear-cut, especially given the relatively coarse-grained chronological control that typifies later prehistory. We may also surmise that, in this, as with other military changes, responses may become disproportionate to the apparent threat. Although it is now apparent that hill-fort defences served other purposes as well as, or indeed instead of, defence, the military dimension of these sites may still be ignored at our peril, even if its centrality to present-day thinking is much less than when it was cogently described by Wheeler (1952, 74):

> Let us not forget that these fortifications are urgent things, dynamic reactions, possessing the anxious effort of men from age to age in a foredoomed struggle to keep pace technically and tactically with the changing art of attack. They have, often enough,

little to do with the less instant and more local vagaries of brooches and crockery, with the petty wanderings of tribesmen and traffickers.

Such non-military considerations are here held over for discussion in subsequent chapters, but that is not to belittle their significance.

PALISADES

Of the recognised features of later prehistoric fortifications, the fence is the most straightforward to envisage and to discuss. More usually styled 'palisades' in the English literature, or occasionally 'stockades' when the topographic setting in which they are identified means that their originally defensive function is more clear-cut, the usual archaeological trace of such features is the negative, below-ground trench, or series of individual post-holes, in which the vertical timbers were placed (*colour plate 10*). In most areas it is this reliance on pre-dug slots, into which the earthfast timbers were set, and then the posts sometimes chocked with packing stones, that gives these features their continuing archaeological visibility.

Palisaded enclosures are known from the Neolithic onwards, with lines of wooden fencing representing some of the earliest enclosures or fortifications known, from the Languedoc of southern France to Denmark (Varndell & Topping 2002; Delétang 1999 for aerial photographs of French examples). They are, however, also a feature of the first millennium BC where often, but by no means universally, they surround some of the earliest enclosed sites of later prehistory in several regions. Some of these places subsequently developed rather more elaborate defensive enclosures, either incorporating or entirely replacing the palisade, during this period. In upland settings, in areas of particularly intractable rock, palisades may have been set in small upcast banks rather than fixed into below-ground slots containing packing-stones, but such arrangements are likely to have been less sturdy from the outset. They are also less likely to have survived centuries of subsequent attrition. Palisades also occur in some other settings: they edge some of the first millennium BC lake-margin sites in the Swiss lakes, and here their function may have been partially defensive, but it is equally likely that they served as breakwaters (*brise-lames* in French terminology). Palisades and fences are also used in other, subsidiary roles on later prehistoric sites, for example as stock enclosures and as internal subdivisions within settlements, as has already been noted at the Goldberg in Germany, and is apparent too in the rock-cut negative features within the fully excavated promontory site at Altburg-bei-Bundenbach near Trier. Such uses are not considered further here. At later times, in particular circumstances, lighter enclosure might again become appropriate, so it is not surprising to find palisades still used on first millennium AD enclosed sites. Single palisades achieve the basic function of clearly separating within from without by a vertical feature that is relatively simple to construct. They do not generally provide an adjacent elevated fighting platform (as is the case with wall-heads) from

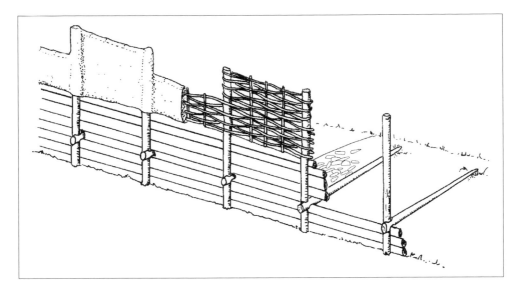

15 The first defence at la Chesle de Bérismenil in the Belgian Ardennes (La Roche-en-Ardenne, Luxembourg province), datable to about the fifth century BC, shows an all-timber face with its vertical elements tied back into a small bank to the rear. *Drawn by Samantha Dennis after Papeleux and de Boe 1988*

which defenders can dominate attackers, unless they were accompanied by an adjacent level-topped bank, as is proposed in some instances (*15*). Their durability is determined largely by that of the species of timber of which they are constructed, with the wood at the ground surface – particularly likely to get repeatedly wet and then to dry out – perhaps especially prone to rotting and decay.

In numbers of cases, notably in the Anglo-Scottish Borders but also elsewhere in Britain, twin palisades, marked archaeologically by two parallel slots usually set around 1m apart, have been recognised: quite how such arrangements functioned in practice may be interpreted in a number of ways. If they were simply two parallel but independent palisades, the logic is that the outer one, perhaps intended to keep livestock – or indeed attackers – away from the more important inner line, may not have been as high as that on the inside. Although a rule-of-thumb frequently advanced is that one-third of the original length of an earthfast post may have been buried in the ground, there seems every likelihood that this concept was never applied strictly in prehistory. The present writer does not know of any cases where the outer of two palisades seems incontrovertibly to have held a slighter stockade than its inner pair. One practical problem ensuing from twin palisaded arrangements is that the narrow gap between the two sets of posts, if open to the sky, must have been prone to colonisation by opportunistic vegetation such as weeds and would have been difficult to access for cleaning.

It is thus possible that in at least some instances the two continuous slots originally marked not the lines of two essentially separate palisades, but rather the front and back vertical faces of narrow timber-built walls. Whereas a spacing of less than 2m between the palisade lines is usually taken to indicate twinned palisades, measurements in excess of this figure are contrastingly interpreted as the positions of the front and rear facings of narrow timber-framed walls, sometimes termed 'box ramparts' in England: amongst the earliest and slightest of the latter was that encountered on the fort of Ivinghoe Beacon (Buckinghamshire) in the Chilterns.

Palisade lines can also be confused with marker trenches in surface inspection; the latter are features usually linked to the setting-out of fortifications and discussed below in relation to unfinished forts (Chapter 4). On excavation, the former might be anticipated to hold chocking stones to maintain vertical timbers in position, whereas the latter would not. But there are cases where the two functions can become confused, particularly where palisades are subsequently replaced by more substantial works. At Braidwood, Midlothian, for example, Piggott suggested the construction of a wall with a timber face, otherwise very rare in the north of Britain; further work at this site suggests the timberwork was more likely to represent a palisade line that had been enveloped within the subsequent wall constructed on the same alignment.

WALLS

Narrow box ramparts of the kind just mentioned would thus represent some of the slightest examples of a large family of temperate European fortification types, comprising walls with vertical or near-vertical external faces, and in some cases a similar feature on their inner margin (but in some cases a sloping ramp). Many of the most elaborate of these are composite constructions employing a range of materials. Infilled with rubble, earth, clay or other fine material, stone and timber were used in varying combinations and in varying conditions for the wall-faces: the whole series can be grouped as 'wall-and-fill' constructions (*16*).

Stone might be either surface-gathered or quarried and sometimes roughly shaped; whereas timber was either used as roundwood, sometimes with the bark still adhering, or shaped into beams or planks. In some instances there is evidence of jointing in the timberwork. In all cases, although most critically (for the issue of dating) in the case of timber, this might be reused material.

The varieties of walls built of these three materials (in German known as *Stein-Holz-Erdemauer*) offer an almost bewildering complexity in terms of the details of their architecture (*16*). In the modern world we have grown used to very considerable similarities in buildings over greater and greater distances; in the ancient world local idiosyncracies in constructional styles seem likely to have been much more common, making it possible to argue that similar materials were deployed slightly differently almost on a site-by-site basis.

Walls using these three materials occur widely in temperate European later prehistory, occurring certainly in areas known to have been peopled by Celtic speakers, as well as others – east across the Dacian sphere (*17*, Glodariu 1983) to areas near the Black

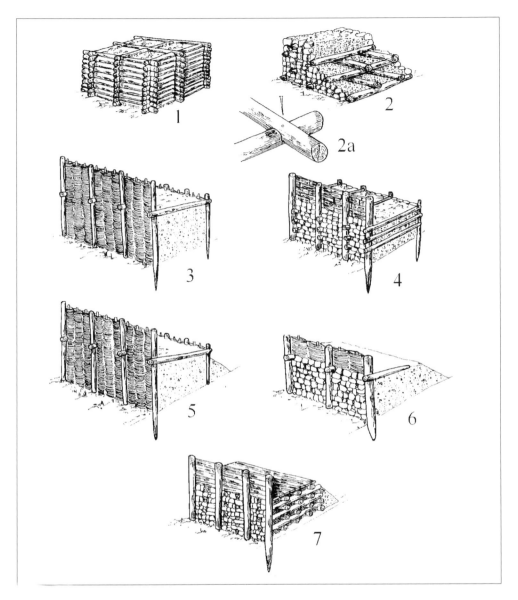

16 Isometric drawings of various styles of wood, earth and dry-stone walls found in the temperate European Iron Age. 1: *Kastenbau* type; 2: Horizontal timber lacing penetrating front and rear dry-stone faces, the Ehrang type; a variant (2a) has long iron spikes inserted, probably in augered holes and is called the *murus gallicus*; 3: box rampart with earthfast vertical timbers in front and rear faces and timber/wattlework face; 4: box rampart of Altkönig-Preist type with transversal beams linking front and rear vertical timbers, termed *Pfostenschlitzmauer* in German terminology; 5: Hod Hill variant of box rampart – the rear timbers are no longer earthfast, and an internal sloping ramp has been added; 6: the Kelheim type – vertical timbers and panels of stonework in the external face, but the transversals no longer anchored into the ground; an internal sloping ramp is usually present; 7: the elaborate wall at the Cathedral Hill, Basle, Switzerland, combines traditions with horizontal timber-lacing and vertical posts in the outer wall face. *Drawn by Gordon Thomas from Ralston 1995*

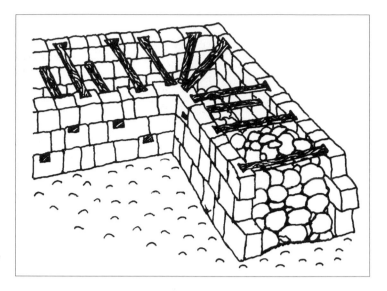

17 A late version of a wall with internal timberwork: the 'Dacian wall'. *Drawn by Jem Heinemeier after Glodariu 1983*

Sea, and west to the southern half of Portugal – where they are unlikely to have been present. There are numerous examples in the British Isles, in parts of which broadly similar styles of walls continued to be constructed well into the first millennium AD, as they did in Slavic areas of the Continent. Nor are at least some of the architectural forms that have been recognised completely innovations of the last millennium BC; some types have pedigrees – although usually not incontrovertible evidence of continuous development – stretching back to the Neolithic period. An example was excavated by Roger Mercer at Hambeldon Hill, Dorset, for instance, whereas the central French Late Neolithic site of les Châtelliers at Moulins-sur-Céphons in Berry has a wall with an elaborate horizontal timber framework, datable to the later third millennium BC, and architecturally close to much later – Late Bronze Age and Iron Age – sites in central and east-central Europe. This is the *Kastenbau* type, as known, for example, at Biskupin in Poland and the Wittnauer Horn in Switzerland. Further variants have been recognised in excavations in particular in the former East Germany and Poland (*18*). That said, there are parts of temperate Europe where the use of timber in defences is rare, albeit not absent, during the Iron Age: Ireland on present evidence falls into this category, as does much of the Iberian peninsula.

The Mediterranean coastlands of Southern France also fit into this set of regions where sites with structural timberwork in their defences are remarkable for their rarity. Examples do none the less occur, occasionally with timber deployed in elaborate arrangements not readily to be paralleled elsewhere: the recently-excavated Peuch de Mus at Sainte-Eulalie-de-Cernon in the Languedoc region of southern France provides some exceptional evidence from the fifth century BC (*19*, Gruat *et al.* 2003). Such areas where a few sites markedly do not conform to local patterns are an intimation that the will of individual members of past elites needs to be superimposed on the search for architectural generalisations.

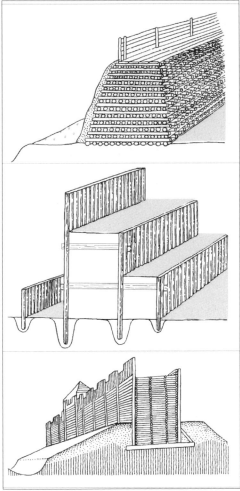

18 Left: Timber-built walls of the end of the Bronze Age and the Early Iron Age in the former East Germany and Poland. From top: *Rostbau* construction, essentially of horizontal logs: Podrosche, Kreis Weisswater, occupied in the Early Iron Age, Herrmann 1989 C16; Vertical timbers deployed in solid faces (German: Palisaden-Schalbauweise) of ultimate Bronze Age at Lübbenau, Kreis Calau; and *Kastenbau* construction at Biskupin, Poland. *Drawn by Karen Clarke after Herrmann 1989*

19 Below: One of the reconstructions proposed for the rapidly evolving fifth century BC fortifications at the plateau-edge fort of Peuch de Mus (Ste Eulalie, Aveyron), comprising an external wall with horizontal timber-lacing and a sloping wall-head, backing onto a stone wall with separate vertical timber face. Such an arrangement, unknown in temperate Europe, intimates that considerable variability in defences remains to be discovered. *Drawn by Samantha Dennis after Gruat* et al. *2003*

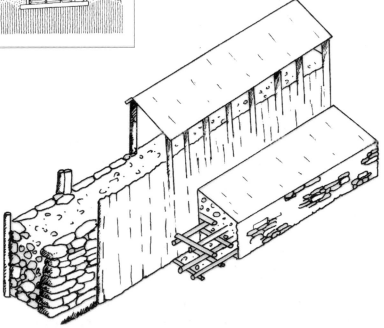

What are the key components of the architecture of such fortifications? It is usual to first consider the external wall-face, since it seems that this was the key element of these walls – that first encountered by outsiders whether hostile in intention or not. Such wall-faces are normally dry-stone-built, but can have set into them vertical posts (their former presence detectable from the existence of generally regularly-spaced post-holes on the alignment of the wall-face, and/or from slots running vertically up through the stone façade of the wall). In other instances, the timberwork within the wall is laid horizontally, often both transversally and longitudinally, and in these cases there may be a pattern of small rectilinear beam-holes, usually covered in each instance by a key-stone, apparent in the dry-stone wall-face, and representing the ends of the horizontal timbers which have long since rotted away. Walls with entirely timber-built facings are also known; these include some English 'box ramparts'; their width often helps distinguish them from the paired palisades considered above. Again these may be of individual timbers set vertically, or predominantly horizontally, it often being suggested that the latter styles are more common in areas where particular softwood tree species, especially conifers, were employed as structural elements (*16, 18*). Another conditioning factor in how the timber is deployed is the suitability of the locally-available stone for building façades; some less resistant rocks, notably chalk, may only be usable as hearting material. In some cases the horizontal timbers of the external wall-face form one side of timber casements, which can be fitted together using half-checks or other relatively simple lap-joints, the boxes so made being subsequently infilled with rubble or other detritus. It is likely that in many instances these external wall-faces were continued upwards into breastworks to protect defenders making use of the raised fighting platform provided by the wall, but the survival of the evidence for these is rare. More difficult to discern from excavation evidence is the frequency with which such exposed timberwork – clearly a fire risk – may have been covered with a skin of laid turves, though Michael Avery has argued for this on evidence from some southern British sites, notably Rainsborough in Northamptonshire.

The wall-cores normally consist of irregular rubble, earth, clay, sand, turf or other readily accessible materials, sometimes including recycled domestic rubbish. In some instances these materials seems to have been carefully packed and tamped down and thus rendered stable; in others, less so. The inclusion of some unexpected elements within wall-cores poses the question as to whether some constitute 'special deposits'. The recovery of human skeletal material in a few cases falls into this latter category, considered below in Chapter 6. The archaeological recovery of all such materials is, as will be appreciated, largely a matter of chance: rampart excavators may have a variety of hypotheses to test in selecting where they place their incisions into lines of fortification, but an anticipation of the contents of the core is generally not one of these. The recovery of such unpredictable deposits is thus all the more noteworthy.

In defensive styles where there are vertical posts in the outer wall-face, it is usually assumed that such posts would have had to be secured using horizontal wooden ties anchored into the core materials, but such transversal timbers, albeit logically required, can be very difficult to detect in excavation since in general they will have long since rotted away. The settling through time of the adjacent core materials can mean that there are no readily apparent 'negative ghosts' apparent in excavation, from which their former presence can be argued. In general, it has proved rather more straightforward to identify other styles of timber-using walls, where frameworks of longitudinal and transversal timbers were set horizontally within their wall-cores. These contributed to the strength and stability of the structures, and the significant quantities of wood sometimes involved assists in making the excavation evidence readable. Clearly, the existence of beam-holes in the façade of the wall provides an excellent indication of the former position of transversal timbers. Assuming the complete decay of the wood itself, other elements that may be detectable in excavation to help the archaeologist reconstitute the original form of the internal timberwork include changes in the constituency of the wall-fill, and the presence of lines of chocking or packing stones which may have contributed to holding the timbers in position as the wall-fill was progressively raised.

In some instances, too, particularly in defences dating to the very end of the pre-Roman Iron Age, the presence of iron nails may help considerably. In the most famous cases, these nails are iron spikes 20–30cm long, which must have originally been augered into the intersections of longitudinal and transversal timbers, but in other cases they are very much smaller nails which seem to have been related to a former use of the timber, which had been subsequently reused in the core of the wall. Despite the fact that the nails are thus essentially redeposited, they are none the less useful proxies indicating where pieces of wood had been laid within the wall-core. This indication that strengthening timbers in the cores of walls may have been reused is a salutary reminder that radiocarbon dates – or indeed dendrochronological determinations – obtained from such contexts are not necessarily securely related to the constructions in which their final use occurred.

In all these cases, it is clearly much simpler to discuss the timberwork where direct evidence of this has survived. In some circumstances, waterlogging may have intervened, and timbers maintained in anaerobic conditions are immensely helpful in making Iron Age structural arrangements much less ambiguous than is ever the case when archaeologists are forced to rely on the evidence provided by 'negative' traces, particularly within materials prone to settling, such as those employed in wall-cores.

The other helpful circumstance is where the immediate environment around timbers which have burnt in a conflagration is such that they have become wholly carbonised in the fire, whilst retaining their shape and in some instances other details such as evidence for jointing. Such indications of the woodworking capacities of Iron Age craftsmen as can be gleaned in these ways of course do not stand entirely alone, and support can be derived from other contemporary structures such as trackways across bogs, domestic architecture in which timber can also be well preserved (as around the margins of lakes and other water bodies), and bridges, perhaps most famously the collapsed structures at the site which gave the Second Iron Age of temperate Europe its name – La Tène on the Lac de Neuchâtel, Switzerland.

As a result of the number of cuttings that have now been made across such timber-framed and timber-laced walls, a wide range of structural variants have been recognised in use in later prehistory (*16, 18*), although by that period some types – as discussed above in relation to the *Kastenbau* type – had already acquired a considerable if discontinuous pedigree. Some examples in other styles also very definitely precede the Iron Age: for example, the wall of Nitriansky Hrádok in Slovakia, consisting of front and rear revetments of vertical timbers interspersed with panels of wattling, belongs early in the local Bronze Age cultural sequence. Margarita Primas (2002) has summarised the burgeoning evidence for Middle and Later Bronze Age wall-ramparts in Switzerland and central Europe, and examined an example with carbonised horizontal beams delimiting a 2.5ha promontory fort at Rhinsberg (Zurich canton, Switzerland). Although there are numerous exceptions, including the fort just cited, the broad pattern discernable amongst the excavated examples is that walls containing vertical timbers tied into their front wall-faces (and to a lesser extent the rear equivalents) tend to be central and eastern in Continental Europe and southern rather than northern within Britain, whereas walls with internal frameworks of longitudinal and transversal timbers are predominantly found to the west on the Continent, and are more common in the north than in southern Britain.

The earliest literary description of any of these is of interest, because it touches on various matters that will emerge during this survey. In the latter stages of his campaigns in Gaul in the first century BC, Julius Caesar gives us a famous account of the defence of the principal settlement of a central French tribe, the *Bituriges* (*de Bello gallico* Book VII, Chapter 23). He described a dry-stone-fronted wall, in which the beam-ends of the transversal elements of a horizontal internal timber framework were visible. These beams served to hold in place the wall-fill, consisting of earth and stone. This type of fortification has been named the *murus gallicus* (the term Caesar himself used = Gallic wall) and this has, since the 1860s, been recognised as a distinctive series constructed mostly during the first century BC and, in some instances, the preceding century. Especially numerous in non-Mediterranean France,

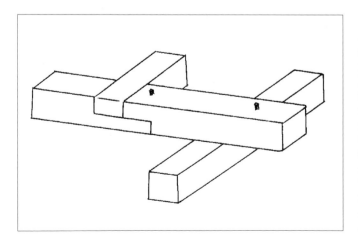

20 At the *oppidum* of Murcens (Lot), Buchsenschutz and Mercadier were able to recover detail of the wall construction, including inferentially the presence of jointing in the timberwork of the *murus gallicus*; nails were added as required to increase stability. *Drawn by Samantha Dennis after* Aquitania 7 1989, fig. 25

but with a northerly outlier in Belgium at Rouveroy, Swiss examples, and an eastern case in Bavaria at Manching, the 'classic' series of *muri gallici* is now recognised archaeologically by the long iron spikes set into the intersections of their timber framework – presumably by auger – a detail not of course visible to Caesar. In fact, the evidence for some forts that are claimed instances of *muri gallici* consists only of the diagnostic metal spikes, rather than structural details recovered by the examination of the wall itself. Caesar tells us that such walls (their internal faces could be either a vertical wall or a sloping ramp) were resistant to attack by battering ram and by fire – the latter a claim that needs to be considered in relation to the evidence of vitrified walls, discussed in Chapter 7 below: a very few sites in this latter category, but including La Courbe in Orne, have produced evidence of nails.

Muri gallici could be massive constructions – that at Murcens in Lot, for example, was estimated to have been 15m wide and 5m high, and can display considerable variety in the way the timbers within them were assembled. In the case of Murcens, for example, half-checks and lap-joints (*20*) are proposed (Buchsenschutz and Mercadier 1989). At his most enthusiastic on the subject, Sir Mortimer Wheeler (1952, 72-3) was prepared to view these defences as the 'sovereign remedy' to the weaknesses of preceding forms of stone, earth and timber walls to fire and battery. He was even prepared to envisage them as 'the inspiration of one man or at any rate one planning-committee, and Vercingetorix and his staff are the obvious candidates'. It is now known, however, that some *muri gallici* would have been decades old by the time Vercingetorix marshalled the resistance to Caesar at the end of the Gallic War. Such nailed timber-laced walls made a late re-appearance in Scotland, at Dundurn in Perthshire and Burghead in Moray, in the Early Historic period, in what appears a clear case of independent reinvention.

Very considerable archaeological efforts have gone into schemes to categorise the varying architectures of this broad family of walls incorporating structural timberwork. A review of some of the main variants is offered here, but this makes no pretence at completeness. It should also be acknowledged that the architecture of individual sites may vary along the length of particular wall, as a result for instance of the differing efforts of different work gangs, or of particular engineering problems, such as those posed by the need to carry walls across minor streams that could be in spate. In particular, the vicinities of gates may be marked by the presence of additional timberwork, especially vertical posts, not least from which to hang the gate furniture and, in some cases, to support a bridge or more elaborate structure set across the entrance passage to enable the defenders to pass from one side to the other without losing height, and thus to retain their advantage. In southern Britain, gateways with substantial amounts of exposed timberwork seem to have been particularly characteristic of the earlier part of the Iron Age.

Since the *murus gallicus* has just been described, it is reasonable to begin with variants, generally earlier in date, of this tradition, marked by the presence of longitudinal and transversal timber frameworks within the wall, but lacking vertical elements in the outer wall-face. Closest to the *murus gallicus* is the Ehrang type, named for a west German fort that had a single wall constructed in this style. The significant difference here from the *murus gallicus* is the absence in these sites of the long iron spikes just mentioned, and generally taken as indicative of a construction of the former type. A note of caution is required however. In extensively dug *muri gallici*, or those prospected geophysically using electromagnetic techniques, it is far from normal for every intersection of timbers necessarily to be nailed; it thus follows that the Ehrang series may be a product of the placing of excavation trenches, and the chance that these simply missed nailed sectors of the circuit. That said, since it is considered that the nails add little, if anything, to the engineering qualities of the structure, the nail-less Ehrang type makes perfectly reasonable structural sense.

In Britain, a broadly similar structural tradition is known especially in the north of the country, where it is usually known as the 'Abernethy' tradition. Here too, the dominant feature is the internal horizontal latticework of longitudinal and transversal timbers, with beam-ends usually projecting through the outer, and sometimes the inner, wall-faces. The type-site, Castle Law, Abernethy (Perthshire and Kinross) was dug in late Victorian times, and the excellent survival of the beam-holes in the well-preserved inner face of the inner wall here (*21*) allowed early commentators to make a comparison with the gun-ports in an old-fashioned man o' war.

Another tradition is that of walls with their outer face marked by vertical posts (presumably originally carrying up to the wall-head and additionally supporting a breastwork), interspersed with panels of dry-stone construction. For these the generic term used is frequently the German *Pfostenschlitzmauer*, in recognition of

21 Castle Law, Abernethy, Perthshire and Kinross: beam-holes showing in the inner wall-face of the main enclosure of this tiny fort in the Ochil Hills after Christison, D. and Anderson, J., Proc Soc Antiq Scot 33, 1899, opp. p. 19. *Courtesy: Society of Antiquaries of Scotland*

the fact that many of the classic variants of these were first systematically recognised there (*colour plate 11*). The Altkönig-Preist series has wall-faces of this type front and back, and evidence of rather varying standard for cross-beams through the wall-core materials which served to tie the vertical posts in both faces to each other. In the Kelheim variant of the series, the external wall-face is to all intents and purposes identical with that just described: the internal stone-built revetment is absent and is replaced by a sloping ramp. Logic demands that the vertical timbers in the external wall-face were anchored into the wall-core, although excavation evidence suggests that such arrangements did not involve further earthfast posts.

Whilst it is usual to consider such walls as being characterised by vertical external wall-faces, in fact many of them were built for practical reasons related to their stability with the external face at a slight batter. This is apparent not only by examination of some of the wall-faces themselves, but also from the nature of exceptional surviving posts, notably ones from the external face of the fortification excavated at Yverdon-les-Bains, Vaud, in Switzerland. In this instance the timbers too have been trimmed at a slight angle, such that they would have remained flush with the wall-face batter along its length.

Wholly timber-built external wall faces have also been identified. In these, numerous variants are possible. The *Pfostenschlitzmauer* tradition of vertical earthfast posts interspersed with stone panels can be contrasted with examples where the dry-stone infill is replaced by horizontal wooden panelling. Such timber-framed walls are recognised in various areas, notably in the Lausitz tradition of north-central Europe and in southern Britain. Of relevance here, are the narrow walls postulated on the basis of near parallel arrangements of twin palisade lines. Such walls differ fundamentally from the *Kastenbau* series, in that their structural strength still derives substantially from earthfast timbers set in the front and rear faces and inferentially tied to each other by cross-pieces.

Although it has already been described, the *Kastenbau* series is worth considering further, because of the fundamental differences in the way this series is engineered. Firstly, and most critically, walls of this series are provided with an external vertical timber revetment that derives its structural strength not from the presence of earthfast vertical posts, but from an assemblage of horizontal elements that can be built up purely from ground level. This style of construction, wholly reliant on at least semi-rigid frames of horizontal timbers, and to which the German term *Blockbau* is sometimes applied, has the benefit that it is suitable for constructions using softwoods, although it is by no means used exclusively for such structurally-weaker timber. It is also suitable for use in areas lacking good building stone to erect stable wall-faces. Sometimes the negative traces of the frames used in this style of construction can be recognised because their lowest courses have been set in prepared trenches, as in sleeper-beam construction, and this has the great advantage – to the archaeologist – of making their presence much clearer: a case in point is offered by the entrance to the beautifully excavated and published Altburg-bei-Bundenbach near Trier in western Germany (Schindler 1977).

DRY-STONE WALLS

While walls built with a combination of the three components of dry-stone, timber and earth are a recurrent feature of temperate European later prehistory, they are by no means ubiquitous. Simple dry-stone walls, again with near-vertical faces, are also present in considerable numbers. The most sophisticated variants on these, with supplementary towers and bastions, and in some instances with clay used as a mortar, are found in areas relatively close to the Mediterranean. Further north, later prehistoric sophistication in terms of dry-stone built architecture is best exemplified by the suite of circular structures labelled as Complex Atlantic roundhouses (*colour plate 12*) and including the broch towers of that Scottish region; these have been considered in particular by Ian Armit (2003). Although these forbidding towers with their blank external walls are defensive in appearance, and have sometimes – in Euan MacKie's phrase – been seen as 'an aberrant form of hill-fort'; a case can be made for considering them fundamentally as aggrandised, monumental houses, rather than fortifications, and they certainly exhibit some constructional devices – notably the hollow wall construction, with two separate walls linked by horizontal lintels – not otherwise widely encountered in later prehistoric fortifications. Other structural features found in brochs, such as stairways, are, however, found more widely in forts built in the dry-stone traditions. Some such traits are distributed much more widely than the Atlantic Scottish zone where brochs are concentrated.

Amongst dry-stone wall constructions, a number of varieties can be seen. Perhaps the simplest form is a wall-face set along the foot of a slope, with the triangular space behind this revetment simply being infilled with rubble or other debris to form a level platform, presumably originally fronted by a breastwork of organic material, or conceivably of stone. Probably the most ubiquitous type consists of a wall delimited by both an internal and an external revetment, with the make-up of its hearting again potentially consisting of a variety of materials that were readily accessible to the builders. These can include soil scraped up from the vicinity and sometimes incorporate remains from earlier settlement or other activity. Such wall fills can thus contain residual artefactual material, artefacts that are very different from the date of the construction in which they subsequently became incorporated, mirroring the problems for dating that ensue from the reuse of wood noted above.

In other instances, dry-stone walls have been shown to contain multiple internal revetments – in effect, built wall-faces that are incorporated within the cores of wider walls. This style of construction is sometimes called the *murus duplex* type (*22*). The term is again taken over from a description Julius Caesar gives in his account of the Gallic War (II, 29). In some of these walls, the extra internal wall-faces seem likely to have been a constructional device employed in single-period constructions as a strengthening feature, but in other cases the additional of extra buttressing to strengthen walls may have resulted cumulatively through time in constructions of this type, perhaps as a response to emerging signs of structural instability, or to provide a wider platform at the wall-head. In some instances, massively thick walls result: 11m in the case of Worlebury in Somerset (*23*).

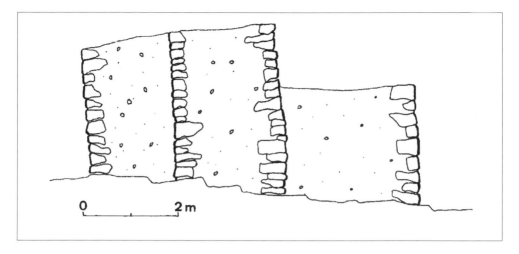

22 Hypothetical cross-section of a wall with internal wall-facings, sometimes termed the *murus duplex* type. Such walls could be constructed thus, or could attain these characteristics as a result of successive additions. *Drawn by Samantha Dennis after Dedet and Py 1985*

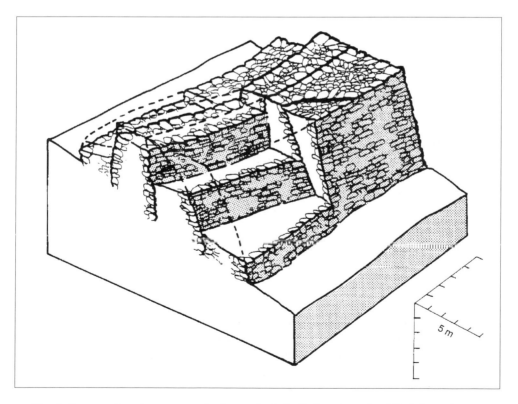

23 Block diagram showing a *murus duplex*: multiple built faces based on Worlebury, Somerset. *Drawn by Gordon Thomas after Hogg 1975*

Although normally referred to in the literature as vertically-fronted walls, to differentiate them from the ramparts discussed hereafter, in fact many of these wall-faces show evidence for slight batters to the wall-face. This trait is also found in the Greek and Hellenistic worlds and, as well as contributing to the stability of these constructions, such batters may have had military advantages. Greek sources, for example, make it plain that scaling walls built with a batter using ladders was more difficult to achieve than climbing vertical ones (Lawrence 1979).

There is also evidence that, in some instances, the inner margins of dry-stone walls may have been tiered in a series of steps, perhaps to facilitate access for the defenders to the wall-head, although in some instances at least the steps appear too large readily to have functioned in this way. The inner and more important defensive line of the bivallate promontory fort of Gurnard's Head near Zennor in Cornwall, some 3ha in extent, provides a clear example, and an Irish example, Dunbeg in County Kerry, is illustrated here (*24*). In general, stepped walls of this kind may indicate structures

24 Dunbeg, County Kerry. Stone wall with stepped profile on inner margin

that were built using larger stones, sometimes surface-gathered, rather than quarried from a fronting ditch, but this is not invariably the case.

RAMPARTS

What unites all the structures discussed above is that the key outcome of the construction of their fortifications was to present, at least originally, a near-vertical face to the outside world, whether hostile or not. This contrasts with the other major building tradition of later prehistory, that of constructing 'dump' ramparts. Ramparts are simply accumulations of material, sometimes carefully amassed and tamped down into position, on other occasions perhaps less so; they are normally without internal structural arrangements such as are found in walls of both the stone/timber/earth or indeed (in some instances at least) dry-stone traditions. Their defining characteristic is that externally they present a sloping face – a glacis. Built elements directly associated with the rampart itself may be minimal; it is usual to propose simply a dry-stone or timber breastwork near the summit as protection for the defenders, although incontro-vertible evidence for these from excavation evidence is rare. Even more than is the case with walls, the earthworks that make up ramparts can vary in scale, with particularly massive ramparts being identified towards the end of the Iron Age when they may have had to withstand assaults mounted using Roman siege equipment. Michael Avery has made a useful distinction between 'low dump', and 'high dump' ramparts from southern British evidence. The latter, generally 4m or more in height, often display a symmetrical cross-section, whereas their lower counterparts often have a steeper external face.

Additional height, for both walls and ramparts, clearly confers defensive advantages, but so does widening the defensive zone, and either of these objectives can be achieved by excavating a ditch in front of the rampart or wall. A narrow level terrace, or berm, may be left between the two, simplifying access to the wall-face for maintenance where this proved necessary, and also minimising the risk of the toe of the fortification slipping into the ditch if erosion began to modify its original profile. In the case of ramparts, omitting the berm may be advantageous in creating a continuous slope from ditch bottom to rampart top. The piling up of a smaller, counterscarp bank on the outer margin of the ditch, running parallel to the original scheme clearly extends the defensive zone still further. This may be a product of the original design, or the outcome of cleaning silt and tumble that accumulated over time on the ditch bottom. Such a requirement for maintenance would have been a recurrent one, although in some cases it appears that it was not carried out and ditches were allowed to infill fairly rapidly. The addition of further ramparts and ditches to such a scheme results in multivallation (*25*), in which a hill-fort is surrounded by a series of generally near-contiguous ramparts interspersed with ditches.

The sloping glacis style of enclosure, low dump or high dump (*26, 27*), conferred a number of advantages. In general it would require much less maintenance than vertical stone-faced walls, would be unlikely to become unserviceable as

25 Low sun highlights this series of small banks, some with accompanying ditches, forming a multivallate system on the accessible north-west side of Evelick, a small plateau-edge fort in the Sidlaw Hills (Perthshire and Kinross)

26 The combine harvester helps give an idea of the scale of this high dump rampart at the Camp de César, La Chaussée-Tirancourt in the Somme département, France

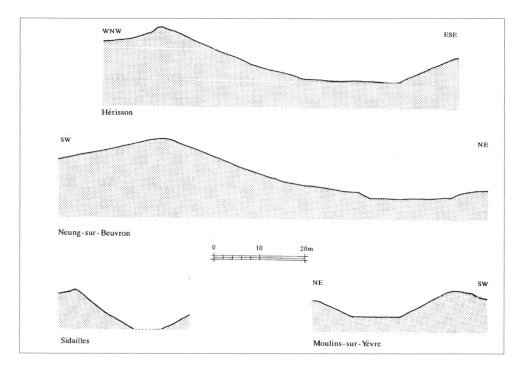

27 Massive dump banks preceded by flat-bottomed ditches in Berry, central France. These belong to the series first recognised by Sir Mortimer Wheeler (Wheeler and Richardson 1957) in Belgic Gaul. *Data: author; drawn by Gordon Thomas*

timber-built walls would have done as their woodwork decayed, and would have been much less prone to damage under any of the mechanised forms of assault that came into use (often following Mediterranean adoption or precedent) during the latter part of the first millennium BC. These included the use of catapults and *ballistae*, as well as battering rams. Faced, too, with the prospect of recommissioning old or decayed walls of the kinds just described, simply incorporating the collapsed wall material within a rampart heaped over its more-or-less decrepit remains must often have seemed the most economical, as well as time- and labour-saving, option.

DITCHES

Compared with the attention focused on the excavation of walls and ramparts, that devoted to the ditches found in front of many examples of such fortification lines has been distinctly less developed. It is clear that ditches in many cases formed convenient quarries for materials used in wall or rampart construction, but in other cases, often depending on the local topography, material derived from the ditch was also cast downslope to form a counterscarp bank on its outer margin. In other cases, the evidence that counterscarp banks contain multiple bands of material, suggesting their accumulation over time, allows the possibility that they were the product of repeatedly cleaning out silts and tumble from the ditch. By no means all lines of fortification were accompanied by ditching, and in some instances wall or rampart fill material was derived from quarry scoops upslope, and thus generally within the hill-fort, or even from off-site locations. Ditch forms and profiles can be very varied, and include sharp V-shaped profiles and, at the other extreme wide (20m plus) flat-bottomed arrangements as cut in sedimentary formations fronting the massive dump banks of north and central French (*28*) and the occasional British site (e.g. Silchester).

Whilst some ditches are only exploited into superficial deposits, others cut into hard rock formations, showing that suitable equipment was available and the necessary labour could be deployed. Like the fortifications themselves, there are some indications that certain portions of ditches were sometimes on a grander scale than elsewhere on the circuit, and such indications of variability can also suggest that the desire to impress could on occasion outweigh the desire to be secure. Most ditches seem intended to have been dry features, although exceptions might include ditches cut across the necks of river meanders. Some examples were at least locally wet, as at Cherbury, Oxfordshire (*29*), and this may have been seen as an additional defensive feature. In other cases, only very restricted portions of the ditch retained water, as at Stanwick in Yorkshire, although here the localised wet deposit at the bottom of a ditch terminal adjacent to an entrance produced a range of finds including a skull and a sword in a wooden sheath, fortuitously preserved, having perhaps tumbled in from a display in the gateway itself.

28 The broad, flat-bottomed ditch in front of the dump bank at the Camp de César, La Chaussée-Tirancourt (Somme département, France) is now cultivated

1 Broxmouth, East Lothian: Peter Hill's excavations of a fort with a complex history of enclosure. Located on a slight rise in the coastal plain, it was completely excavated as a rescue project. *See Hill 1982*

2 The wall of one of Ireland's highest enclosed sites – the promontory fort of Caherconree, County Kerry

3 The mid-first millennium BC princely seat of Mont Lassois, Burgundy, above the upper River Seine

4 A classic contour fort: banks and ditches, and later stone walls, surround the heather-covered Barmekin of Echt, Aberdeenshire

5 Villejoubert, Saint-Denis-des-Murs, the major *oppidum* of the *Lemovices*, occupies the 4km long interfluve between the River Vienne and a tributary (now dammed, hence the raised water level) in Limousin, France. The principal defence, covered in woodland, cuts across the promontory

6 Rock outcrop at the summit of the fort at Dunadd, Argyll, overlooking the lowlands of Crinan Moss bordering the River Add. The main defence here also sits on a rocky ridge, and the site is also famous for the suite of Early Historic carvings on another rock surface within it. *See Lane and Campbell 2000*

7 The western end of the small multivallate fort of the Chesters, Drem, East Lothian, is overlooked from a neighbouring ridge in the Garleton Hills. The ramparts are here picked out by gorse, with the interior of the site on the right

8 The tiny enclosed headland of Dunorroch on the western coast of Wigtownshire, Dumfries and Galloway, beneath the main coastline. The great promontory of the Mull of Galloway is in the background

9 Maiden Castle, Winterborne St Martin, Dorset: the southern defences, looking west

Overleaf

10 A palisade slot shown by the ditch in which the feature was set, and the presence of the chocking stones for individual posts: from the promontory fort at Cullykhan, Aberdeenshire. *Courtesy: Colvin Greig*

11 A reconstruction of the southern *Pfostenschlitzmauer* at the late Iron Age *oppidum* at the Donnersberg, Dannenfels, Rheinland Pfalz. *Courtesy: Ian Shepherd*

12 Right: Upland landscape with stone-footed hut circles of likely Bronze Age date and a broch with tumbled stonework and substantial outworks (top left) in the Strath of Kildonan, Sutherland. The complex Atlantic roundhouses are now more usually considered by archaeologists as grand houses rather than small fortifications, but they none the less have some defensive aspects, not least in their entrances

13 Below: The dry-stone built blockhouse or gatehouse at Ness of Burgi promontory fort, Shetland, looking outwards and showing the lintelled entrance passage and the entrance to one of the three mural cells within the thickness of the wall. Preceded by two ditches and a stony bank, it is debatable whether this ever represented a serviceable defence carried all the way across the promontory. It may rather have served as a platform for display.
Courtesy: Caroline Ashworth

14 Three portal stones, the tallest standing to 1.6m high, probably originally accompanied by a fourth, frame the main entrance to the univallate dry-stone fort at Garrywhin, near Wick, Caithness

15 Entremont, near Aix-en-Provence, Bouches-du-Rhône, France: projecting towers on the second, later dry-stone wall further discussed in Chapter 9

16 Penycloddiau, Flintshire, Wales. Internal quarry scoops flanking one of the banks of this 20ha hill-fort

17 A first partial reconstruction of the Porte du Rebout at Mont Beuvray showed serious signs of collapse within a few years of its erection

18 Some of the Roman siegeworks around Mt Auxois as reconstructed at the Archéodrome on the A6 motorway near Beaune. Excavation has demonstrated the close match between Caesar's descriptions and the traces left in the ground

19 The stone grotto surrounding the Virgin in the church at Bègues, Allier, France is built of vitrified and calcined stones from the local promontory fort

20 Tap o' Noth, near Rhynie, Aberdeenshire, under snow. The unbroken outline of the vitrified fort on its summit, one of several in northern Scotland of this form, doubtlessly contributed to early confusions with extinct volcanoes

21 The East Tullos wall as built. The projecting transversal timbers – of pine – would have been trimmed flush with the wall-face had time allowed, but this does not materially affect the experiment

22 The East Tullos fire seen against the Aberdeen night sky

23 Defences of the Iron Age and the 1940s at Burray, South Ronaldsay, Orkney

24 The castro at Baroña on its rocky headland

25 Oblique aerial view of Ben Griam Beg. *Courtesy: Jim Bone*

26 The Danube, with the Heuneburg on the skyline

27 Part of the elaborate entrance arrangements at the final addition to La Mesa de Miranda

28 The inner end of the gateway; the modern single-track road gives an indication of the overall width. The single massive post at the end of the northern inturn is placed in a post-hole recognised by J.-G. Bulliot in 1868, and is the only feature of this size associated with the entranceway

29 Aerial view of Tap o' Noth in evening sunlight. Within the oblong vitrified enclosure are traces of an earlier fortification. Downslope, at the junction between the crowberry-covered upper slopes and the heather moor below, is the slighter outer enclosure. Above it are sets of platforms and scoops, some likely to be house-stances and others informal quarries

29 The low-lying univallate fort of Cherbury, Oxfordshire, is on an area of limestone surrounded by clays which may once have been covered by marshland. The vegetation shows that the ditch is still wet in places

30 Identified below considerable later accretions during a rescue project in the centre of the modern town of Bourges (Cher, France), the probable ditch of Late Iron Age *Avaricum*, some 10m deep and 25m broad, is amongst the largest known. *Courtesy: Service archéologique municipal, Bourges*

Unfinished forts (see Chapter 4) provide some evidence that different elements extracted from the ditch were separated and stockpiled in informal but distinct dumps for subsequent use. In particular, turf, soil and the altered rock recovered from many superficial deposits might have been stockpiled for use as hearting within the wall-core, or as a capping to, or internal ramp built against, a revetted wall. Such sorting of the available materials is, of course, also an essential component of dry-stone dyking and, as the ruinous remains of some of these works are described, it is as well to bear in mind that the building of them entailed not only the movement of the necessary materials to the construction site, but also undoubtedly its sorting prior to use. Whilst impossible to quantify, such activities need to be taken into account in considering the overall effort for the community concerned implied in the construction of these works.

There are very significant differences in the scale of ditches represented, the biggest known to the writer being that drawn across the access to the promontory at Late Iron Age *Avaricum*, now within the town of Bourges in central France (*30*). The Late Iron Age ditch here was in excess of 10m deep and 25m wide – but even these dimensions do not seem to have particularly impressed Julius Caesar, who famously described *Avaricum's murus gallicus* in considerable detail, but made no mention of its astounding accompaniment.

ENTRANCES

In any fortification, entrances are points of potential weakness. As such, a number of strategies can be adopted to minimise this difficulty as far as is possible. In general, if defensive considerations are uppermost, the number of entrances will be the minimum consistent with other requirements; this is why the multiple entrances into the Brown Caterthun (Angus, Scotland: see Chapter 9) are so surprising and have even led to this site – wrongly, as it turns out – being suggested as a northern version of the Neolithic causewayed camps well known in southern Britain, at Windmill Hill (Wiltshire) and elsewhere. Considerable numbers of hill-forts – like many subsequent castles – only have a single entrance, but others do have more than this. There are even rare examples of hill-forts with no apparent entrances.

The simplest form of gate is that represented by a gap in the defensive circuit. The width of this should be tailored to the likely traffic, whether on foot or in vehicles. If livestock are to be driven into the fort, that too will have a bearing on the characteristics of the entrance. Associated arrangements may include earthfast features to stabilise the rampart ends, to accommodate a single- or double-leafed gate, or to support a bridge across the passage from wall-head to wall-head.

If defence is a priority, other factors need to be considered. One key element of any defensive arrangement at a gate is to maintain the assailants within range of the defenders' firepower for as long as is practically feasible. There are a number of means of achieving this. Ramparts or walls can be turned out adjacent to entrances, therefore funnelling potential aggressors into a confined space, potentially overlooked by defenders on the wall-head, even before they reach the line of the main wall and gate. Alternatively, the entrance can be inturned, thereby forming the same kind of corridor, but now projecting into the site's interior. Again, this has the result of keeping the attackers in range for longer, while maintaining the defenders' height advantage; in this kind of arrangement, the gate may be displaced towards the inner limit of the rampart or wall, and the assumption is that the wall-heads on either side of the gate were linked by a bridge or similar arrangement that oversailed the entrance passageway. The most famous of these formats are the gates often known by their German descriptor as the '*Zangentor* type'. These are marked by inturned passageways flanked by substantial ramparts or walls, and are widely found on the *oppida* sites of the end of the Continental Iron Age (*31*). Other devices employed include additional earthworks set outwith the main fortification line and the gate in it; these include projecting hornworks, and arrangements sometimes termed 'barbicans' in emulation of medieval castellation: these consist of enclosed projections set downslope, again resulting in a lengthened entrance passageway, sometimes accompanied by additional gates.

The same broad principle can be satisfied by overlapping the wall ends, thereby placing the gate in an entrance passage that is effectively at right angles to the main wall-lines, or producing a sort of chicane by off-setting the approach through the

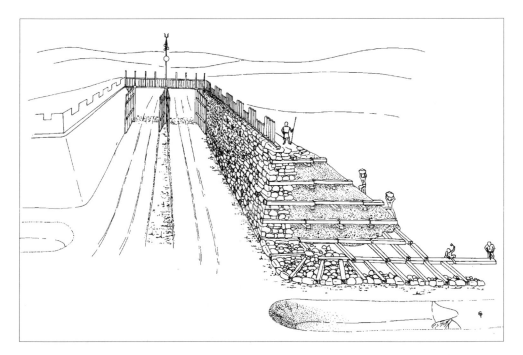

31 Hypothetical reconstruction of an inturned entrance of *Zangentor* type, based loosely on the Porte du Rebout at Mont Beuvray, with a double portal and a bridge carried over the entranceway. *Drawn by Gordon Thomas*

ramparts. In any such arrangement, it is usual for the entrance to be so arranged that soldiers approaching from outside the fort had to expose their right arms, the assumption being that shields would have been carried on the left.

Whilst many of these features noted may have had a military dimension to them, other, more practical, considerations also impinged on gate arrangements: amongst these was the need to drive cattle through them – livestock that, if not properly managed, could have brought about considerable damage in such confined spaces. In general terms, whatever the devices used, however, the result of prioritising defence is conspicuously to lengthen the passage. In exceptional cases, entranceways can exceed 40m in length, and Avery has proposed, following his consideration of the evidence from southern Britain, that all that exceed 20m measured from the aperture in the external face of the rampart to the gate position should be classed as 'Very Long', with other descriptors (Long 10–20m; Short 5–10m; Very Short – less than 5m) for other shorter variants. Avery's scale has the merit of making plain the very considerable diversity in sizes found in these entranceways.

Furthermore, if defence is the primary consideration, another dimension is of critical importance. Entrances should be as narrow as is possible, bearing in mind the kinds of vehicles that will have been required to use them; and the plan of the entrance passage may be otherwise modified both to slow down the progress of attackers and to keep them within range of defenders. Sturdy gates can be inserted; the furniture associated with them may be detected in excavation. Double or multiple sets of gates positioned sequentially within an entrance passage are certainly known in the Mediterranean world, and are feasible in some of the gate constructions encountered in temperate Europe, although most published examples usually only consider a single gate position on the basis of the excavated evidence. Exceptions include the late gates at La Chaussée-Tirancourt in the Somme Valley, and the Phase 3 gateway at Crickley Hill, for which the gate in the main wall-line is preceded by another at the outer limit of the stone-built barbican (*32*). Given that hill-fort entrances are often built on sloping land, reconstructions often depict them opening outwards, but such an arrangement might be considered unusual. In the case of two-leaf gates, it would be normal to imagine them hinged against the side-walls of the entrance passage, although Hawkes and his collaborators postulated in the case of the early phases of the north-east gate of St Catherine's Hill (Hampshire) that this was a two-leafed gate which opened inward with both halves hinged on the central post.

A walkway or bridge over the entrance passage from one wall-head to its opposite number both simplifies the task of redeploying defenders and provides an additional fighting platform for the defenders' use. In some cases, it is suggested that the structure built over the entranceway consisted of more than a bridge, and various reconstruction drawings propose altogether more elaborate towers or gatehouses spanning the entrance passage from wall-head to wall-head, perhaps most famously in the case of the elaborate *Torhaus* (gatehouse) buildings suggested for the excavated eastern gate at Manching (Bavaria), or Gate D at Zavist (*33*, Bohemia,

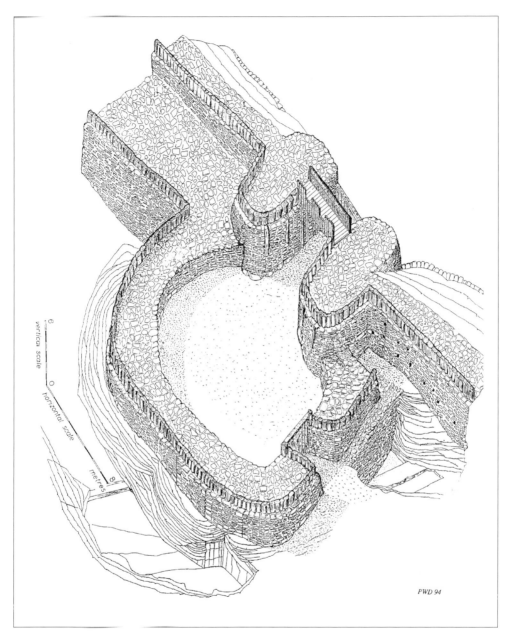

32 Crickley Hill, Gloucestershire: the Phase 3b gate with its barbican and separate gate projecting outward from the main rampart line. *Drawn by, and courtesy of, Philip Dixon*

33 Model reconstruction of Gate D at Zavist, Bohemia. *Courtesy: CAE Mont Beuvray*

Czech Republic). In general, these show a major timber structure built up from the bridge itself, and thus set squarely across the entranceway, but compelling evidence for such complex arrangements may need to await the recovery of a collapsed and carbonised example.

The last major variable in the form of the entranceway consists of the materials of which it was constructed. In some instances, these were essentially the same materials as the remainder of the wall, but in other cases there were marked variations. In southern Britain, as Avery has shown, timber-lined entrance passages seem to have been favoured, in some instances in association with defences where suitable constructional stone would have been difficult of access, but in other cases when this did not apply. It can be inferred that a deliberate choice was thus made to differentiate building materials and, in this instance, to prefer that which would have been at risk from fire. Later in the Iron Age, this trait was abandoned, and some southern British hill-fort entrances were to include some of the most elaborate plans to be found anywhere (*34*).

Whilst the above discussion has highlighted some of the elaborate constructions known, the plans of hill-fort gateways vary considerably, with some simpler arrangements suggesting that defence was not such a significant consideration. The simplest types take the form of a straightforward gap in the wall or rampart; very narrow, usually subsidiary, gaps, suitable only for humans, are sometimes termed 'posterns', broadly equivalent in scale – although perhaps not in function – to the sally-ports found in some medieval castle and town defences. In some areas (Scotland broadly falls into this category), such simple portals seem to be the dominant form, with little effort being devoted to enlarging the 'killing zone' by lengthening the entrance that attackers would be required to traverse within range of the defenders.

The survival of evidence for the gate furniture within the entranceway is often rather uneven. In part, this may be because the very conditions that attract excavators to entranceways – the fact that they are potentially pressure points, subject to a good deal of wear and tear in everyday usage and probably more so in conflict situations – means that they may display complex histories or repair and modification through time. As a result, at least some of the signs of the original arrangements may be removed deliberately, or worn away casually, during subsequent modifications. They are clearly places where successive modifications may be anticipated. Much-modified gates have been identified at sites such as Midsummer Hill in the Welsh Marches, where Stan Stanford identified nearly 20 building phases. Whilst in some cases the examination of gateways has thus proved productive, in others erosion, anthropogenic or natural, has conspired to reduce the amount of recoverable information.

34 Although reducing the amount of exposed timber seems to have characterised later hill-fort entrances in southern Britain, this concern was not shared across the Channel. Reconstruction of the entrance passage at La Chaussée-Tirancourt, Somme. *Courtesy: Stéphan Fichtl*

The positions of earthfast posts are often the clearest signs of where bridges and/or gates were positioned, and the occasional slot set across the access passage suggests that in some cases drop-gates were also sometimes employed. In other cases, both single- and double-leaved gates are suggested. An example of the latter survived in excellent condition at the lowland Polish site of Biskupin (*35*), recovered by excavation since it had collapsed outwards and was substantially preserved in the adjacent marshland. A door, complete with the element on which it pivoted, survives from the *oppidum* of Altenburg in Hessen, Germany (*36*). It is very rare for any iron fitments related to the wooden gates themselves to be recorded, but exceptional evidence survives from a few sites, such as South Cadbury, in south-west England, and at Pech Maho near Perpignan in the south of France. The latter gate seems to have rotated on a domed iron spike set into its base.

In numbers of cases, however, the slightness of the surviving evidence for a gate or associated structures within the entrance passage suggests that arrangements may have been considerably less elaborate. There may have been no permanent gate structure at all in some of the entrance passages; in at least one southern British case, in Kent, it appears – according to Caesar – that trees had to be felled as an emergency measure to block an entrance as the Romans approached. As an alternative, an arrangement such as the piece-gate, constructed of interlocking beams, as proposed by Michael Avery may have been employed (*37*). Finding direct archaeological evidence for such a gate would require fortuitous circumstances not unlike those that preserved the gate at Biskupin, for the nature of such structures means that in normal circumstances little or nothing will survive of them archaeologically. It is even possible that some entranceways were walled up in dry-stone when they were not in service.

35 Some of the details of the reconstructed gate built by Olivier Buchsenschutz at the museum at Moulins-sur-Céphons, Indre, are based on that found at Biskupin, Poland

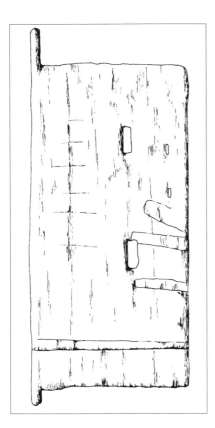

36 The surviving leaf of the Late Iron Age gate from the *oppidum* of Altenburg bei Neidenstein, Hessen. *Drawn by Samantha Dennis from a photograph in Herrmann, F.-R. and Jockenhövel, A. 1990* Die Vorgeschichte Hessens, *277*

37 A piece-gate as envisaged by Avery 1986/1993. *Drawn by Jem Heinemeier*

Other features located within, or close to, entrances seem, or are claimed, to be related to their functions. At Maiden Castle, Dorset, the discovery of an immense hoard of over 20,000 sling-stones adjacent to the eastern entrance, with other smaller collections of such stones on the slopes of adjacent ramparts, suggest an arsenal related to the protection of the entrance. Elsewhere, too, in south-central England, elaborate gateways seem to be designed with defence-in-depth in mind: the case can be illustrated from Danebury (*38*).

Rather more puzzling, however, is the case of so-called 'guard chambers' which are a feature of a number of southern British forts, and occur also in examples in the 'developed hill-fort zone' along the Welsh Marches. These take the form of single or paired recessed features set into the sides of the entrances passages within hill-fort gates; they can be semi-circular or sub-rectangular in plan (*39*). The suggestion that these were, in effect, an early variant of sentry boxes or the porter's lodge of medieval castles is, however, unconvincing in at least some cases. Puzzlingly, they are generally only represented in a single entrance, even in forts with more than one; equally, in some cases it appears likely that even one leaf of a double-leafed gate,

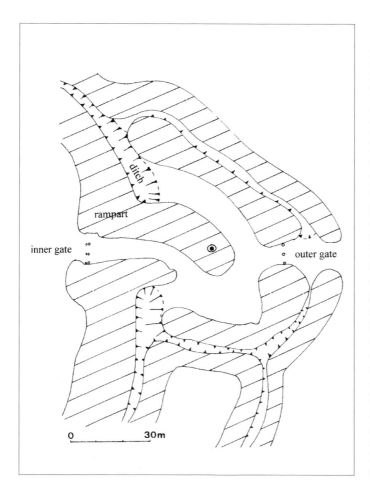

38 The eastern gate of Danebury (Hampshire) in its final (Phase E: Cunliffe 1995, fig. 3) configuration. Modifications included the construction of outer hornworks, and the out-turning of the inner gate passage over the former ditch. A command post is envisaged on the flat summit of the north inner hornwork (marked); this enjoys good line of sight over the entire gateway including the outworks, and could have been used by slingers, for whom the entire gateway and its surroundings, lying within 60m, would have been comfortably in range. *Drawn by Samantha Dennis after Cunliffe, B. 1983* Danebury: anatomy of an Iron Age hillfort

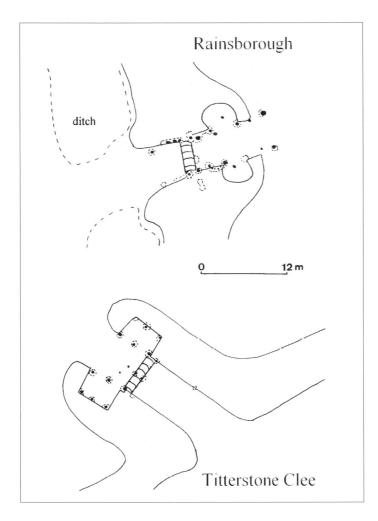

39 Two southern British examples of fort entrances with paired round or rectangular guard chambers: Rainsborough (Northamptonshire) and Titterstone Clee (Shropshire). The possible positions of bridges linking the wall-heads on either side of the entrance passage are indicated. *Drawn by Samantha Dennis after Dyer 1992*

when opened, would effectively block them, rendering them entirely ineffective as recesses in which to position guards. That said, the biggest of them are comparable in size with contemporary houses, and some have produced evidence such as hearths and domestic debris which suggest that they were lived in, at least from time to time.

Entranceways of course fulfil other, more symbolic, functions, discussed in a subsequent chapter, and for this reason their design very rarely seems to have been conditioned entirely by military requirements; indeed in some cases other considerations – perhaps to do with the need to impress visitors with the importance of the site and its inhabitants – means that symbolic perspectives seem to have been to the fore in the design of their layout. Platforms for bombastic display fall into this category: the extreme case of these is offered by the detached lengths of walling termed blockhouses known on a few sites of the Shetland Iron Age, most famously at Clickhimin. These remarkable stone-built features are elaborate but detached structures. In the case of Clickhimin, the blockhouse forms a detached arc of massive walling with a central entrance; whereas at Ness of Burgi, a diminutive rocky coastal promontory is isolated by a massive stone-built wall, bisected by a central stone-lined entrance with 'guard-cells' leading off, and fronted by ditches and a bank. From the description this might seem a formidable arrangement, but for the fact that the blockhouse fails to run all the way across the neck of the promontory on which it is located (*colour plate 13*). In northern Scotland, too, entrances framed by large orthostats, as at Garrywhin, are known: these efforts at monumentality again suggest priorities far removed from defence (*colour plate 14*). Evidence for trophies, nailed up or otherwise shown at the threshold to a site, also falls into this category and is considered in Chapter 6.

Finally, it is worth remarking that some forts show no sings of interruptions in their walls. Those that have most perplexed the present writer are the gateless oblong enclosures of north-east Scotland. Since none of the well-preserved sites of this type displays an entrance, it seems unlikely that the disappearance of any such feature on these sites is the result of systematic collapse, which has effectively disguised them. Theretically, a stone superstructure could have been carried across the original entrance on a timber or stone-lintelled bridge, which, on its destruction or eventual rotting, would have resulted in the stones cascading down and blocking the passage. There is no help to be derived from obvious access routes, such as hollow ways leading to apparently blocked gate positions, such as the previous hypothesis would give rise to. It is indeed possible that in the case of this usual series the original arrangement involved clambering over what can be very substantial walls, but this would be exceptional and, in the surviving remains, there are no signs of any features such as steps (although stone staircases do occur elsewhere) which might be associated with such a procedure.

TOWERS AND BASTIONS

As with numbers of features of temperate European Iron Age fortifications, the appearance of projections attached to fortification walls was not entirely an innovation of the last millennium BC. In western Europe such features had first been constructed in the Copper Age fortifications of southern Iberia, from Murcia to Portugal, at sites such as Vila Nova de Sao Pedro, where it is suggested that they are derived from the east Mediterranean world. Thus their spread is another symptom of the exchanges of commodities and ideas that occurred around the basin of the Mediterranean, which continued in the first millennium BC through the activities of the Phoenicians, Carthaginians, Greeks and Etruscans.

However, such features become much more common in later prehistory, especially in southern France and in Iberia, and it seems easiest to account for their development as an adoption from Greek or later Hellenistic models, entirely separate from any residual influence left over from the earlier contact. In France, such stone-built towers extend northwards to about the department of the Ardèche, to the site of Jastres-Nord, where successive walls had initially solid, towers, rectilinear in plan, and subsequently circular ones (Saumade 1996). The background to the adoption of these features thus in all probability lies principally in the enclosures associated with the Greek colonies that were established along the coasts of Provence, Languedoc and Catalonia, from which it is most likely that they were emulated. It is equally possible that the idea of incorporating such features was a product of Celtic mercenary service in the armies of the Hellenistic kings, but, if so, the restricted distribution of such features within Europe north of the Alps would be harder to comprehend. The role of Phoenician fortifications – as established in southern Spain on at least some of their trading factories – is less easy to distinguish, not least because they have received less attention. Separate influences from the margins of the Greek world at a later date are likely to have inspired equivalent developments in Dacian fortifications further east in Continental Europe.

The distinction between bastions and towers is that the former were normally the same height as the wall-head of the remainder of the wall to which they were attached, whereas towers projected above this level. The surviving elements of bastions and towers are either rectilinear or semicircular in outline. The former normally consist of solid stonework, faced with dry-stone and occasionally by well-shaped blocks. They are integral to the dry-stone walls of some southern French forts from about the fifth century BC to the Roman conquest in the second century BC. Contrastingly, towers, which can project both in- and outside the wall-line, may be independent constructions, incorporated into the wall in due course; they were also standardly higher than the fortification walls they accompanied. Towers furnish, self-evidently, elevated look-out positions, as well as points from which both hand-thrown missiles and those launched from bow or sling can be deployed (*colour plate 15*).

Compared to the hill-forts of temperate Europe, many of these sites in southern France and Iberia are of relatively limited extent; the spacing of the bastions deployed along their walls generally adopts one of two distinct traditions. In one, the distances between these features are regular, and the separation is not influenced by topography, changes in the alignment of the wall circuit and the like; in the other, such local topographic features clearly influence the positioning of these projections. Both styles thus fit with the general military explanation of such features, that they enabled defenders to mount cross-fire on assailants directly attacking the wall. As ever, there is every indication that the size, scale and positioning of these features was not dictated solely by military considerations of tactics and strategy. The size and placing of some examples, most notably the truly massive example subsequently converted into the Tour Magne at Nîmes, suggest that it was clearly there to impress – to provide an imposing, monumental feature which overstepped any concept of military necessity.

It is also worth remarking that at sites like Martigues in southern France, stone-built fortification walls with bastions surround settlements where some of the domestic architecture was built of mud-brick, showing that the two building materials coexisted on settlement sites in Provence. The observation is important, because much attention has been focused on the apparently unusual conjunction of these materials in one of the phases of the fortification of the Heuneburg in south Germany.

Before considering northern outliers of the distribution of towers and bastions in the heartland of the Continent, it is worth remarking that a number of Iberian sites in Levantine Spain demonstrate the adoption of further related features to provide both direct and flanking fire at attackers. These include salients – projections in the line of the fortification wall – as well as bastions (on the fortification's outer margin) and towers. The salient, despite being the most economic form of these projections to construct, consisting as it does simply of an outward deviation in the line of the fortification, in fact appears to be very rare (Moret 1996, 104). Towers included both examples with solid bases, masses of masonry which may have continued as high as the wall-head before providing some accommodation in their upper parts, and others which included usable space at ground level, normally accessed by an entrance facing into the interior of the site.

For much of its life as a princely seat, the defences of the Heuneburg were constructed in an impressive variant of the *Stein-Holz-Erdemauer* type, such as might be anticipated for a very important first Iron Age site in south Germany. It appears likely that the Heuneburg was the subject of repeated attacks during this period, for the main wall was rebuilt on numerous occasions in the sixth and on into the fifth century BC. In one phase, however, a radically different solution to the needs of defending the site and its inhabitants was adopted. This involved placing a number of rectilinear bastions along the outer wall-face, in a tradition altogether foreign to this region. The footings of the bastions were of stone, but much of the surviving structures above these were constructed of unfired mud-brick, a building material generally considered to be suited to more southerly, drier environments. A further noteworthy feature is that the bastions are generally considered to be too tightly clustered along the curtain wall adequately to have fulfilled their function of providing raking crossfire. All these traits have been put forward to suggest that the fortifications of this period at the Heuneburg represent a rather botched adoption of more southerly fortification ideas, in the context of a society in which high-status imports from the south were clearly significant motors in economic, political and social arrangements (see Chapter 9). At the Heuneburg some of the other materials present, such as locally made pottery finished on the slow wheel, suggests either the presence of southern artisans or local craftspeople who have directly witnessed southern technologies and southern traits. A similar explanation seems appropriate for the adoption of the bastions, even if, in this instance, someone's enthusiasm for quantity overran the quality control that would have been provided by stricter adherence to military considerations in deciding on their separation.

Towers attached to fortifications (as opposed to the regionally-specific broch towers of Atlantic Scotland) are otherwise rare but by no means absent in temperate European later prehistoric architecture. That they were constructed hastily in times of war, we know from Caesar's description of the siege of *Avaricum* in 52 BC. But

40 Model reconstruction of a
tower surmounting the defences
at the Bois de Boubier, Hainault,
Belgium, and considered to date to
the fourth century BC or earlier
(Bonenfant in Papeleux and de
Boe 1988). *Courtesy: Pierre-Paul
Bonenfant*

at other times and places evidence for such features is increasingly forthcoming, as excavations increase in scale. One was identified on a Belgian site: at the 5ha promontory fort of Bois de Boubier near Charleroi in Hainault (*40*), excavation directed by Pierre-Paul Bonenfant revealed evidence interpreted as the remains of a burnt and collapsed tower structure partially draped over the surviving wall. At the *oppidum* of Mont Vully in Switzerland, set at the end of the hill ridge south of the Lac de Neuchâtel and the site at La Tène itself, a tower was proposed by the excavator, Gilbert Kaenel, on the basis of massive post-holes encountered in a gap in the inner margin of the principal wall that did not constitute an entrance, the breach not extending to the outer face (*41*). This example raises the interesting possibility that other irregularities in the longitudinal profiles of ramparts elsewhere may also correspond to the former positions of such features. Further examples are suggested in the area of the former East Germany, as at the Early Iron Age fort of Nieder-Neundorf near Dresden (Herrmann 1989, 475). In Britain, some of the four-post arrangements identified within hill-forts have been suggested as towers, rather than granaries or exposure platforms for the dead, on the basis of their proximity to wall-lines, as at Crickley Hill (see Chapter 6).

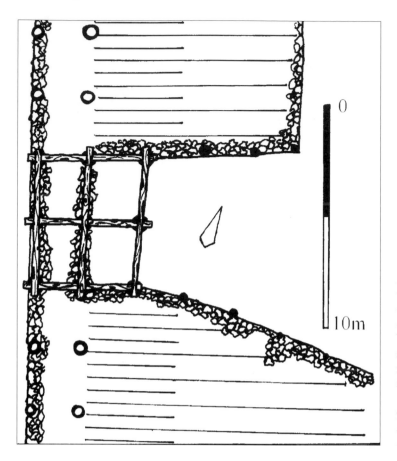

41 A proposed tower over the outer wall of the *oppidum* of Mont Vully, Switzerland, set over a gap in the bank in its inner margin (see also Chapter 9). *Drawn by Jem Heinemeier after Kaenel* et al. *2004*

In other cases, towers have been proposed directly related to the positions of gates. The gate of the 3ha lowland fort at Biskupin is a celebrated example. Elsewhere, the excavation evidence from which the towers have been proposed is only a little less convincing. At the Altburg-bei-Bundenbach, near Trier in western Germany, the detection of a rectilinear grid of sleeper-beam trenches excavated into the bedrock within the entrance passage of this univallate walled fort (*42*) seems a strong contender for a tower of some kind. The grid arrangement recalls the much more extensive ones found within the Heuneburg, which form the groundworks for some of the biggest individual buildings found in temperate European protohistory. Such rigid and elaborate foundations allow the possibility that the structures based on them may have been of considerable complexity, and it seems fair to remark that, in proposing reconstructions, the archaeologist is confronted with a much wider range of structural possibilities than when dealing with (say) a simple ring of post-holes defining a roundhouse. Towers were thus certainly present, albeit as yet still rare, in Continental forts some distances removed from the direct influences of the Mediterranean world; bastions, apart from the unique case of the Heuneburg, and salients seem, however, to be entirely absent. And none of these features of wall

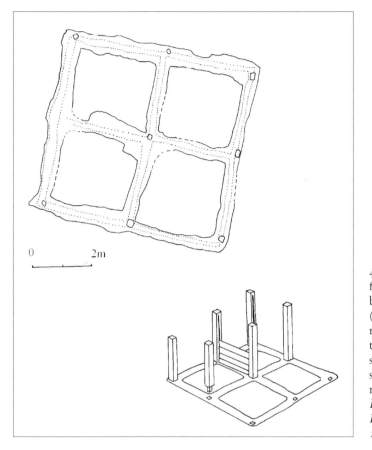

42 Evidence for the first gate at the Altburg-bei-Bundenbach (Rhine-Palatinate). The rock-cut sleeper-beam trenches could have supported an elaborate superstructure, partially reconstructed here. *Drawn by Samantha Dennis after Schindler 1977*

construction seems to be encountered on any Iron Age fortification in Britain or Ireland, although in Britain free-standing four-posters, as found immediately behind the defence at Crickley Hill, Gloucestershire, have been suggested as towers (see Chapter 6).

MANCHING, MONT BEUVRAY AND OTHER GRAND GATEHOUSES

Of all the buildings associated with ramparts, the most elaborate and imposing structure is the *Torhaus* or gatehouse proposed on the basis of excavation evidence for the great east gate of the lowland *oppidum* at Manching in Bavaria. The excavation evidence for this consists of five rows of massive post-holes set within and on the margins of the inturned ends of a *Pfostenschlitzmauer* (replacing an earlier *murus gallicus* on the same alignment). There are other features not easily explained in the vicinity, not least a rectilinear cavity straddling the approach causeway to the site, but for present purposes it is the superstructure proposed for the gateway that is the focus of interest. It is clear that the structure is symmetrical, with two wider passages, perhaps initially edged by two narrower ones (although these were later encompassed within the wall), suggesting roads for vehicles in and out, and separate pedestrian access along the margins of the structure. This is an arrangement also noted, for example, in many Roman town gateways. The alignment of the post-holes would allow for a two-leafed gate spanning the main carriageways, and this is what reconstruction drawings show. As is conventionally the case in many hill-fort reconstruction drawings – and what makes sense in sites where the gates are situated on a slope (not in fact the case at Manching's East Gate) – these are depicted opening outwards, contrary to usual practice in fortifications of other periods. At Manching, since the *Torhaus* position is essentially level, such an arrangement is not necessary. More problematic, however, is the superstructure that is proposed to have traversed the entrance based on the five rows of posts. That this was something substantial is not disputed and minimally a bridge spanning the gap between the two wall inturns is called for (cf. *31*). The preferred reconstruction (van Endert 1987), however, shows a two- or three-storey timber building, which the present writer believes is excessive in relation to the surviving archaeological evidence. Imposing as its appearance would have been, it would have contributed little to the defensibility of the gateway, whilst presenting a mass of exposed wood which, if ignited, would surely rapidly have rendered the immediate surroundings indefensible.

Such images have been transferred to other sites, where the evidence does appear to support their existence – as at Gate D at Zavist in the Czech Republic (see above), but also in cases where the likelihood of such elaborate gatehouses seems even more remote. The classic instance is the Porte du Rebout at Mont Beuvray where, despite the publication of the modern re-excavation of this entranceway, an illustration of a truly gigantic *Torhaus* (*43*) clearly modelled on the Manching example continues to find favour despite the lack of any compelling archaeological evidence for such a structure at this position uncovered during the complete excavation of this gateway. At the Porte du Rebout, the wall-faces of the two inturns of the gateway as it was originally constituted were separated by over 19m, almost double the distance between their equivalents at Manching. The Beuvray entranceway, set on a relatively steep slope, had been eroded in a variety of ways: by subsequent use having created a hollow way across part of its breadth, by modifications to the entranceway during its period of use including the insertion of ditches running parallel with its wall-faces, and by other, natural erosion through run-off of surface water from the slopes above it. None of these detrimental impacts, however, would be sufficient, alone or in combination, to account for the complete disappearance of all the rows of massive post-holes that would have been necessary for an elaborate gatehouse set between the inturns of this huge gateway (*44*). Furthermore, allowing for an identical arrangement to that encountered at Manching – two passages for vehicles, and two for pedestrian traffic on the margins – the central pair of outward-opening wooden gates shown on the Beuvray reconstruction drawing would have been excessively heavy to manoeuvre. Whilst this difficulty could be addressed by proposing an

43 Watercolour reconstruction by J.-C. Golvin of the gate at the Porte du Rebout prepared in advance of the modern excavation and frequently reproduced. Based on the reconstruction suggested for the East Gate at Manching, there is no indication that any such elaborate structure occupied the much wider entrance passage at the Porte du Rebout. *Courtesy: CAE Mont Beuvray*

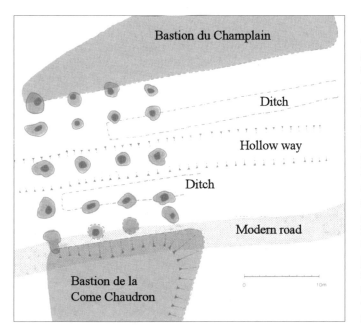

44 The Porte du Rebout gateway at Mont Beuvray, showing various features – Iron Age ditches, a medieval and later hollow way, and a 1950s road – subsequently inserted through the passage. These would have been insufficient to eliminate all the major earthfast posts of a gate arrangement like that identified at the East Gate of Manching, the posts of which are here scaled up to fit the width of the Beuvray entrance – approximately twice that of Manching

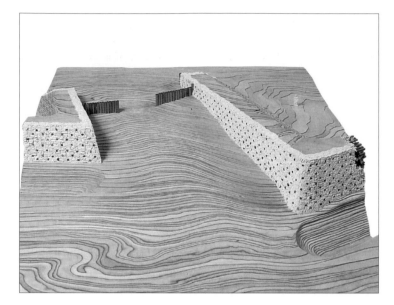

45 The Porte du Rebout entrance early in its existence – a proposition. *Courtesy: CAE Mont Beuvray*

individual two-leafed gate in each half of the structure, the fundamental problem – that the surviving archaeological evidence suggests altogether flimsier structural arrangements across the entrance passage – is harder to dissipate.

In contemporary British terms, a width of 19m is easily sufficient for the passage of an A-class road, but not for a motorway. Such a width for the gateway (one of several) into an *oppidum* hardly suggests that in this case defensibility was uppermost in the original architect's mind or indeed brief. Elsewhere, Olivier Buchsenschutz and I have suggested that this gateway, through which Julius Caesar may have passed towards the end of the Gallic War, was more a monumental entranceway for show, a symbolic limit perhaps to the juridical scope of the settlement's elite (*45*). An analogy for the disproportionate difference between flanking works and blocking arrangements in the gateway itself is suggested by Horace Vernet's painting, now in the Louvre, showing one of the gates of Paris towards the end of the Napoleonic Wars as that city prepared its defences: the wide access between the monumental flanking towers is occupied by a relatively feeble and apparently hastily-constructed wooden stockade. In the apparent disproportion between massive flanking works and apparent absence of any substantial gate barring the intervening passage, the Porte du Rebout is not unique. In southern Britain, for example, Sir Mortimer Wheeler's excavations at one of the largest forts in the country, Bindon Hill, near Lulworth Cove in Dorset, failed to find any uprights for a gate in the 13.5m wide, inturned entrance through the main rampart of that site; it can, however, be argued, that this entrance was unfinished.

Elaborate arrangements at entrances can however be traced far to the north. The most northerly claimant for a bridge across the entrance passage known to the present writer is at Castle Point Troup (or Cullykhan) on the north coast of

Aberdeenshire. The evidence for the former presence of this arrangement consists essentially of the scale of the spaced vertical posts set in the external wall-faces of the elongated entrance-passage here – such a use of vertical posts in any case being rare in Scotland. Other narrow entrances in the north – as in the Shetland blockhouses – were clearly lintelled over, and it is possible other dry-stone walls could have had timber bridges which were not anchored on vertical uprights, but archaeological evidence is lacking.

OTHER SUPERSTRUCTURES ON WALLS

Arrangements on the wall-head of fortifications are generally not well attested from fieldwork or excavation, because of subsequent settling, collapse or decay. Some structural arrangements lend themselves to the creation of breastworks, notably the walls with vertical posts in their outer face built in post-and-panel style. Fire-steps may also survive on some dry-stone walls as at Tre'r Ceiri (Carnarfonshire: see Chapter 9) and at Mither Tap o' Bennachie (Aberdeenshire).

Other kinds of evidence are generally more ephemeral, although some remarkable survivals can be noted. During her excavations of the fort at Bonchester Hill, Roxburghshire (Scottish Borders), Mrs Piggott noted that the outer bank displayed traces of two parallel lines considered originally to have held stakes running along the summit of the wall. Scottish cases of surviving traces of breastworks have also been recorded as at Balloch Hill in Kintyre, Argyll, whereas at the Brown Caterthun, Angus, the examination of one of the earthworks revealed a collection of carbonised timberwork on top best interpreted as a burnt wattle fence or breastwork (Dunwell and Strachan forthcoming).

CHEVAUX-DE-FRISE

One supplementary element in defensive schemes which shows an interesting, discontinuous distribution is the presence of sets of upright, jagged stones arranged in irregular rows; these occur in restricted patches, generally outside, but in close proximity to, fortifications. The term is alleged to have been coined to describe spikes implanted in the ground to impede enemy cavalry by Frisian troops of rather more recent date. The archaeological distribution of stone examples related to hill-forts is much more western, almost entirely Atlantic, and there is absolutely no reason to associate the structural form described here with the southern coastlands of the North Sea Basin nor, in date, with the Frisians.

Numerous examples of *chevaux-de-frise* have been recorded in inland northern Spain, notably on the margins of Galicia and in the province of Soria (where they have been inventoried by Alberto Lorrio 1997) (*46*), being relatively rare in the Iberian culture zone; and a much more sporadic distribution occurs in the

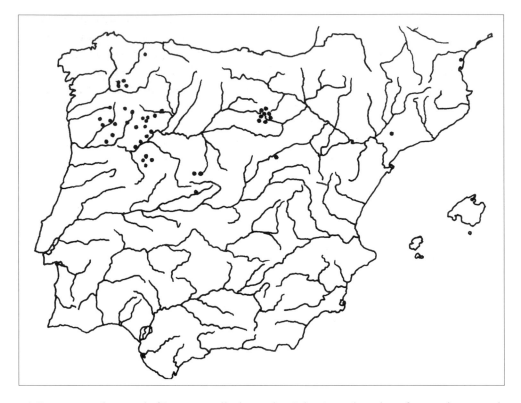

46 Dry-stone chevaux-de-frise occur all along the Atlantic seaboard as far north as south Barrule on the Isle of Man, the Aran Islands off County Kerry, Eire and Scotland, but they are most numerous in Iberia. Drawn by Jem Heinemeier after Lorrio 1997

British Isles, extending west to the Aran Islands off Galway, and north into lowland Scotland. In a number of British instances, they are clearly not the latest structural feature on site. At Dreva Craig above Broughton in Peeblesshire, for example, one set has had many of its members extracted when it was converted into a series of stone-walled roundhouses, although another patch at the other end of the same site was not so affected. Contrastingly at the Carnarfonshire site of Pen-y-Gaer, the southern spread of these stones is bisected by the outermost rampart at the site, suggesting that the *chevaux-de-frise* here is probably older than that fortification line. That is also manifestly the case at Castel Henllys, Pembrokeshire, where Harold Mytum's excavations have revealed the surviving elements of a stone *chevaux-de-frise* underlying a later fortification line.

Chevaux-de-frise – the French term originally applied to pointed pieces of wood and not the upright stones identified in Iron Age contexts – remain rare in that material in the Iron Age, and desultory efforts to make the stone examples of Atlantic Europe simply lithicised versions of a widespread, but rarely detected, wooden tradition of central European origin fail to convince. Whilst timber examples have been recognised at the forts of Le Fou de Verdun in Burgundy, and the Bois de

Boubier in Hainault, these are most likely of La Tène date, and thus more recent than the probable initial date for the stone examples. In Spain, dating evidence is hard to assemble for many examples, although some appear to be early: at the tiny lowland site of Els Vilars in Lleida (*47*) the upright stones were placed directly outside a *murus duplex*-variant style wall and tower of local limestone, suggested to date to around 600 BC. In the case of La Mesa de Miranda at Chamartín de la Sierra (Avila Province), the existence of bands of *chevaux-de-frise* (*48*) outside two conjoined enclosures suggests that they were built successively, in tandem with the expansion of the site, thereby implying at least some time-depth to the use of this technique. The *chevaux-de-frise* in the shallow ditch outside the principal bastion of the outer enclosure at Pech-Maho 2, in Aude, Languedoc, appears to be distinctly more recent, perhaps close in date to the destruction of the Middle Iberian site around the third century BC. The datable examples in Soria province, Spain, seem to belong to the first Iron Age but, further west, in Galicia, the most recent example (at Sierra d'El Caurel) is attributed to the first or second centuries AD, although others are most

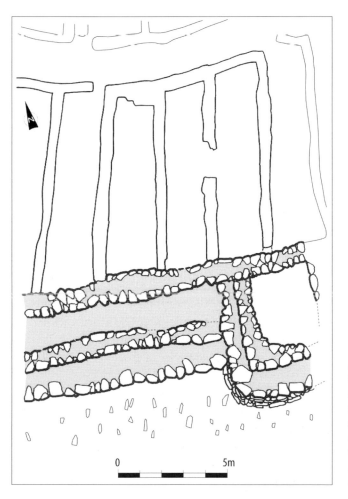

0   5m

47 Els Vilars, Lleida. Considered to be one of the earliest examples of a *chevaux-de-frise*, this Iberian example is set immediately outside a *murus duplex*-style wall with flanking bastions. *Drawn by Karen Clarke after Moret 1996*

48 Chevaux-de-frise at La Mesa de Miranda, Chamartín de la Sierra, Avila Province, Spain: see also Chapter 9

probably considerably older. Whilst some examples in Iberia appear tardy, it none the less seems possible to argue, as Hogg did many years ago, for a north Spanish origin for this predominantly Atlantic innovation.

Whilst it is certainly true that evidence for cavalry warfare emerges widely in temperate Continental Europe during the La Tène Iron Age, *chevaux-de-frise* have nothing (or very little) to do with the use of mounted troops against permanent fortifications, in any case a manoeuvre of very debatable logic. Their purpose is to disrupt infantry assaults, as is borne out by the locations in which they occur – on the berms immediately outside walls, and indeed on that between two ditches. Such a view would tend to be supported by the fact that at least some examples also seem to be rather earlier than the upswing in evidence for cavalry, which in temperate Europe is mostly a feature of the last three or so centuries BC.

WERE HILL-FORT DEFENCES DESIGNED BY SPECIALISTS?

Given what a major feature they were of many of the societies with which the generals and travellers from the Mediterranean World came into contact, there is surprisingly little contained in the classical sources about the construction and use of hill-forts. What we know from such sources is predominantly about their role in warfare and sieges and a selection of this evidence is considered in Chapter 5.

Faced with the question of whether these fortifications were the work of full-time teams of specialist architect-builders, it is hard to give a definitive answer. The Early Irish literature, contrastingly, contains evidence for specialists in the building of the small fortifications of the first millennium AD in that country, and it is certainly possible that equivalent specialists existed in the first millennium BC. This would be entirely in keeping with the general evolution of craftsmanship at this time, which indicates a widening range of specialist crafts during this period. Not all such craftwork need have been full-time.

To point to the increasing evidence for skilled craft-working, however, is not to imply that all fortification works were necessarily designed, still less constructed, by specialists; and at least some of the evidence points to much of the work being done by non-specialist labour, some of it perhaps supplied by children. Whilst indisputable evidence seems to be lacking for their use in such tasks, it is manifestly the case that they laboured in some of the salt and other mines, such as the Dürrnberg in Austria, where the preservation of small leather shoes underground provide eloquent testimony. Such building works may perhaps also have been undertaken by slaves, or by subservient members of the population.

It is certainly also clear from the ancient texts that armies on campaign, or the citizens and forces besieged within a particular site might, if and when the need arose, either build or modify a fortification. In the case of the siege of *Avaricum*/Bourges in 52 BC, for example, wooden towers were apparently added on the wall-head by the defenders during the siege, but such evidence is ambiguous: these need not have been erected by the general populace for, amongst the numerous groups sheltering from Caesar's assault within the *oppidum*, may have been the relevant specialists. Close similarities between fortification types and similar detailed arrangements at features such as gateways in particular regions might betoken the involvement of specialists, but numbers of other mechanisms could account for such similarities. As in medieval times, the practice of fosterage may have been significant, with returning sons bringing news of innovations in fortification styles seen elsewhere. Equally, too, mercenary service in the armies of the Hellenistic kings, or participation in other raids southwards, might have provided sight of, even experience of, combating some of the features of more southerly fortifications. The result has been that some distinguished colleagues have hypothesised that traits found in Late Iron Age walls, such as the addition of sloping ramps against their inner faces, may have been adopted from the south, but in this case indebtedness is perhaps harder to demonstrate than in the case of towers and bastions.

In sum, despite manifest contacts with the Mediterranean world, most of the essentials of Iron Age fortification in temperate Europe are best envisaged as the products of local ingenuity and endeavour.

4

CONSTRUCTION, MAINTENANCE, REPAIR AND MODIFICATION

The design, building and maintenance of hill-fort defences provide some of the best archaeological evidence for the scale of collaborative effort that Iron Age societies in temperate Europe could achieve. Encoded in them are indications about the abilities of these communities to mobilise resources and to utilise manpower. They thus provide indirect indications of the amount of labour that could be deployed on such tasks although, sadly, since we do not know over what timescale most of these fortifications were built, it is generally not possible to be certain about how many people were labouring, whether forced or as volunteers, on the erection of these structures. Clearly, the longer the period over which any given task was accomplished, the smaller the tally of individuals who would need to have been employed on the work. The likelihood is that many in the labour force would have had to make their contributions at slack moments in the agricultural year, or those of other activities. Furthermore, these fortifications not only required to be built; in some instances at least it seems likely that maintenance, and sometimes upgrading, may have been tasks undertaken on a near-continuous basis. In all probability, some of the complex wall-and-fill ramparts, with their admixtures of different building materials, must have been very demanding in this regard, if they were to be kept in a serviceable condition. In other cases there are indications that individual defences were allowed to decay fairly rapidly, and their accompanying ditches to silt up.

CONSTRUCTION

Constructing a new fortification would have required a multitude of tasks to be accomplished. Some of these can be surmised by inference from a consideration of the nature of completed works; but others are best considered by looking at the evidence of forts which are apparently unfinished. In these, intermediate, even preparatory, stages in their laying out and construction can sometimes be recognised

– evidence which might well be obliterated in finished defences, or at least be much more difficult to discern in them. In this chapter, the reasons for the incompleteness of some hill-fort defences, whether the initial defences on a particular site, or *addenda* to already existing structures, are not the key concern. Clearly a whole raft of causes, social, political, economic, religious, could be invoked: in some instances, however, more prosaic causes related to local physical conditions – the intractable nature of the bedrock, or unexpected characteristics of the water table – may have played a part.

By the last few centuries BC, the range of iron hand-tools available for constructional tasks had increased markedly from those for which we have evidence in copper alloy at the beginning of that millennium. To open the publication of the iron tools from a major Late Iron Age settlement – that produced by Gerhard Jacobi (1974) on the equipment recovered from the early campaigns at Manching is a classic – suggests not altogether the voluminous hardware guides of today, but something in which there are already signs both of a considerable range of tools, and of a range of varieties of a particular tool, each designed for a specific task.

Generally speaking, more direct evidence survives for the tools that would have been required for some of the more detailed work and the finishing tasks required in building a fortification, rather than the heavy-duty gear implied by the scale of some of the rock-cut ditches or by the number of trees that would have required to be felled. Amongst the equipment for wood-working for example, a range of iron socketed axes and carpenter's adzes with splayed blades are found, as well as the occasional shaft-hole iron axe. Different sizes of adzes, which fall into recognisable sets, suggest they were employed in a variety of specialist ways for trimming and shaping wood. Wood chisels occur in a variety of sizes, and specialist types too are represented. There are also punches. Spoon augers, which could be used to drill out sizeable holes occur, and would have been necessary to prepare the holes into which the great iron spikes known from the timberwork in the *murus gallicus*-style of fortification were inserted. A selection of gouges, useful for a range of paring tasks including examples suitable for cutting out blind recesses, are also known. Saws are rare in the metalwork recovered at Manching, but examples resembling modern pruning saws, with a curved blade, are known from other sites including La Tène itself, and at Glastonbury in Somerset. Draw-planes or draw-knives, with both flat and curved blades (sometimes termed inshaves) are also identified. Analytical evidence from elsewhere in the Continental Late Iron Age suggests that at least some of these items would have been made of hardened steels. Not all the items in the toolkit were of iron, however; leaving to one side perishable equipment of wood or horn, generally little known, a range of hammer-stones and other heavy stone equipment is also known.

A range of iron tools is also present for working the land, and thus potentially of service in site preparation: these include sickles and – by the end of the Continental Iron Age – scythes, as well as rare mattock and pick blades, and bill-hooks. Some types, rare at Manching, occur elsewhere, for example at the Celtiberian stronghold of *Numantia* in Spain, where a variety of shaft-hole pick-heads, some relatively heavy-duty, have been discovered. Other tools are found at much earlier dates: there is, for example, a shaft-hole sledge-hammer amongst the extraordinary deposits within the Byci skala cave in Moravia, and this must date to around the sixth century BC. Some of these tools would obviously have been appropriate for preparing the site of a proposed fortification for construction, depending on what the preceding land-use was, and for other tasks, such as cutting wooden poles from pollarded trees for hazel and other withies for wattlework for use in superstructures. Overall, however, it remains true that relatively little heavy equipment, such as picks for breaking stone, has apparently been identified in the Iron Age record, although there is an example of these at the site of Tronoen, St-Jean-Trolimon, Finistère. Whilst much of the Iron Age toolkit thus indicates specialisms and skills, there are additional indications pointing the same way. Stephan Fichtl has, for example, commented on the quality of the trimming of the pink sandstone slabs used to face late fortifications, such as at the Fossé des Pandours on the border between Alsace and Lorraine in eastern France. This had been rather expertly done, often on five faces of the same block, thus enabling a close fit to be achieved during construction; but other stone trimming was less expert.

Such iron hand-tools would have been complemented by other, wholly organic ones, of the kind that survive in some of the salt mines of central Europe, such as at Hallstatt and the Dürrnberg in Austria, or in wetland sites, such as the wooden mallets recovered at Glastonbury. Basic pulleys and similar mechanical devices would have been available, although direct evidence for these from later prehistoric fortifications is absent: wooden elements surviving from wells, as within the south German enclosure at Fellbach-Schmiden in Baden-Wurttemburg indicate something of the possibilities. Most endeavour probably relied on human muscle power, although heavier traction in the form of bullocks would have been available. Wagons and slide-cars, depending on terrain, could certainly have been used to bring some of the material to site; smaller quantities of loose material were probably shifted in baskets and similar containers: that useful device of the modern building site, the wheelbarrow, is however a medieval invention.

The excellent preservation offered in some of the salt mines, where small sizes of leather shoes have survived in some numbers, make it plain that at least some societies at this time had no hesitation in making use of child labour in such gruelling environments, and skeletal abnormalities in their cemeteries indicate that women were routinely and repeatedly carrying heavy loads. It would therefore be entirely reasonable to imagine that women and children also laboured in the gangs building fortifications, and the occasional female skeleton found in the build-up of a rampart, as at Maiden Castle, Dorset, may represent the remains of a casualty of this heavy labour.

In other instances, direct historical testimony suggests that other, less suitable equipment could be pressed into service when the need dictated. An attack by the *Eburones, Nervii, Aduatuci* and their allies on a Roman winter camp in northern Gaul in 54 BC included the construction by the Gauls of a substantial circumvallation (*de Bello gallico*, V, 38-49). Caesar tells us that this work was done under instruction from Roman captives, an interesting example of the Roman-Gaulish interplay in military tactics at this time; and that it was achieved at what appears to have been an impossibly breakneck speed. Lack of suitable iron tools meant that the besiegers had to cut the turf with their swords, however; and move earth in their cloaks.

Some of the materials used in constructing walls and ramparts would have been collected effectively on-site, including those extracted from the ditches that often accompanied such features. Evidence for such practices is clear at a number of the unfinished sites discussed below. Others could have been stockpiled from the clearance and levelling of the immediate position of the wall, where this was done: turf and soil was sometimes, but perhaps not invariably, stripped to provide a more solid base on which to erect the wall or bank. Yet more materials were often obtained from quarry scoops located immediately within, and often slightly upslope from, the line of the fortification. These can often still be identified as slightly scalloped indentations, generally with relatively level bases, or less regular hollows, close to the wall-line (*colour plate 16*). Other materials would need to have been brought in from further afield. This would be the case with the posts and other timber beams where these were used, although theoretically, in some cases at least, initial clearance of the site might produce enough usable wood to incorporate in the fortification. As well as major structural timbers, much slighter pieces, whether split or used as roundwood, would have been required for hurdling and similar purposes. This is likely to have come from managed woodland, coppiced deliberately for the

49 Indications of blows struck with an iron tool (highlighted with chalk) on a rock-face in a quarried area within Mont Beuvray

purpose. On other forts, the stone used in the facings of walls in particular was not simply locally obtained rubble, but deliberately quarried material, sometimes from nearby (inside the inner enceinte in the case of Mont Beuvray for instance: *49*) or from further away (as Sir Mortimer Wheeler noted was the case with the stonework used in the eastern gate at Maiden Castle). At the Colline des Tours at Levroux, Indre, the limestone small rubble used to construct the dump bank over the *murus gallicus* would have had to come from the plain below the site. The use of stone from different geological formations than those of the site is of course a clear indication that material has been carted there, but in other instances the condition of the stone itself can also indicate such practices: at the Caterthuns in Angus, for instance, the rounded, water-rolled character of the stones strongly indicated that they had come from a riverine setting.

THE EVIDENCE FROM UNFINISHED SITES

Since its publication in 1931 by the late Stuart Piggott, the southern English site of Ladle Hill in Hampshire has remained the classic unfinished hill-fort, still remarkable as Richard Feachem (1971) has described it for its 'spectacular incompleteness', and for the clear implications it provides of different sectors of the circuit having been worked by different gangs of labourers (*50*). Evidence from other sites, more-or-less unfinished, adds to the tally of traits that tell something of the process of construction, although it has to be acknowledged that at least some of this evidence could be interpreted differently, particularly if it is allowed that individual rampart circuits could have been of variable construction around their perimeters. For example, had a particular circuit been conceived as lengths of bank and ditch set at the most accessible points, joined by either a living or a dead thorn hedge across intervening, less approachable, stretches, the surviving lengths of earthwork might well be interpreted as indicating an unfinished scheme when, in effect, the present-day appearance is solely a product of factors of survival and detection. Other combinations could produce a similar effect – where earthworks were complemented by palisades, now not detectable on the surface, for instance.

It is also true that many of the initial means of indicating the future course of a fortification will have left no discernable trace, no more than do their modern equivalents such as bamboo canes, ranging rods, or even fluorescent tracer paint. There are, however, exceptions. It has been suggested, for example, that stake-holes noted by Thalassa Hencken at two locations under the inner fortification at Bredon Hill, Worcestershire, a glacis bank most likely later in date than the outer wall at the same site, may have been an indication of such an initial planning exercise.

'Unfinished works' as a concept effectively groups together fortifications abandoned in a variety of different conditions. In the case of those that were almost completed, it can be extremely difficult to decide in their now-decayed condition whether this was indeed their history. At the other end of the scale are those sites

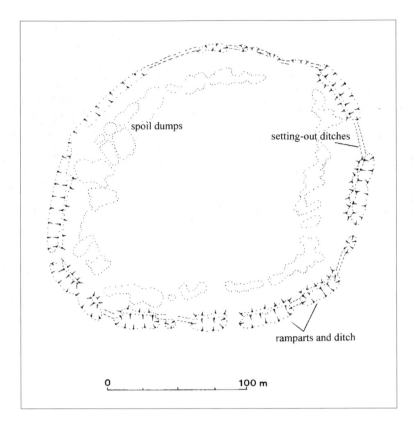

spoil dumps

setting-out ditches

ramparts and ditch

0   100 m

50 Ladle Hill, Hampshire, the unfinished fort. Evidence for the setting-out ditch, gang work in the digging of the main ditch, initial rampart construction, and dumps of superficial material from the ditch for re-sue in the wall-core. *Drawn by Samantha Dennis after Piggott 1931*

where little more than the intention to build is signalled, by marking-out features. Arguably amongst the most informative of sites, however, are those like Ladle Hill, abandoned during construction. In such circumstances, expedient devices that would have been buried within, or swept away by, the completed works can still be present, and can also be related to those sectors of the site where the scheme has been pursued and the banks and ditches built. And the patterning of this evidence, and any indications of different styles of work, can be used to propose different work gangs present on the project.

    Where a recognisable marker bank or ditch (or indeed both) occur, the implication that completion of the major work might take an extended period may be put forward. Other indications include earlier man-made features, such as pre-existing linear earthworks: such a bank was also incorporated into the Ladle Hill scheme. A variant on these is offered by fortifications that replaced earlier lines of palisading: in some cases, the subsequent enclosure lines ran approximately parallel to these, as at numerous sites in the Scottish Lowlands and Northumberland. Castle Knowe in Midlothian, with palisade line matched by an incomplete external ditch offers a good example. In other cases, the earlier palisade line was sealed directly below the fortification which succeeded it. Another indication of a scheme being unfinished is the occurrence of irregular heaps of building material, such as the low spreads of stone which intermittently overlie a marker ditch around the conspicuous hill of Little Conval near Dufftown in Moray (*51*).

Ladle Hill displays almost all of these traits. A pre-existing ditch, accompanied by a bank actually on the side outwith the future hill-fort ran around a portion of the intended circuit. Elsewhere a ditch half a metre deep had been cut on the line, and the material extracted from this thrown up on the ditch's inner margin to form a small bank. Gaps in these features, notably on the south-west and the east were probably intended to have been developed as entrances. At a number of points around the circuit, work had begun to deepen the ditch, normally just outside the line adopted by the marker features. The superficial deposits, soil and turf as well as the disaggregated upper parts of the underlying chalk, had been moved inside the fort and stockpiled for subsequent use, most likely as hearting or capping for the wall or to serve as an internal ramp. Once harder chalk that could be extracted in usable blocks from the ditch was reached, these were employed directly to build the wall. Still with substantial parts of the scheme unstarted, this building project was abandoned.

The pattern of the evidence recovered at Ladle Hill very much indicates that the work was being carried out by a series of work gangs, and in this instance as many as 12 of these have been suggested. The evidence of incomplete fortifications at other sites lends support to the idea of construction gangs, each with a length or lengths of the work to complete. On the northern side of the fort at Elsworthy Barrows in Somerset, for example, there are two segmented quarry ditches, set at a rather awkward angle to each other, and flanked some distance from their inner margin by a slight bank made up of the superficial deposits extracted from them. Evidence

51 Slight marker trench and informal rickles of gathered stone on a hill that also has palisade ditches: Little Conval, Moray

of gang work can be discerned elsewhere, including in more than one phase of the complex promontory enclosure at Winklebury Hill in Wiltshire, with segments of both unfinished ditch and rampart apparently in all three of the constructional schemes evident on this site.

One of a pair of enclosed sites at Hardings Down in Glamorgan demonstrates another variation on evidence both for gang work and for schemes abandoned before their completion. Both the site considered here and its neighbour seem to have been designed as multivallate hill-forts, with widely-spaced ramparts, of a type well known in south-western Britain. The East Fort, on the summit, has an incomplete inner enclosure, of which significant portions of the eastern end have been apparently completed, but where only a single detached length of bank is apparent at the western end. Where finished, the bank seems to have had an inner stone revetment, although in places this has subsequently been robbed out. A detached length of outer bank is most clearly marked adjacent to a simple gap entrance through it; an accompanying ditch is only visible at the south end of this feature. None of the unbuilt sections now show marker features of the kind discussed above. Dr Hogg remarked that some of the gangs here had 'completed the work, even to building an inner revetment of large blocks; others (of a kind not unknown today) did nothing'. One is tempted to say: it was ever thus. The western fort here sits slightly off the summit, and is rather different in character: it includes both a well-marked inner univallate enclosure and two outer lines, doubtfully unfinished, on the eastern side.

At one time, unfinished forts were explained as evidence for responses to invasion or other attacks that were made redundant by the course of events, with hurried construction in the face of the arrival of the Romans being a preferred hypothesis in some cases. Numerous alternative explanations are of course possible and unfinished forts cannot simply be read off as intimations of an unsuccessful defensive strategy.

It is now also possible to suggest that in at least some cases relatively slight lines of fortification are not evidence for schemes being incomplete, but rather that the function they were designed to fulfil was non-military – perhaps defining a space for ritual – such that the scale of the boundary works was of lesser importance. One indication that sites may have been conceived in this kind of way comes from a famous example that is very much an exception: Emain Macha near Armagh in Ulster. Here the substantial ditch of this remarkable enclosure lies, exceptionally, inside the line of rampart: it can be suggested that the reason was to contain what was represented by the remarkable features on that hilltop, and not to repulse attackers. Like the other 'royal sites' of Ireland this may not have played any conventional defensive role whatsoever.

Without entirely accepting that position in every case, it is possible to propose that some works were essentially token undertakings, not more elaborate schemes that had been abandoned before completion. An indication of this is the number of sites which have somewhat more substantial works, or additional lines near the positions of entrances, as at Dunnideer Hill near Insch in Aberdeenshire; and sites where surrounding works are apparently unfinished, but the interiors contain evidence for houses, as is the case at Charge Law Plantation in Peeblesshire. In the former cases, the variability in the nature of the enveloping works might have been intended, and not a symptom of incompleteness; in the latter, whilst the preferred explanation is that the site is simply unfinished, it could be that the site's boundaries were sufficiently defined to satisfy those living within them.

HOW MUCH LABOUR WENT INTO BUILDING FORTIFICATIONS?

There have been a number of attempts to gauge how much labour, over what sort of timescale, may have been involved in the construction of defences. Most have begun by calculating the physical resource requirements – tonnes of earth, quantities of stone, lengths of timber – implicit in the construction and using such figures as a basis, however shaky, to proceed to an estimate of labour. By the later stages of the Iron Age, almost the full gamut of hand-tools used in medieval times would have been available, but it is reasonable to assume that fewer mechanical aids in the form of machines to lift materials would have been used than in the contemporary Mediterranean world. It is assumed that animal traction was used primarily to haul materials to site. Nor have we any direct information on likely working practices, so that the figures that are suggested are very much 'guesstimates', and no more than that.

Digging and transporting material on modern experimental reconstructions – notably the building of the experimental earthworks in southern England – provide another insight into what could have been achieved using the available equipment. Using simple organic tools (rather than the iron ones to which at least some will have had access) on chalk, it is suggested that breaking up and moving a cubic metre of chalk per labourer per day is a reasonable average to use in calculations of this kind. Different rock types, and different distances over which materials were to be displaced, would clearly impact significantly on this figure – as would labour practices, and a raft of other variables which in essence are not known in detail. Such figures thus need to be regarded as giving very tentative orders of magnitude for tasks.

Clearly other insights can be gleaned from working through the routines of erecting such structures experimentally, including some inkling of organisational routines, as has been suggested too in the case of reconstructing houses. Some results from such endeavours help to provide colour on how the building of ramparts and walls may be considered.

Who constituted the labour force and who directed them? Any remarks on this need to be prefaced by the comment that practices are likely to have been very different over the geographical and chronological ranges across which hill-forts were built. The occurrence of comparable styles of building over substantial areas suggests shared architectural traditions, perhaps evidence, too, for some fundamental engineering understanding attained pragmatically and held in common. Such arrangements most likely entail the existence of specialist architect-builders and, given the range of specialist artisans otherwise apparent in at least some temperate European cultures during the Iron Age, and the existence, indeed celebrity, of some architects in contemporary Mediterranean societies, the existence of 'master builders' may be assumed. There is, however, no direct testimony of their existence in temperate Europe; it would be unreasonable to assume that the ideas and expertise of such a specialist necessarily lay directly behind the layout and construction of all hill-fort walls and ramparts. By the end of the Continental Iron Age, as Caesar's text makes plain, the building of at least temporary defences on campaign was following southern precedents and even being achieved (as in the Nervian works in front of Cicero's camp in 54) with Roman guidance. The first direct reference to specialists of this kind in the 'Celtic world' itself belongs in the first millennium AD (Graham 1951).

The labour forces deployed in the building of fortifications are unlikely to have worked uniquely on such tasks. A number of different mechanisms by which they could have been assembled can be proposed. It is likely that work was carried out by a system akin to *corvée,* whereby the provision of labour was part of a social or economic obligation. It is also a reasonable assumption that much of the labour was fitted into convenient periods of relative calm in the basic rhythm of the agricultural cycle: this is perhaps especially the case when the provision of load-bearing vehicles and animal traction for the transport of materials was important. In other instances, different mechanisms might be employed. One of the elements of life in Iron Age Europe that has become much more apparent in recent years is the evidence – from the analysis of collections of animal bones, or the existence of quantities of discarded wine amphorae apparently representing the product of single events – that feasting was a feature of life for some people, undoubtedly, and for some of the time only: it is certainly possible to envisage work feasts, of the kind discussed by Michael Dietler from a wide consultation of the anthropological literature, being produced to recompense those who had assisted in major labour-intensive manoeuvres associated with the construction of fortifications, such as – notionally – erecting major gates. In some cases too, it is known that modifications to defences – and even the building of some earthworks – were directly related to campaigning, and were thus the product of a labour force brought together primarily to fight and not to build. Inevitably, the mechanisms which have just been rehearsed are largely speculative, but they highlight the fact that it is to be expected that the products of such variable working arrangements might themselves be expected to show considerable architectural variety, and considerable variation, too, in the competence with which they were built.

RESOURCE REQUIREMENTS

The construction of major fortifications undoubtedly used substantial resources. In the case of the inner, 135ha enclosure at Mont Beuvray, the surrounding wall is over 5km long. Assuming, like the sections excavated to date, it was all constructed in *murus gallicus* style, some idea of the quantities of material required can be estimated. Discussion with colleagues from the *Office national des Forêts* suggests that the internal horizontal timberwork in the wall could have been obtained, given the density of trees in central France in near-natural circumstances, by clear-felling of the order of 60ha of mature oak forest – a substantial figure admittedly, but considerably less than the enclosed area of the site. In this instance, too, it is apparent that not all the timbers so used were in fact newly-felled; some had clearly been reclaimed from previous structures. Substantial quantities of slighter wood must have been needed for the breastwork along the top of the wall, although no direct evidence of this survives and it might have been dry-stone built. The initial height of the external wall-face is not known, but may be estimated to have been minimally 4.5m high. Whilst some of the facing stone could have been obtained from the ditch, much of the material extracted from this source seems to have been unsuitable, and most of the 7,500 cubic metres of facing stone required would have had to be quarried on, or close to, the site: traces of toolmarks at some of the quarried areas within the enclosure are still visible (see above). Some stone used apparently in small quantities in detailing (e.g. granites) had to be imported from lower ground nearby, but off the hill which the site occupies. The core of the wall would have required of the order of 100,000 cubic metres of hearting; at Beuvray, this is most likely to have been obtained from the ditch, by excavating quarry scoops adjacent to and upslope from the rampart line, and by redepositing domestic rubbish scraped up elsewhere. The last major element in the wall were the iron nails augered into the intersections of the structural timbers. Each of these weighs about 150g, or about 6,500 such massive spikes per tonne. These may have been contained in the wall at a rate of say 10 per linear metre, suggesting that there may have been some 10 tonnes of these diagnostic items in the original make-up of this circuit. Such a figure, which has to be advanced with very considerable caveats, given that only a miniscule proportion of this inner wall has been examined in any detail, none the less makes it plain that the iron production necessary demands work on an 'industrialised' scale. For the construction of a wall-and-ditch like that of the major *oppidum* of the *Aedui*, it seems reasonable to imagine that a substantial labour force was mobilised by the use of some or all of the mechanisms listed above. It is, however, interesting to note that some very much smaller enclosures in central France are surrounded by impressive fortifications built in this style, so that in some instances the elite seem to have been able to deploy significant resources on surrounding what may have been their key residences and main farms in a similar style.

LABOUR REQUIREMENTS

Given all the uncertainties surrounding working practices in the past, it is perhaps unsurprising that very different figures have been put forward for particular tasks, and for the overall effort involved in building some of these defensive works. Mortimer Wheeler, for example, suggested that the rampart at the great coastal fort at Bindon Hill, Dorset, could have been built by about 60 men in a fortnight, admittedly using modern tools and excluding the preparation and transport of timber. Given that its rampart is over 2800m long, this seems an impossibly high work-rate, with the squad erecting about 200 linear metres a day, and Hogg's estimate – that it may have taken 20 times longer to build with the equipment available in the Iron Age – appears intuitively much more probable.

Dr Hogg calculated the effort required in the construction of a number of forts, and these are worth reiterating as a way – albeit very approximate – of getting some idea on the effort that would have been required and, potentially, on the order-of-magnitude that may be surmised for the numbers involved in the construction process. Had the 680m long bank at Ladle Hill (Hogg 1975, 56) been completed to a height of 4m, and a basal width of 7m, some 11,000 cubic metres of chalk would need to have been moved. On-site observations make it plain much of this chalk would have required double-handling, as it was stockpiled for subsequent use in the bank pending the extraction of more solid blocks. Some 1,000 saplings would also have been required for the timberwork, Hogg estimated, and these he guessed might have taken 500 man-days to fell, strip and transport. In all, reducing the daily work rate to take account of the double-handling, somewhat less than 20,000 man-days might have gone into its construction. To arrive at the potential labour-force involved, Hogg used as a rule-of-thumb an estimate that hill-forts may have been intended to hold some 60 people per hectare of their internal space, so that the possible population of some 200 in this fort of a little over 3ha might have been capable of 150 man-day equivalents per working day, allowing for lesser contributions from children, the elderly and the infirm. On this basis a figure of some 80-120 working days can be derived for completing the univallate defence of this site, so that had all the population worked on it full-time it could easily have been completed within half a year.

It will be plain from the series of guesses and approximations just executed that calculations of this kind have little by way of solid foundation. For this reason, many archaeologists are altogether sceptical about citing them, but the present author believes that, as a rough-and-ready means of approaching what these monuments may have meant in terms of sheer human effort, they have a value. Enclosed sites which show no sign of permanent inhabitation – the so-called refuges – clearly pose extra, perhaps insurmountable, problems in regard to where the labour that built them may have originated, and how it was organised. Leaving this conundrum aside, a number of general tendencies can be extracted from such figures, namely that elaborate defensive schemes on small sites made proportionately the heaviest demands on their inhabitants, and would thus have benefited most from being able to call on additional labour from elsewhere. That said, the scale of work can be less demanding than appears at first sight: some of the smaller works can be shown to have been relatively manageable undertakings even for small-scale communities. Hogg's example was the small, trivallate contour fort on Camp Tops at Morebattle in the Scottish Borders, a site containing – from surviving surface evidence – eight houses and thus perhaps a labour force of some 30 from a total population a third or so larger. On this basis, the 900 cubic metres of material contained in the inner rampart might have required 30 days of labour for the community; the slighter, middle bank some 19 days to move its 570 cubic metres; and the least substantial, outer bank could have been built within a fortnight. Such figures tend to show that whilst ramparts and walls were indeed major investments for the communities that built them, and included ranges of tasks that would have had to be fitted into the agricultural year and doubtlessly programmed against all kinds of other demands on people's time, they were generally not of Herculean proportions. For all the shortcomings encoded in such calculations, they may help to bring into slightly sharper focus on the one hand their significance as fortifications, and on the other ideas of these features as monuments and symbols.

HOW DURABLE WERE HILL-FORT DEFENCES?

It is one thing mobilising the labour and resources required to construct the circuits of fortifications surrounding hill-forts, and clearly in some instances these represented very major undertakings that may have taken some years to achieve, but the maintenance of these works, generally little considered in the literature, must have represented a major commitment.

Freeze-thaw, displacement through surface run-off, the consequences of accumulating leaf litter and other plant debris, colonisation by weeds, damage by animal and other biological activity, the presence of wet-rot, dry-rot and other forms of timber decay, insect infestation, normal wear-and-tear, flash floods, settling and subsidence, correcting original substandard building, fire-, storm- and wind-damage, more cosmetic aims such as maintaining or enhancing their appearance – there is a host of reasons why many components of fortifications would have required both routine and, on occasion, special attention from maintenance squads. Of course requirements would have been very variable, depending on such things as the architecture of the defences, the quality of the materials used, and a raft of local weather conditions including humidity and exposure, and to that extent the frequency of the need for repair and how widespread the problems encountered were, will too have shown very considerable variation (*colour plate 17*). A well-built dry-stone wall, constructed of durable granites on a stable and free-draining subsoil on a levelled terrace in a relatively sheltered location, that was, in addition, lightly used is likely to have posed far fewer problems than, for example, a timber-framed wall, built using reused wood of varying quality and age, and interspersed with wall-faces of very mixed geologies, including rock types prone to exfoliation at low temperatures. This would especially be the case if the latter was built on a slope over an impermeable subsoil in an area subject to torrential rain. Such a comparison simply highlights variability; the first wall would not have been maintenance-free, as it would have been desirable on the one hand to keep it free from colonisation by shrubs, and on the other the exposed timberwork of the breastwork would have been subject to weathering and other kinds of decay and would thus have required periodic repair or replacement.

Of course, although useful insights can be gleaned from the anthropological literature, archaeologists have very little real knowledge about how such maintenance work may have been carried out in organisational terms, and this has a profound bearing on the durability of some at least of the series of fortifications that have been discussed above. This is perhaps particularly the case with those mixing materials in their construction, where structural timbers may have been exposed differentially to weathering and, for example, to contact with water-retaining clays in the wall-core.

Thus whilst some defences, perhaps particularly dry-stone walls, or well-built dump ramparts, may have remained basically serviceable for extended periods, others may have started to cause problems almost from when they were completed, and certainly within a decade or two. Such difficulties would of course have been exacerbated by what can be considered defective workmanship in their original construction; and clearly in this consideration the issue of damage sustained in any attacks has been set to one side.

In some instances, the outcome of maintenance work would have been highly visible over extended areas around the hill-fort. As originally built, for example, the fresh chalk-white ramparts of a multivallate site like Maiden Castle, Dorset, must have been an imposing spectacle, visually far more stunning than their current subdued grass-green hue suggests. The brilliant white of their initial appearance would have diminished as weathering occurred, and as vegetation began to colonise wherever it could establish a foothold. It is thus possible to suggest that on the one hand extending, and on the other repairing, these earthworks must have been a very visible activity, and thus, as Niall Sharples has suggested, an effective means for those commanding this work and mobilising the labour necessary to signal their importance visually to all who could see the multiple lines of rampart.

LATER MODIFICATIONS

In a number of cases, the earthworks of hill-forts were subsequently remodelled or repaired for use in the Late Roman period, or indeed during the centuries of the Early Historic period. Some have mottes added to, or set within, their circuits, and the sites of yet others are also occupied by masonry castles. An excellent example of the former is the substantial Norman castle mound within 'British Camp', or the Herefordshire Beacon in the Malvern Hills. Generally speaking, the later these modifications, the more distinctive the traces they leave, such that separating out what are or may be the traces of the earlier earthworks is more readily achievable.

It is worth remarking as a codicil to this discussion, that some hill-forts have been the target of much later modifications, of an altogether different nature. Sometimes these make good damage, inadvertent or otherwise, but in other cases they modify sites in order to make them conform better to anticipated characteristics at the time. One of the sites that attracted the attention of the Emperor Napoleon III in the middle of the nineteenth century was the major fort of some 26ha at Vieux-Moulin at St-Pierre-en-Chastre in Oise, France, a site with a particularly important final Bronze Age occupation. As elsewhere, Napoleon ordered this site to be excavated, and in this instance the work was carried out under the direction of Viollet-le-Duc, celebrated for his exuberant restoration work on medieval architecture. In the case of the Vieux-Moulin, it appears that Viollet-le-Duc had the ramparts entirely rebuilt if not wholly created 'avec beaucoup de fantaisie', according to Jean-Claude Blanchet. The entrances, too, were remodelled, and double ditches fronting the earth-and-dry-stone wall edging the summit plateau were probably added at this time, most likely in an effort to persuade Napoleon that the site was Roman.

The idea that each generation of archaeological researchers interprets sites according to the precepts and models of their day is a well-known one. But to that truism needs to be added the odd case where the field record has been physically reshaped to conform to such concerns.

5

HILL-FORTS IN WAR

Despite reasonable doubts about the military effectiveness of some examples, hill-forts, it has been claimed with justification, were 'the ultimate defensive weapon of European prehistory…of the first millennium BC' (Avery 1986). In recent years there has been a revival in the acceptance amongst archaeologists and anthropologists of strife and warfare as a component of Iron Age life, as part of a wider trend away from rather pacified perspectives on the lives of our predecessors (e.g. Leblanc and Register 2004 review recent literature), and in this chapter I will consider some of the material that is directly relevant to Celtic fortifications.

Evidence for conflict at hill-forts takes two principal forms: archaeological and literary. Exceptionally, they may coincide, sometimes in a very detailed way, as at Mont Auxois in Burgundy, *Alesia* of the *Mandubii*. Here, Caesar's text (in *de Bello gallico*, Book VII) can be matched in detail with the archaeological evidence, more particularly of the siege works that he commanded to be built in 52 BC. Since the literary accounts tend to relate to a period when warfare with the Romans was underway, it is sometimes uncertain whether tactics that are mentioned in these documentary sources are long-established native procedures, or ones adopted in emulation of, or response to, the practices of the late Republican army. In most cases the sources discuss Roman attacks on native sites; or – outside the scope of this volume – native attacks on Roman encampments. Few accounts describe native attacks on native sites. Even in post-Roman times in Britain, literary evidence for assaults on fortified sites is rare: detail is often absent both in the early literature of Ireland and in sources such as the Annals which, whilst they make mention for example of sieges at strongholds and their outcomes, do not generally provide extensive detail on the conduct of the conflict itself.

It is also worth bearing in mind that by the time accounts such as that of Julius Caesar become available, there had been a prolonged period of contacts, including military ones, between the peoples of the European heartland and their southern neighbours. The nature of these had been varied: there were raids south and south-east; and efforts to consolidate these into permanent annexation and settlement in some regions; and there is also evidence for mercenary service. Whilst at least some of the set-piece battles about which we have classical accounts were fought in open country, there must have been plentiful opportunities to observe and participate in attacks on fortified settlements. Of these, perhaps the first, almost certainly the most famous, albeit somewhat mythologised in the version that has survived, is the account of the Gaulish attack on Rome itself in 390 BC.

It is certainly clear that even by the time of the expansion of the Roman republic into the areas of Cisalpine Gaul, Gaulish strategies of resistance could involve the occupation and defence of their principal enclosed sites, their *oppida*; but elsewhere such sites seem to have been given up in favour of resistance based in the countryside rather than marshalled behind walls. Such a pattern fits well with Alain Deyber's analysis (1987) of the conduct of the Gallic War in the first century BC. Whilst there were certainly sieges and set-piece battles at hill-forts, at this time represented by *oppida* such as *Alesia*, *Gergovia* and *Avaricum* discussed below, much of the military resistance to the legions was based on what might be considered a guerrilla-style willingness to profit from the opportunities offered by the landscape, and in particular by forest, and through hindering the enemy's progress by scorched earth policies to deprive them of supplies. In these special circumstances, too, the existence of fortified places did not necessarily entail their defence. Indeed, in some instances – for example in the territory of the *Bituriges* in 52 BC – the decision was taken deliberately to destroy enclosed sites, rather than to seek to defend them against the Roman army. Caesar tells us that more than 20 *oppida* in that territory were deliberately torched; *Avaricum*, which was defended – unsuccessfully – was the exception to the rule.

LITERARY SOURCES AND TACTICS

In the documentary sources, unsurprisingly, the conflicts considered worthy of note are generally those between Roman and native. Accounts of warfare describing assaults on hill-forts by native tribes thus rarely occur. There are, however, rare examples in Caesar's *de Bello gallico*, helpfully enumerated in translation for us by Leo Rivet (1971). One of the most famous refers to an attack by a substantial force of Belgae and Germans in the initial stages of the Gallic War in 57 BC. This native assault occurred at *Bibrax*, an *oppidum* of the pro-Roman *Remi* lying north of the Aisne River in north-east Gaul. A passage (one that cannot be regarded as wholly uncontentious, as Leo Rivet has detailed 1971, 189), in Caesar, as translated by Peter Wiseman, uses the occasion to provide more general information, recounting that:

> The Gauls and the Belgae use the same method of attacking such places. They begin by surrounding its entire wall with a large number of men and hurling stones at it from all sides. When this has stripped the wall of its defenders, they hold up their shields to provide a protective shell, set fire to the gates, and begin to undermine the wall. (*de Bello gallico*, II, 6)

In this instance, although the first part of this strategy was launched, and Caesar tells us spears too were thrown, in fact the arrival of Roman legions brought the attack to a premature halt. Neither the firing of the gates, nor the sapping, actually occurred in this attack. There is, however, plentiful evidence that fire-raising was a preferred tactic, not only used by the Iron Age inhabitants of Gaul against Roman siegeworks (see below for *Uxellodunum*), but also, in his assault on the *oppidum* of *Cenabum*, present-day Orléans, by Caesar himself. Michael Avery (1986) has, however, seen in this description an indication of a style of warfare he believes to be implied by the counter-measure represented by the development of inturned entrances with long, largely stone-lined, passages and gates at their inner margins, as are characteristic for example of areas of southern Britain in the later phases of the Iron Age. These (and other late elaborations of entranceways, such as the last phases of the gates at Maiden Castle, Dorset) he sees as a response to assault techniques using slung and/or thrown stones – and stones lobbed in quantity – as the means of clearing the defences of troops to enable the gates at the inner extremity of the entrance passage to be approached, quantities of tinder to be positioned and ignited, and then the attack in due course to be mounted through the smouldering debris of the destroyed gateway. Whether or not one accepts the detail of this scenario, Caesar's description just quoted does indeed suggest the use of an organised sequence of tactics in which numbers of troops were engaged, some way removed indeed from the ideals of heroic warfare, and perhaps indicative of a change in military procedure and etiquette.

Details of the evolution of hill-fort architecture may thus bring indirect testimony of such changes in the objectives of warfare and the means of achieving them. It may also be remarked that, whilst numbers of southern British hill-forts in particular, but also some Continental examples such as the Puy du Tour in Corrèze, have produced caches of sling-stones, the present author knows of no instances in which suitable stones have been recovered distributed in quantity through an entranceway in the manner that Avery's hypothesis of their use in conflict might imply, although very substantial stockpiles – as noted for the eastern gate at Maiden Castle in Dorset – do come from their vicinity. Contrastingly, the evidence for the use of archery against forts is altogether more muted, certainly in temperate western Europe, at least until the later stages of the La Tène Iron Age. One exception to this is a relatively recent series of finds of weapons, including numerous iron arrowheads of approximately (La Tène B2/C1) third century BC date, on the back of the rampart of the upland promontory fort at Bourguignon-lès-Morey in Burgundy; this may well be evidence of an assault on the site.

Were specific assault tactics borrowed or not? It is sometimes difficult to be sure. An example is provided by a description of the infilling of ditches with brushwood or wattles, something, as Leo Rivet noted (1971), only described by Caesar in use by the Gauls for attacks on Roman works, but conceivably a strategy that they had adopted at an earlier date, if not one developed locally. Rivet hypothesises that the tactic of infilling ditches to facilitate assaults may have been a contributor to the development of multivallation, generally proposed as a response to the advent of sling warfare.

LITERARY SOURCES, FIELD REMAINS AND AN ARCHAEOLOGY OF BATTLES AT HILL-FORTS

Since the nineteenth century, particularly in Gaul, ancient *Gallia*, there has been a major antiquarian and subsequently archaeological effort to try to identify the various sites mentioned – in some instances in considerable detail – by Caesar. Particular attention has been paid to those where battles occurred. Such exercises have tended to combine topographic studies, the use of place-name evidence, and the results of archaeological survey and sometimes excavation. Sites associated with events described in Caesar also occur in Belgium, Switzerland and southern England. Whilst not all the settlement sites that Caesar recorded were the locations of battles, some certainly were. The approach has also been taken elsewhere: *Numantia* in Spain and (at a slightly later chronological horizon) *Masada* in Israel are other famous instances where this type of Iron Age 'battlefield archaeology' has been pursued with considerable success.

Not all identifications resulting from this approach are of course uncontroversial, and in some instances competing claimants have been proposed and supported with vehemence, passion and a lesser or greater degree of convincing archaeological and topographic support, over decades and indeed longer. This last factor has long been the case with the site of the attack on *Gergovia* (52 BC), with a number of claimant sites, especially in the hinterland of Clermont-Ferrand in the Auvergne, having produced vociferous advocates. The confirmation during recent evaluative excavations of the existence of the two Roman camps used in the siege below the plateau de Merdogne – the site renamed as the *plateau de Gergovie* during the Second Empire of Napoleon III in the third quarter of the nineteenth century – demonstrates that, in this instance, the hypotheses advanced in the pioneering work done then were essentially correct (Guichard in Goudineau 1998). Relatively little material culture was found to support these views compared to the quantities of evidence from *Alesia* for example, but it does include two iron catapult bolts as well as prepared stones for use in other artillery pieces. There now seems no reason to doubt that the plateau de Merdogne, a site of some 70ha settled progressively from a generation or so before the Roman conquest, is indeed the *Gergovia* in and around which Vercingetorix camped his troops in 52 BC, rather than alternative claimants such as the upland sites of Corent or the Côtes de Clermont.

A CASE STUDY: *ALESIA*

Still the most remarkable of these locations in at which conflict took place around a hill-fort is the *oppidum* of *Alesia* of the *Mandubii* at Alise-Sainte-Reine in Burgundy, France (52). In this instance, major new research, its publication directed in exemplary fashion by Siegfried von Schnurbein and Michel Reddé, has amplified in considerable detail the results of nineteenth-century work on the site and its surroundings; but here the primary link between Caesar's text and the locality had been made long

52 The upland plateau of Mont Auxois. *Courtesy: Stéphan Fichtl*

before Napoleon III's associate, commandant Baron E. Stoffel, carried out fieldwork from 1861. The fit between the lengthy text Caesar provides us with in Book VII of the Gallic War, and the archaeological details of the siegeworks on the ground is very close, although the evidence from Mont Auxois itself, the site of the *oppidum* and subsequent Gallo-Roman settlement of *Alesia*, is a less positive element. For instance, the position of the *murus gallicus* around the Mont Auxois at the time of the decisive events in the summer of 52 BC is less clear-cut, some elements of what may have been a complex system appearing to be more recent in date.

Key elements of Caesar's text describe the building of two lines of earthworks around the *oppidum* site in and around which Vercingetorix and the Gaulish army were established when Caesar caught up with him. In outline, the works consisted of the *oppidum* enclosure (itself never directly implicated in the fighting), an outer wall and ditch on the eastern side of the fort, behind which further elements of the Gaulish army were encamped, and the Roman siegeworks erected over a period of some two months in 52 BC. These, built sequentially, consisted of two lines: the first usually termed the circumvallation, investing the *oppidum*, was some 11 Roman miles in length and equipped with numerous camps and strong-points; additional features, notably a major ditch some distance in front, were subsequently added. The second line was a response to units of the Gaulish cavalry managing to steal away from Mont Auxois to raise a relieving army from the other Gaulish *civitates* or states and is usually called the countervallation. Three Roman miles longer than the first, its purpose was to block the new army's progress towards the Roman positions around the *oppidum*.

In archaeological terms, the landscape around the *oppidum,* as cultivated ground, is in the main a zone of destruction, in which surface traces of the investing works have long since disappeared. Considerable elements of Caesar's scheme were identified by the troops at Stoffel's command (*colour plate 18*), essentially by an assiduous programme of trenching, and quantities of Roman and native equipment was recovered, notably at the foot of Mont Réa, one of the neighbouring plateaux, and in the plain of Laumes immediately below the site. The newer work was able, however, to profit from the cropmark imagery produced by René Goguey's repeated aerial surveys of the vicinity, and was of course attuned to pick up finer detail in the archaeological record – small pits, post-holes and the like – than the fieldworkers of the Second Empire had been able to note. More examples, and more detail of those already known, were added by the 1990s fieldwork. In essence, Caesar's scheme worked: Vercingetorix and the Gaulish army placed within and – initially – on the eastern slopes of the *oppidum*, failed to break out, with the exception of the escapade mentioned above, whereas the relieving force, again despite some initial successes, did not manage to penetrate the entire Roman system. In the end, as the possibilities of the two Gaulish armies linking up evaporated in the clash of arms, Vercingetorix surrendered some years later to be strangled at Rome in Caesar's triumph, and the *oppidum* itself is not mentioned as having been directly attacked by the Roman forces.

The catalogue of finds from all the fieldwork around the Mont Auxois gathered in the recent definitive publication provides an excellent introduction to the armament of the mid-first century BC, and makes clear the importance of projectiles – javelins, arrowheads and slingstones (double-pyramidal lead examples being found in some numbers by metal detectorists) – as well as swords. Some of the elements relate to artillery, and iron caltrops – otherwise rare outwith the immediate Mediterranean basin at this time – would have served to break up cavalry charges. These are multi-pointed iron devices, designed always to have a point projecting upwards whichever way they are laid or fall, to maim horses. Two brief observations may be added: first, attributing particular series of arms to one side or the other is made harder by the fact that weaponry was clearly thrown back and forward between the adversaries; and second, amongst the La Tène swords, one or two were of middle La Tène type, and thus of some considerable antiquity by the time the battle took place. Whilst, in general, it may be reasonable to assume that each warrior usually fought with a sword designed, measured and made for him, here the presence of a few rather elderly weapons may be evidence for one or two fighters going into conflict perhaps clutching their grandfathers' blades'.

UXELLODUNUM OF THE CADURCI

Of the several Gallic War sites where we have literary testimony and where direct evidence of warfare is known, there is one case where the provision of water was critical to the way the conflict unfolded. During the extensive 'mopping up' operations that took place in 51 BC after the defeat and capture of Vercingetorix at *Alesia*, a Roman force was sent in pursuit of an irregular Gaulish army whose leaders intended to invade the immediate hinterland of the Mediterranean coast − the original Roman *Provincia*. This latter force halted on its route south and occupied the Cadurcan *oppidum* of *Uxellodunum* − identified most usually with Puy d'Issolu near Vayrac in the department of Lot (Quercy). Under the command of one of Caesar's lieutenants, and then latterly Caesar himself, camps and a circumvallation were started around the upland plateau near the River Dordogne on which this *oppidum* was set (53). Gaulish troops despatched outside the *oppidum* to obtain supplies were eventually defeated, and their leaders captured or driven off. The defenders still inside the *oppidum*, however, appear to have been adequately supplied with foodstuffs. In these dry limestone uplands, Caesar's attention turned to cutting the water supply as the prime means of bringing matters to a conclusion. First, artillery, archers and slingers were put in position to prevent the defenders scrambling down the steep side of the hill from the fort, which was set on an upland plateau at about 310m and 80ha in extent, to the nearby river. Attention now focused on the only remaining source of water: a spring located outwith, but close to, the main fortification line of the *oppidum*. Caesar set out to deny the defenders access to the spring, by building a mound and a massive tower as a platform for artillery. Resistance continued: this and neighbouring structures were ignited by the Gauls, who tossed flaming tallow-filled barrels downslope. Feigning a general assault on the *oppidum*, Caesar managed to divert attention from this sector, and the fires were extinguished. But still the besieged held firm. The *coup de grâce* was provided by Roman sapping: the water supply from the spring was diverted by tunnelling, at which time the defenders capitulated. Once victorious Caesar had the hands cut off his Gaulish opponents, as a gruesome means of demonstrating his power.

Recent excavations around the location of the spring provide detailed support, much amplifying the results of the limited excavations of the 1860s by J.-B. Cessac, and thereafter Stoffel, which swung Napoleon III in favour of this, rather than a number of other possible sites in Quercy advocated for this battle. Such a selection cannot be made, of course, without others taking different lines; before the new fieldwork directed by Jean-Pierre Girault got under way, a literature review identified some 2,000 items written by protagonists of one or other proposed site for this, the last great battle of the Gallic War. The site of the battle that saw the end of the siege has been confirmed around the spring called the Fontaine de Loulié. Although the terrain has been much disturbed by early excavators and by the attentions of *fouilleurs clandestins* equipped with metal-detectors, Girault and his colleagues have identified over 200 arrowheads in context, and 15 iron catapult bolts to add to the quantities (over 700 arrowheads for instance) recovered in less secure circumstances since the nineteenth century (54). Surviving elements of stratification examined by the team have also produced pottery, Roman amphorae, and further armaments, along with copious indications of severe fires, and tunnels of the kind to be anticipated from the

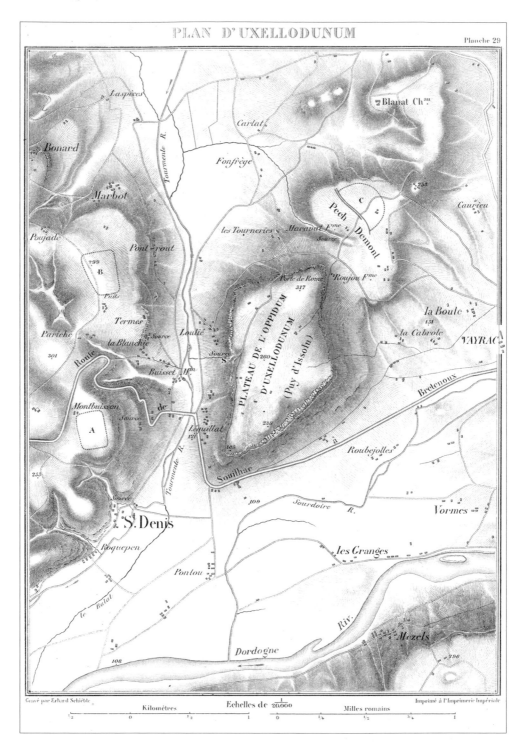

53 The setting of the plateau of the Puy d'Issolu near the Dordogne river (Quercy); after Napoleon III's original publication. *Courtesy: Stéphan Fichtl*

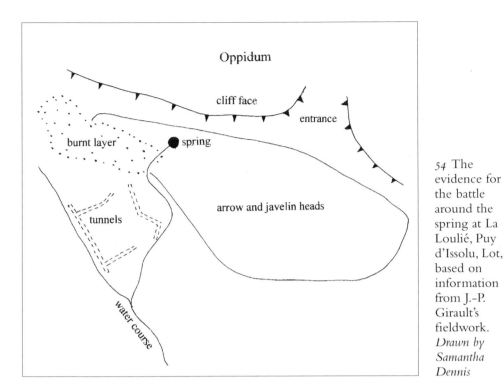

54 The evidence for the battle around the spring at La Loulié, Puy d'Issolu, Lot, based on information from J.-P. Girault's fieldwork. *Drawn by Samantha Dennis*

literary account. In this instance the localisation of the battle seems incontrovertible, although the positions of the camps associated with the Roman works remain uncertain, and the nature and extent of the native occupation on the hilltop and its fortifications have still received little attention.

OTHER EVIDENCE FOR WARFARE

Recognising indications of warfare at a particular hill-fort site is not, of course, uniquely dependent on there being literary records, but in their absence archaeological evidence can be more difficult to interpret, and is in some cases not unambiguous.

In the absence of modern provisions to bring them under control, evidence for widespread fires within forts is to be expected. Whilst undoubtedly testimony to destruction, burnt deposits and layers are difficult to sustain as necessarily evidence for warfare, in the absence of supplementary indications from other kinds of data. Thus, a gate burning down could be evidence for its deliberate firing, but is not forcibly so. Clearly such evidence of destruction is strengthened by the recovery of weapons suggesting hostilities: at the Iberian site of Pech Maho, near Sigéan in Aude, Languedoc, for instance, evidence for widespread destruction by fire is matched by the recovery of stone bullets from catapults, and by a substantial collection of

Greek types of arrowhead, triangular in cross-section, picked up between the two enclosing walls of the site. In this instance, it seems reasonable to read the evidence as suggesting an assault, leading to the destruction of at least part of the site.

In other cases, a straightforward reading of the surface evidence on or around a hill-fort may lead to a potentially spurious conclusion about the nature of the activity at a particular site. At the foot of Annandale, a river that drains southward into the inner Solway Firth in south-west Scotland, a conspicuous isolated hill is crowned by the grass-covered remains of one of the most extensive hill-forts in the country. At the foot of the hill, along both of its long sides, were laid out two substantial Roman camps; conspicuous mounds attached to their perimeters on the sides nearest the hill-fort are interpreted as stances for pieces of artillery, from which stones could be lobbed upslope into the hilltop fort. At first sight, then, the disposition seems not unlike that just described at *Alesia*; the hill-fort at Burnswark must therefore, it has been suggested, be the site of a siege related to one of the campaigns of subjugation that periodically saw the Roman army roll northward into lowland Scotland. Given the incompleteness of the literary record detailing the history of Roman involvement in Scotland, the absence of a corresponding source specifying the event is, in itself, untroubling. Closer inspection of the field record, coupled with excavation evidence, suggests, however, that the interpretation arrived at superficially can be questioned. The first element of doubt arose as a result of small-scale excavations by the late George Jobey on the hill-fort, traditionally seen as a 'minor *oppidum*' of the *Novantae*, the tribe who occupied south-west Scotland at the beginning of the first millennium AD. The designation of the site as a minor *oppidum* was a recognition that none of the major hill-forts of Scotland reached anything like the scale of their southern counterparts, but carried the assumption – now known not always justifiable – that the biggest examples in the local environment would be chronologically amongst the latest, essentially the culmination of the series in social and political terms.

On the one hand, Jobey's intervention demonstrated that the initial enclosure of the summit, by a double palisade – taking in potentially about the same area as the subsequent fortifications – occurred much earlier in the Iron Age than the first or second centuries AD, the most likely dates here for Roman activity. Jobey's work also indicated that the subsequent fortification was equally to be attributed early within the local Iron Age, although the evidence available to fix it chronologically was rather slender. Tentatively, then, Burnswark can be fitted into an emerging pattern in southern Scotland, whereby some at least of the big forts seem not to be the outcome of increasing centralisation and hierarchisation during the Iron Age, and thus pale northern equivalents of the *oppida* of Late La Tène found some hundreds of kilometres to the south. Rather it is argued that they would have been a feature of an earlier stage within the Iron Age, perhaps even of the end of the Bronze Age. The fortifications on Burnswark may thus have been dilapidated for some considerable time, possibly centuries, before the Roman troops constructed the camps around its skirts. On the other hand, Jobey concluded on the basis of his rampart cuttings that the stones projected by the Roman catapults had been launched at a defence that had already collapsed. Although small finds are generally not prolific on many Scottish hill-fort sites, material close in date to the Roman period is often amongst the most recognisable and this is rare but not entirely absent at Burnswark. And so, in recent years, the prevailing view has been that the Burnswark camps do indeed testify to a military event; that, however, was not a battle as part of a siege, but rather the testament of the manoeuvres of an army in training, as the sweating troops 'took their turn in repeated assaults upon the derelict ramparts under cover of a hail of sling-shot and arrows' (RCAHMS 1997, 182). Not everyone is, however, convinced that this scenario reveals the whole story: a small Roman fortlet in one corner of the larger camp, and indications that the larger camp may have been modified, suggest that the time-depth of Roman activity at this site may have been greater, with only a second, Antonine phase being explicable by the hypothesis just given.

DEAD BODIES AND WAR CEMETERIES

So rare are Iron Age burials in many, although by no means all, cultural settings in temperate Europe, that those found in association with settlement sites in general, and with the defences of hill-forts in particular, need to be regarded as something distinctly out of the ordinary. Some of the latter may be dedicatory and thus directly related to the construction of the earthworks which overlay them; others may be much more straightforward burials, once placed *extra muros*, but subsequently enveloped as a particular site expanded or was later enclosed. Others may even be the result of deaths, accidental or otherwise, during construction, conveniently disposed of within accumulating banks like the unfortunates interred in poured concrete in more recent time. Overall, discerning the motives lying behind the disposal of the dead in such intances may be less than straightforward: some of the evidence is thus considered in a subsequent chapter, where practices interpretable as ritual in intention are the focus.

If the human skeletal remains found in the immediate environs of fortifications are examined in closer focus, further issues require to be taken into account. In particular at locations where, for example, the hanging of trophies may be likely, such as entrances, the interpretation of some kinds of finds, notably skulls, needs to be reviewed cautiously. Even if these had been severed on the battlefield, it can be argued that the fighting could have taken place well away from the hill-fort on whose portal they were eventually displayed. The association between the place of death and that of the display of these human remains is thus not secure; in sanctuary sites in Continental Europe it is not unknown for crania to be under-represented relative to other remains which are in some instances at least interpretable as battle casualties: the implication that the skulls ended up elsewhere is clear.

In other instances, contrastingly, the evidence does suggest that complete skeletons, and sometimes parts of bodies, related to fortifications, may less ambiguously be considered as casualties of war in or around the earthworks at which they were eventually interred. Some of these occur in more-or-less recognisable graves; the context of others suggests that, had their deaths not been related to the destruction and abandonment of a particular site, their remains would not have lain undisturbed at their particular style.

Maiden Castle's 'war cemetery' probably remains the classic example of the formal series of graveyards found in close association with fortifications. During Sir Mortimer Wheeler's celebrated excavations of this Dorset fort, a considerable number of burials was found in the eastern gateway, in pits cut through an ash or charcoal layer related by him to the destruction of the gateway, and from the vicinity of which a number of Roman projectile points – considered by Sir Mortimer to indicate the use of artillery *ballistae* – were also found. Associated objects suggest these burials could belong to the campaign directly following the arrival of the Roman army in southern England in AD 43, but overall, these interments are part of a wider series of Durotrigian burials around this entranceway, and are not in many respects different from other examples from Dorset of Late Iron Age/Early Roman date. Some, however, did show clear signs, in the form of skeletal damage, of injury from weapons, including one male skull with a disc of bone entirely detached from its left front, damage entirely consistent with a heavy strike by a right-handed swordsman (Wheeler 1943, plate LVC). In general it was skulls rather than limb bones which showed the most severe wounding, and some of the cuts and blows may well have been rained on the heads of already-dead defenders. There are adult and adolescent females amongst the nearly 40 dead interred here, but, as Niall Sharples has pointed out, less than half show definite wounds, and in a few cases wounds have at least partially healed over. Of course, the latter could have been from an earlier conflict; and many fatal injuries will not be registered on the skeletons. All in all, the evidence that this 'War' component of the cemetery is an unambiguous indication of hasty burial following a massacre here in the eastern gate is less than clear-cut, although the death of numbers of those buried from injuries sustained in fighting (albeit perhaps elsewhere) is beyond debate.

At Sutton Walls, Herefordshire, the skeletal evidence seems rather more diagnostic, although the circumstances of its discovery were very different. At this 11ha univallate fort a series of skeletons of males, generally middle aged or younger and including young teenagers, was found: some displayed weapon cuts that had penetrated bone. These remains were discovered in the ditch terminals at an entrance and were lying in its last, flat-bottomed, recut. There was no weaponry with them. Although some had been wholly or partially decapitated, there is no evidence that they were other than buried quickly, but at no great depth however (55). The burials in the upper layer showed signs of disturbance by dogs or wolves. It may be entirely reasonable to see these as casualties of a battle related to the Roman expansion into this area around AD 75, as Kathleen Kenyon (1953) envisaged. Certainly, the site's major univallate enclosure was modified somewhat before this time, with material scraped from internal scoops being used to heighten an earlier glacis bank. Parts of this

55 Some of the skeletons in the final ditch recut at Sutton Walls. *Courtesy: Royal Archaeological Institute*

bank seem to have been pushed down to inter these corpses, but there seems no compelling reason in the apparent absence of any diagnostic equipment to suppose that the casualties were involved in fighting the Romans, rather than another native British force. Those that had been beheaded may either have been so treated *post mortem*, or could have been executed for no better reason than having been on the losing side.

A number of southern British sites, notably South Cadbury, Somerset, but also including Bredon Hill, Gloucestershire, have produced partial remains of individuals who have either been hacked to pieces or left to decay on the surface before ending up, wholly or partially disarticulated, in their findspots within gateways. Not least as a result of the varied and extended post-mortem treatment of the Iron Age dead identified by Jean-Louis Brunaux (2004) at sites across the channel in Picardy like Gournay-sur-Aronde (within a hill-fort) and Ribemont-sur-Ancre (set in open country), it should not be automatically assumed that the incomplete remains of people found in gateways are necessarily informing us of where they died. Hill and Woodward's thorough interpretation of the human remains in the south-western gateway at South Cadbury in the final report of the excavation (in Barrett 2000) make plain how complex it can be to try to disentangle precisely what is represented by remains that can be initially characterised as 'massacre deposits'. This South Cadbury evidence is considered further in the following chapter.

The structural sequence of the gate through the inner massive dump rampart (probably the more recent of the two lines of fortification represented) at Bredon Hill, culminated in the construction of an elaborate and very long inturned passageway, some 7.5m wide and 40m long. This had a gate at its inner end, supported on three posts, and along its length a bridge carried on upright timbers set in the revetments of the inturns, complemented by two massive posts in the entranceway. This entranceway had received at least two layers of paving, above which excavation revealed the presence of many incomplete skeletons, some still partially articulated. At least 64 individuals were represented. The original excavator regarded these remains as the casualties of a massacre propagated by arriving Belgae, one is tempted to add with all the hallmarks of the fully berserk. Not all the human remains here, however, can be accommodated in this perspective, regardless of whom the adversaries may have been. Six human skulls were found roughly aligned in the charred remains of the gateway, and they are likely to be trophies from earlier activity, perhaps but not necessarily conflict. These, it appears, had been displayed at the gate by the site's inhabitants some time before the conflict betokened by the other skeletal material, but ended up mixed in with the latter during the carnage and destruction indicated during Thalassa Hencken's fieldwork (1938).

In other cases, the character of the human remains seems to have been rather different. The laying of a railway line that cut through the ditch of the fort at Spettisbury (Dorset) produced the remains of about 100 skeletons, seemingly from a pit, but in this instance with an admixture of metal objects (Gresham 1939). The southern British evidence reviewed by Whimster (1981) and others points to very variable practices, in which expediency and haste in the disposal of the dead seem to be recurrent traits. If circumstances like those argued for here related directly to warfare, such variations are perhaps to be anticipated.

OTHER MILITARY USE OF HILL-FORTS – CASE STUDIES IN THE ROMAN ARMY

Both literary and archaeological evidence make it plain that, on occasion, during wartime, or in its immediate aftermath, native fortifications could be used by the Roman army. Caesar, for example, regularly seems to have quartered some of his legions in the *oppida* of pro-Roman tribes – sometimes ones whose loyalty at the time might have been considered questionable. In some cases, and *Bibracte* of the *Aedui*, where Caesar and some of his troops overwintered in 52/51 BC, is a case in point, some of the plentiful Mediterranean imports recovered from such sites might have been to nourish the Roman forces, but such evidence is not unambiguous, for these commodities were also sought after by the native elite. This is especially the case with the consumption of wine, an activity accompanied by the discarding of the amphorae in which it had been transported. Probably less ambiguous as evidence for the Roman army's presence would be the recovery of distinctive Roman military equipment from a 'native' hill-fort; or even better, evidence for the construction of military works in Roman style within, or conjoined to, a native fortification. Examples of both can be put forward.

LA CHAUSSÉE-TIRANCOURT, SOMME, FRANCE

Examination of this impressive fort, set on a flat-topped promontory between the main Somme valley and a small but steep-sided tributary, close to the SAMARA archaeological park in northern France, has added a new dimension to the consideration of the use of hill-forts in relation to Roman military activity. The Camp de César here is, from its superficial appearance, a classic example of a fortification belonging to the Fécamp series characterised by Sir Mortimer Wheeler (1957) and marked by the construction of massive dump bank, preceded by a wide, flat-bottomed ditch (see *28*). It thus belongs to the series of fortifications that Wheeler originally considered as a specifically Belgic style of response to the new types of military threat arising from the deployment of artillery by the Roman forces in particular.

Whilst relatively small-scale excavation has not radically changed the first century BC date Wheeler proposed for this site, it does suggest that the inhabitants were not altogether the local tribespeople that might have been anticipated. The dump rampart itself was a two-stage construction, with a dry-stone built revetment at the front itself seemingly tied back into a smaller dump bank. In itself, this sequence is hardly surprising, as there are numerous cases where gigantic dump banks are the culmination of a series of constructions (as at the Porte du Rebout at Beuvray), or the replacement for earlier, often timber-laced, walls that had fallen into disrepair or been slighted in an attack, as at the Colline des Tours at Levroux in Berry. A little more surprising is that the sequence revealed in the complex gateway to this site suggested to Jean-Louis Brunaux that its occupation occupied a very restricted period, in essence only a couple of decades after Caesar's conquest. There are, however, numerous other sites in Gaul where major occupation seems to be concentrated in the decades after the conquest – the *oppida* did not of course go out of use immediately following military conquest, indeed in some cases they did not do so at all. Altogether more exceptional, contrastingly, is the character of the small finds discovered in the gateway through the massive bank (the sole portion of the site to have been the subject of area excavation). These are substantially dominated by non-local material, most readily paralleled in southern France, in Provence. Brunaux and his collaborators are convinced that this material betokens troops – probably auxiliaries, and perhaps recruited amongst the *Volcae Arecomici* – for service with Rome. In this instance, rather than simply troops quartered within a pre-existing native stronghold, the case can be made that this Camp de César was substantially modified, if not entirely built, by auxiliary troops.

Given that there are, as Wheeler and Richardson noted, a string of these promontory forts extending down the Somme valley including Mareuil-Caudert, much later the scene of fierce fighting on the outskirts of Amiens in the Second World War, and Liercourt-Erondelle, the intriguing hypothesis can be put forward that this line of sites represents a first Roman effort at a *limes*, not in this instance marked, as subsequent Imperial ones would be, by recognisably Roman installations whether signal towers, forts, or linear barriers, but by the use of hill-forts essentially similar in design to those otherwise constructed at that time in the local area. The evidence, however, is not compelling, and other defences of this specification elsewhere seem certainly to have been erected in a native context.

HOD HILL, DORSET

Although aerial photography indicates the presence of a temporary Roman camp by a cropmark on the plateau outside the great rampart at la Chaussée-Tirancourt, there are no incontrovertible signs of conflict in the evidence so far recovered from the promontory fort itself. A rather different case is offered by the results of the excavations at Hod Hill in Dorset, for here there are substantial remains of a Roman auxiliary fort built into the north-west corner of an earlier, Iron Age fort, one from which the native population seem to have been driven to allow the Roman construction project to go ahead. Excavation directed by Sir Ian Richmond showed that the present configuration of the defences of the site – less strongly defended on the western side where the scarp of the chalk on which the hill-fort was situated was steepest – is the outcome of at least four successive constructional episodes, broadly altering the defences from timber-framed wall, to massive dump bank, fronted by a counterscarp bank, the latter ultimately crowned by a wall walk of flints, and edged by a parapet of the same material. The incomplete state of some additional defensive works around the periphery of the site suggests that the latest programme of modifications was still underway when the Roman attack came. The most graphic evidence for this consists of direct evidence of accurate Roman fire-power: 11 iron bolts, evidently fired from a *ballista* set up outside the south-eastern defences, had rained down on, or close to, a roundhouse set within its own compound. Richmond suggested that this display of missile warfare was enough to convince the local chief to capitulate, since the extensive excavation of a portion of the interior produced no other signs of conflict.

HILL-FORT ARCHITECTURE, THE DEVELOPMENT OF ASSAULT STRATEGIES, AND MEANS FOR DEFENCE

It is extremely questionable whether there is any straightforward correlation in general between what is known about styles of warfare and the nature of Iron Age fortifications, although some points of interest can be noted. Most attention has been devoted to the potential impacts of missile warfare, whether dependent on human muscle power such as archery or the use of slingshot, or by the deployment of artillery (for temperate Europe essentially by the Romans) and of the use of fire. In terms of effective ranges, both arrows and slingshots can hit targets in excess of 100m distant, although accuracy may be assumed to decline with increasing range. A figure of that scale order is none the less worth bearing in mind in relation to the overall width of the defensive zones of some of the more elaborate hill-forts.

Sling warfare may have been something mercenaries recruited amongst the Celts from temperate Europe learned in the armies of the Hellenistic kings or elsewhere in the Mediterranean area in the fourth century BC or later. The Balearic tribes from Mallorca and neighbouring islands enjoyed a high reputation as slingers and it may be from this source that this style of fighting derived. Wheeler saw the sling not simply as a weapon for use on land, but also at sea; for the coastal *Veneti* of Brittany, he argued that the sling could be the most convenient and the most economical of weapons, given the ready supplies of suitable pebbles that can be found on many beaches. But in temperate Europe there is evidence that use of the sling was not confined to this purpose. At South Cadbury, Somerset, for instance, caches of slingstones are of different materials and different weights: alongside pebbles weighing around 150g, certainly sufficient to bring down a man, are much smaller items of unfired clay, some 20g in weight. The latter may well have been used to shoot birds, but such training in hand-eye co-ordination and precision would clearly have been readily transferable to the military sphere. An alternative explanation may be that, heated, these clay pellets were shot in an attempt to ignite fires: a variant of this tactic is recorded on the Continent during Caesar's conquest of Gaul.

It has long been suggested, first by Sir Mortimer Wheeler, that multivallation, most elaborately seen on southern British sites such as Maiden Castle, Dorset, a device which serves radically to widen the defensive zone on the perimeter of sites, may have been a response to the development of missile attack of this kind. On the one hand it would have kept attackers at a distance, but on the other it would have conferred considerable advantages to the defenders, enabling them to profit from the field of fire offered by the sling across the defensive zone of successive sloping glacis-fronted banks that could be raked by their slingstones. Wide zones of sloping banks, with little by way of vertical features to dislodge, would also have had advantages against the more mechanised styles of warfare practiced by the Romans, in making various assault techniques they used — *ballistae*, battering rams and sapping — harder to deploy effectively. Indeed, the only evidence for the use of the sling by the *Veneti* he was able to identify was the fact that many of their coastal promontory forts indeed exhibited multiple ramparts.

Although the bow was used in assaults on enclosed sites as early as the Neolithic period, evidence for archery is relatively rare for much of the Iron Age of western temperate Europe. As a general rule, arrowheads are not part of the warrior panoplies — dominated by swords and spears by way of attack weapons — that occur as a component of La Tène cemeteries across Europe. By its end, however, when funerary evidence is altogether rarer, iron arrowheads in a variety of forms, some socketed, some tanged, are relatively common. Their presence is particularly noteworthy at sites of conflict like the Puy d'Issolu or *Alesia*, from which they have been recovered in sizeable quantities.

The issue of setting fire to defences will be considered more fully below (Chapter 7), although it seems self-evident that styles of fortification with substantial quantities of exposed timber must have been the most prone to attack by fire. Wooden gates, too, as Avery (1986) has emphasised, would be likely features to attempt to torch. Battering rams could have been deployed against gates, and to destabilise walls, more particularly by dislodging material from their external faces.

The archaeological evidence from Iron Age temperate Europe can be read to suggest that conflict and warfare were recurrent features of this period: recurrent, undoubtedly, but not ubiquitous. Aggression was both potentially a feature of social and political relations internal to these societies, as it was of their relationships with their southern neighbours. It would therefore be reasonable to conclude that, as the main enclosed places of the relevant centuries, hill-forts would be locations considered on the one hand worthy of attack and on the other necessary to defend. Estimating the frequency at which such conclusions were reached is altogether more hazardous, but the available evidence, some of which is rehearsed above, indicates that is impossible entirely to decouple hill-forts from ideas of aggression.

6

SIGNS AND SYMBOLS IN THE ARCHITECTURE OF HILL-FORT DEFENCES

In Northern Ireland, the great enclosed 'royal site' of Emain Macha *c*.3km west of Armagh in County Armagh, datable to the last centuries BC and part of the Navan complex of monuments that emerged in the later Bronze Age, differs in a number of ways from a conventional hill-fort (see also Chapter 9). These differences include not only the scale and character of the internal buildings recovered there, but also the fact that the arrangement of the enclosure on this remarkable site is the inverse of normal practice. Here the massive ditch, which locally retains water, sits not outside but within the enclosing bank, in much the same way as is known on much earlier prehistoric monuments, notably the henge monuments of Britain (Harding 2003). The arrangement may be because, as Professor Jim Mallory and others have suggested, the real purpose of this remarkable and securely Iron Age feature, was not to contribute to the defence of the site from external attackers, but to stop the spirits held within the enclosure from escaping into the surrounding world. Given the immediate context of Emain Macha – including the earlier King's Stables site (effectively a small enclosed wetland) and the nearby lake at Loughnashade from which bronze trumpets and human skulls are recorded – such an explication seems all the more feasible. Here is a site for which defence simply makes no sense as the *raison d'être,* and for which alternatives must thus be sought.

This high-profile example is a useful pointer to the fact that, alongside more prosaic functions ranging from safety and defence on the one hand to the regulation of exchange and the delimitation of property and legal rights on the other, the lines of enclosure around hill-forts and kindred sites are likely to have fulfilled a number of other roles. In recent years, these have – perhaps especially in the English-language literature – attracted considerable attention. Coupled with this is the realisation that, conspicuous and resource-consuming though they were as architecture and as structural engineering, lines of enclosure do not simply delimit a hermetically-sealed space capable of archaeological analysis in all its splendid isolation, but rather offer a number of possibilities for envisaging how the hill-fort may have fitted into its wider landscape, both physically and culturally. It is thus necessary to go beyond the military imperative to attempt to approach the wider *mentalités* of the communities that commissioned and used these places. Such inquiries have been to the fore for some years now.

In this chapter, some of these newer perspectives will be introduced. The available evidence falls into a number of categories. Some of these develop themes considered elsewhere here, such as the nature and scale of the architecture represented in a particular fortification, notably in relation to how effective it might have been defensively. Such concepts are always difficult to consider with precision, but it remains possible that the scale, nature and elaboration of defensive works became disproportionate, and 'like other military concepts throughout history…dominated the minds of the planners of fortifications…even if it required overinvestment' (Mazar 1995, 1528), as has been noted in another context. A tendency towards an excessive monumentality might therefore attract attention; alternatively, some earthworks might be envisaged as too slight, too discontinuous, too oddly set into their landscape readily to be viewed as straightforward functional defences.

A second theme focuses on the setting of individual lines of enclosure, more particularly as a means of permitting or impeding visibility of hill-fort interiors from the surrounding countryside, as has already been discussed (Chapter 2). A further field of interest is the recovery of special deposits in association with fortifications: notable amongst these is the presence on a few sites of human bodies in close relationships with lines of enclosure; in considering these, a distinction needs to be drawn with more conventional cemeteries or less formal deposits of skeletal remains related perhaps to warfare (as discussed in the previous chapter) in the vicinity of defences. More generally, in contrast to most work on fortifications which tends to consider the upstanding earthworks as being the most significant elements, some contexts within ditches – often accorded scant attention since they may be dismissed as a simple quarry for building materials or as supplementary defence – in particular seem to have been the arenas for 'special deposits'.

THE SCALE AND SETTING OF LINES OF ENCLOSURE

For some areas, and for some sites, it has been suggested on occasion that the slightness of the enclosure line or lines around an apparent hill-fort indicates that defence was not a prime consideration in the minds of its builders. In relation to some of the Irish sites, for example, Bernard Wailes has written of 'token ramparts', perhaps only a metre or so high. It is assuredly unsafe, however, categorically to dismiss even relatively slight works (which may originally have been crowned by some form of wooden breastwork, now archaeologically invisible) regardless of their topographic setting. A number of sites on conspicuous summits in the steep-sided hills of the Scottish Borders, for example, now display very slight banks, which cannot simply be accounted for as the product of intensive erosion in a relatively high-energy environment. Despite this, their settings, around prominent hilltops such as the White Meldon, near Peebles, strongly suggest that defence was at least one of the functions of a site which, in Avery's terminology (1976) has to be described as a 'high eminence'. In other instances, the deliberate placing of lines of enclosure well down slopes, as at Scratchbury in Wiltshire, contrastingly suggests a markedly different intention (56). The fact that at Scratchbury much of the interior is thus visible from the surrounding countryside diminishes the defensive capability of the site, since external observers could readily follow the deployment of forces within the enclosure. The counter-suggestion may be put forward: a key purpose in locating the enclosure downslope was to allow external spectators to witness events within the hill-fort without being direct participants in them, with the enclosure

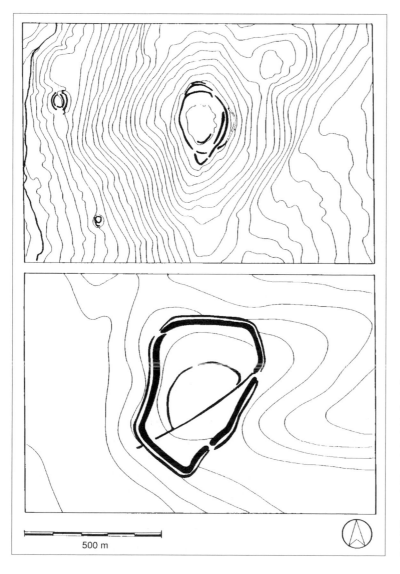

56 The contrasting settings of the rampart lines of White Meldon, Peeblesshire (upper), and Scratchbury, Wiltshire (lower), in their surrounding landscapes. *Drawn by Gordon Thomas*

thus effectively acting as the limit to a kind of open-air arena from which certain spectators were excluded. Such ideas have been pursued more widely using south-eastern English data by Sue Hamilton and John Manley (2001), and have been outlined in an earlier chapter.

Another aspect of this issue is evident in small forts or other enclosures, which mimic the defensive styles of major sites, but on an altogether different scale. Perhaps the clearest example to consider is in the case of *muri gallici*. Generally, these highly resource-consumptive walls are a feature of major sites of the end of the La Tène period and, in some instances, the very beginning of the succeeding Gallo-Roman horizon. Individual walls of this style extend to hundreds of metres, and often kilometres, in length. What, however, should be made of the construction of walls constructed to this specification in much lesser fortifications, for example at the small (2.4ha) promontory fort of Beg-an-Aud, St Pierre Quiberon, in Armorica, where a wall only some 50m long was built in this style? Even more remarkable is the case of the territory of the *Bituriges Cubi* in central France, where a succession of small sites of Late Iron Age date, in an area otherwise not noted for enclosed farmsteads as an element of the settlement pattern, have been dug or re-examined recently. In each case, these provide evidence for the construction of defences in *murus gallicus* style, complete with long iron spikes. Is it reasonable to see the adoption of this configuration as essentially an extravagant symbol, signalling an elite residence, whose owner is deliberately emulating the fortification style of neighbouring places, including Bourges, reputedly – if Caesar is to be believed – the most beautiful settlement of Gaul?

MONUMENTALITY

From the foregoing descriptions, and much of the remainder of this book, it will be plain that the defensive systems considered here were clearly intended as signs and symbols to the societies that built them, as well as, even in some instances rather more than, straightforwardly functional fortifications. In numerous cases, in a tendency paralleled in other contexts, it may be argued that the defensive works ended up being out of all proportion to, or otherwise inappropriate against, the threats they were supposedly designed to face. In other cases, even structures that at first sight seem imposing, may be argued to be inappropriately sited in their local topographies, to have been built to inadequate standards or only to be built on an imposing scale for limited sectors of their enclosure – next to the entrance for instance (Collis 1996). Despite the resources that went into their construction, and the labour mobilised to erect them and therefore directed away from other tasks, it may be suggested that what seems to have been uppermost in the minds of their architects and those that commissioned them was that they looked imposing, perhaps only for a relatively brief time, rather than that they were serviceable and could be maintained as 'fit-for-purpose' over extended periods. Les Porcins at Luant in Indre, for example, takes the 'miniaturised *oppidum*' perspective almost to the limit; not only has it a nailed timber-laced wall surrounding an area a little over a hectare in extent, but the sole entrance conforms to the *Zangentor* type.

It can thus be argued that at least some of the defensive architecture of later prehistoric Europe comes close to fulfilling Trigger's (1990, 119) definition of monumental architecture: 'Its principal defining feature is that its scale and elaboration exceed the requirements of any practical functions that a building is intended to perform'. In the case of hill-fort enclosures, however, it may be preferable to replace 'exceed' with 'fails to match', for here the evidence points not only to constructions being erected on a scale that is altogether grandiose, but also in some cases being put up in unnecessarily resource-consumptive architectural styles, and then not even well built. In temperate Europe, perhaps with the exception of the roads and bridges, about which relatively little archaeological evidence has yet been amassed, a disproportionate amount of constructional effort went into the construction of the boundary works around forts. Other linear boundaries, including major divisions like those traversing parts of Ireland, and – to a lesser extent – boundaries enclosing other sites, such as sanctuaries, certainly occur: the impression none the less is that much of the effort devoted to architecture as sign and symbol in the temperate European Iron Age, went into fortification works. In general terms, then, it seems reasonable to assume that, during the currency of the European Iron Age, a variety of messages were encoded in such structures.

Still the most staggering evidence in support of such a view in quantitative and scale terms is that produced by some of the late *oppida* sites, not least the massive territorial *oppida* of southern Britain. Their apparent structural excesses highlight this issue. In the present writer's view, it is the *oppida* most resembling gigantic variants of the older contour forts that make the case most strongly.

Consider Mont Beuvray: it has two successive lines of *murus gallicus*-style defences, each fronted by a rock-cut ditch, enveloping an inconveniently high massif on the north-east fringe of the Massif central (57: see Chapter 9). The outer, and stratigraphically the earlier, fortification takes in some 200ha and achieves this by running at relatively sharp angles across steepish slopes at a number of points. It is some 10km in length. This line was subsequently and perhaps rapidly replaced by another, distinctly shorter but none the less still somewhat over 5km in length, and punctuated by a number of gates. Of these, the most fully excavated example indicates at least five major constructional phases within a span of use of about a century. It represents a very long entrance (on Avery's 1986 scale it reached some 46m in total length) that was for some of these phases nearly 20m wide. For much of that time, this entrance does not seem to have had any coherent gate structure across its entire width. Massively resource-consumptive in terms of timber, iron nails, hearting materials and quarried stone for the retaining walls (much of this was quarried elsewhere on site and did not derive from the adjacent rock–cut ditch; and some of it, latterly at least, was imported granite), this wall was built for most of its phases in an architectural style that was militarily outmoded (58). It is impossible

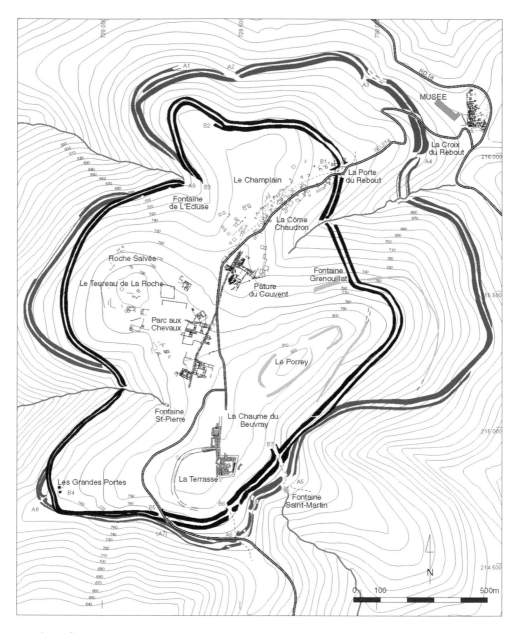

57 Plan of Mont Beuvray, Burgundy, France. The main lines of enclosure, with their fronting ditches, are shown in black; other ramparts are in grey. *Courtesy: CAE Mont Beuvray*

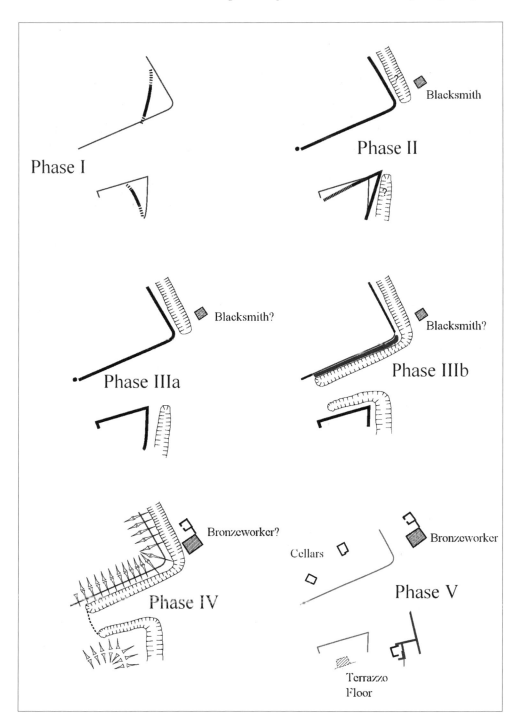

58 A diagram to illustrate the successive constructional phases of the Porte du Rebout at Mont Beuvray in the last century BC. *Based on Buchsenschutz* et al. *1999. Courtesy: CAE Mont Beuvray*

to avoid the word 'monumental' in describing these works. As Trigger has noted in relation to complex societies elsewhere, this monumental architecture demonstrates, as anticipated, first a stylistic continuity with what had gone before in the Celtic Iron Age and second the building of a very limited range of forms – essentially in this case boundary works – but ones implying considerable architectural and engineering capabilities. Like the walls of Uruk many centuries earlier, this Gallic Wall around Bibracte was designed above all to impress all those who gazed upon it: 'monumental architecture makes power visible' (see also Chapter 9). Zipf's principle of least effort has been utterly discarded in favour of conspicuous consumption made plain by the very visible mobilisation – on not less than several occasions in less than a century it might be argued, if building and maintenance were not in fact all but continuous – of labour and resources to build walls, and latterly a dump rampart of stone. In this sense, these fortifications framing this entranceway are manifestly symbols of power, even if their efficacy as defences seems now, and may have seemed then, distinctly questionable. One difference may be noted from many other early manifestations of monumental architecture: there is little indication that these structures – unlike for example megalithic chambered cairns – were meant to endure. At one stage, the Porte du Rebout even had substantial timberwork inserted in its entrance passageway to hold back the adjacent collapse tumbling in from the rampart inturns.

In the case of the repeated rebuilding of the Porte de Rebout, tight chronological precision on the timing of the event is lacking. The recurrent calls on labour and resources to rebuild or refurbish it may be essentially generational, or related purely to practical factors of decay. Highly speculative as it would be to suggest it, it may be worth remarking that the periodicity of the renewal is not far removed from that of around 16–18 years noted for the causeway at Fiskerton in East Anglia, where the dendrochronological pattern shows close attention to years marked by lunar eclipses. Martin Almagro and Jean Gran-Aymerich (1991) have suggested that other features of Beuvray, notably a stone-built basin set astride the main road into the site that passes through this gate, are laid out precisely in astronomic terms, albeit on the sun, not the moon. Such speculations on the precise arrangements of these grand sites need to be tempered by the fact that identical styles of building these elaborate walls were also employed in defining at least some smaller, perhaps essentially private, spaces, as well as the major *oppida*.

Whilst this discussion has focused on forts of the pre-Roman Iron Age, it is perhaps reasonable to note here that they continue to be an aspect of the building of defences in the post-Roman centuries too. In Scotland, for instance, the tradition of building major forts (albeit of a much humbler physical extent than their late prehistoric predecessors) still in styles mixing the same elements as the *murus gallicus* is maintained in the great enclosed Pictish site of Burghead (Alcock 2003; Ralston 2004). Another intimation from this time that appearance and monumentality continued to matter is the reuse in some forts of Roman masonry, perhaps especially in those cases, as at Clatchard Craig in Fife, where such stone would have needed to be brought some distance to the site. The latter trait may represent a continuation or a revival of the earlier practice of incorporating elements of older monuments into hill-fort defences, as represented by the massive cup-marked slab, presumably dragged from an earlier monument and placed on the outer earthworks of the White Caterthun in Angus.

ORIENTATIONS OF, AND SPECIAL FEATURES AT, ENTRANCEWAYS

As key points for conveying messages both to new arrivals at a site as well as its inhabitants going about their daily routines, entrances were undoubtedly a focus for display in later prehistoric hill-forts, as they have been in many other kinds of architecture. In general terms they were significant thresholds, and are therefore likely to have been positions for the display of significant and telling material culture. They may perhaps have served, too, for personal display, as has from time to time been suggested, for example for the Shetland 'blockhouses': but such showmanship is unlikely to leave straightforwardly readable archaeological correlates. Because they have a propensity to contain complex sequences of building, repair, use and abandonment, hill-fort entrances have often proved to be a magnet for excavators. Equally, it has long been recognised that it is necessary to excavate on quite a significant scale to make sense of them stratigraphically and structurally, and so some of the clearest evidence for other than wholly mundane activities comes from these features.

A number of aspects of entrances can be interpreted as intimations that they had symbolic significance and were locales for the advertisement of power and status. These include their orientation, particular elements of their architecture, and some of the finds associated with them. Entrance orientations have attracted particular attention in southern Britain, as part of an approach which also set out to examine the directions in which roundhouse doors were set. It has been argued that the interest in particular orientations can be interpreted in terms of wider cosmological concerns. In southern Britain for example, numbers of hill-forts have entrances aligned due east and west, and it may be argued that such a deliberate pattern is due to interest in the daily passage of the sun, which may have been more widely echoed in the belief system of the inhabitants.

In some cases, the function and the message particular gate arrangements were intended to convey may elude us. For instance, a number of sites on the north Scottish mainland and in Wales have an arrangement of upright orthostats set within the entranceway. It is clear that the architecture of the orthostatic 'four poster' edging the single entrance to the fort at Garrywhin, Caithness (*colour plate 14*), is not a device for supporting any form of practical gate arrangement; but the significance of this very calculated arrangement is altogether less clear.

Interpreting deposits in entranceways can be less than straightforward. The excavated inturned entranceway through the *murus gallicus* of the plateau fort of the Camp de Mortagne at Vernon, in Eure in Normandy, offers a case in point. This is a classic entrance of its type, some 24m long and a manageable 7.5m wide, with the posts for a two-leaf gate and a bridge towards the inner rampart ends. Metalwork from the entranceway includes a number of military items: fragments of swords, arrowheads, spear-butts, shields, a helmet and coats of mail. The gate itself shows no sign of violent destruction, however, and the route through the gate seems to have been used to access the interior even when the fortification itself was dilapidated. Further, the weapons show signs of having been disassembled and twisted deliberately, and this perhaps indicates that here the remains signify the former presence of a trophy set at this conspicuous position within the site, and are not the by-product of a battle at the entrance itself.

HUMAN REMAINS IN ASSOCIATION WITH RAMPARTS, GATEWAYS, DITCHES AND DITCH TERMINALS, BUT NOT BETOKENING WARFARE

It is well known that the treatment of the dead is very variable during the European Iron Age, with some areas and cultural traditions being marked by extensive cemeteries, by the practice of both inhumation and cremation, and by the accompaniment of the dead with a range of grave-goods which extends in some cases to elite weaponry and jewellery, vehicles, and drinking and feasting equipment. In other areas, including many parts of the British Isles, such evidence is much less common and 'funerary archaeology' plays a much lesser role in regional Iron Age syntheses.

Given that in many regions of temperate Europe for much of the Iron Age burials are far from a normal occurrence, instances of burials near or under fortifications are particularly unusual and merit consideration as another indicator of non-mundane practices associated with such works. As will become clear, complete or partial human remains associated with lines of defence fall into a number of categories, other than those already considered as potential casualties of warfare in the previous chapter. Not all are readily interpretable.

Burials have been discovered apparently placed below or in close proximity to ramparts. In some instances, the deliberate nature of the association seems clear, and the unusual nature of the burial itself strongly endorses the idea that this is an instance of a special, perhaps votive, deposit. In other cases, archaeologists may have to allow for an element of serendipity: for the existence, for example, of sets of burials whose apparent association with a fortification may have come about by chance, as when interments initially located outside the defensive zone were subsequently overwhelmed when this was extended outwards.

In southern Britain, a classic instance of an apparent foundation burial was that encountered during Leslie Alcock's sectioning of the ramparts of South Cadbury, Somerset. Here, sealed beneath the last Iron Age rebuild of bank 1 was a pit

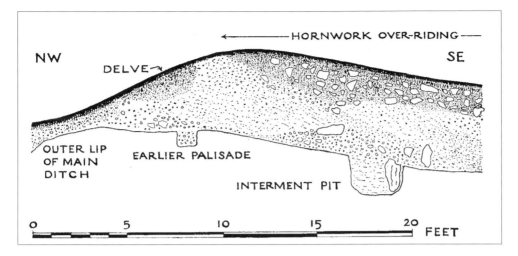

59 Hod Hill, Dorset: outside the Steepleton Gate. The original publication drawing makes it plain that the mound covering the interment pit containing a female inhumation was an upstanding feature when the counterscarp bank was erected over it; the locale was subsequently the point at which this construction was met by the later hornwork. *From Richmond 1968, fig. 10a. Courtesy: Trustees of the British Museum*

containing the unaccompanied skeleton of a man in his early twenties, crammed head-down into a pit, in a tightly flexed position, in fact the only complete adult skeleton from the site (Alcock 1972). It is possible in this case that the body would have to have been bound in order for it to fit within the tight confines of the pit. At Hod Hill, Dorset, contrastingly, an assessment of the significance of the tightly flexed burial of a young woman immediately outside the Steepleton gate in relation to the earthworks there is more contentious. Her interment there may have had more to do with the proximity of the gate than with the erection of the substantial counterscarp bank that was subsequently placed directly over the top of her grave, but it is none the less noteworthy that the mound overlying her grave was adsorbed directly within that bank (59). Equally contentious is another southern British case: at Maiden Castle, during the Wheeler campaigns, a burial of a young man was recovered in a pit – perhaps even a reused storage pit – in Sector H at the junction of two separate rampart builds. Were it not for that fact, and that the fill of the overlying rampart could not be readily distinguished from that of the subjacent pit, it would be possible to envisage this juxtaposition as wholly due to chance – a deposition in a storage pit that happened to be covered by a later rampart build.

Other burials seem to have been inserted during the construction of a wall or rampart. At first sight, the most gruesome, from their frequent republication, for example in Stuart Piggott's *The Druids*, are the skull and bones of an upper torso, apparently showing the remains of a man walled up in the dry-stone fortification, but visible through its outer wall-face, at l'Impernal, in Lot, south-western France. Re-examination of Viré's original publications by Olivier Buchsenschutz, however,

60 Viré's original publication drawing of the skeletal finds within the wall at L'Impernal, Lot, France, demonstrates that they were not exposed in the wall-face

makes it clear that this body (and also those of two children, apparently found close by) was placed on its back within the thickness of the wall and was not exposed in the wall-face (*60*). If the Impernal examples seem to have been set in position with particular care, in others it may be suggested that they were dumped apparently with less ceremony, during the erection of the rampart. Instances of the latter would include the burial of a woman at depth in the mass of one of the ramparts at Maiden Castle, Dorset (Wheeler's trench CXI), and the recovery of the skeleton of a man from the principal rampart at Sutton Walls (Herefordshire).

Amongst the most astonishing discoveries from a ditch was that made by A.E.P. Collins (1952) in his excavation of the western rampart and ditch at Blewburton Hill, an outlier of the North Berkshire Downs, just after the Second World War. Towards the base of a relatively narrow, flat-bottomed ditch cut into the chalk to a depth of about 3m outside the main rampart, were encountered the remains of a dog, a horse and a human skeleton. Set some way above the initial fill, the horse and rider seem to have been buried before a standstill phase in the accumulation of the ditch fills marked by the development of a thick organic horizon. The beast seems to have lain across the width of the ditch on its left side, its rump against the inner cut in the chalk, and its forequarters towards the outer edge of the ditch; its head was bent back over its shoulder. The vertebral columns of man and mount were recovered on the same axis, and the evidence seemed to point firmly to the man having been astride the horse. Beneath the horse lay an iron carpenter's adze-head, and below this, and just above the bottom of the ditch fills the complete skeleton of a dog was uncovered. Sherds of pottery found with the dog and with the horse suggested that all three had been buried in a single event, apparently disturbing ditch fills already *in situ*. Collins speculated that the man might have been tied onto the horse at the time it was pushed into the ditch, and that the man's skull and jaw may have been mutilated subsequently, although the evidence could been accounted for simply by secondary settling of the fills. The horse was young – some five years old – and really a small pony, estimated at only 10 hands. Further horses from the western gate of this site are considered below. It may be remarked that the burial of horses with their riders seemed to be very rare in the western European Iron Age, at least until the recent discovery of an important and remarkable grave discovered during an INRAP excavation containing seven adult males, an adolescent, and eight 12-hand horses some 300m outside the lowland promontory fort of Gondole in the Auvergne. Apparently datable to the second century BC neither ponies nor horsemen show signs of injury; a major difference in this case is that the men were not mounted on the horses when they were put in the grave.

Other discoveries in ditches are generally less spectacular, but none the less point to ritual or related practices, giving rise to special deposits. These would include the child's skull, complete with sword hack, found in the south ditch of the low-lying fort at Stonea, Cambridgeshire, along with other human remains (Malim 1992). It is in fact surprising, particularly in southern Britain, how many hill-forts produce human skeletal material from their ditches, sometimes along with other traces from the immediate vicinity of their earthworks. Thus at Wilbury Camp, Letchworth, (Hertfordshire) the remains of one adult male were recovered from the bottom of the ditch and two others were encountered in pits cut into the rampart close to one of the gates (Applebaum 1949). Aylesbury, Buckinghamshire, contrastingly, is a long-established borough on the site of an earlier Iron Age fortification, in this case, too, showing an apparent association between ditching and human – and in this instance animal too – remains. In one sector, a human skull was found in the bottom of the ditch, with the adjacent part of the interior producing human and animal skeletons, with further fragments in a neighbouring pit (Farley 1986 and *pers comm*). Radiocarbon determinations suggest that these deposits were made early in the Iron Age.

In other cases, it may be suggested that human remains – particularly skulls –found in or close to entranceways may originally have been displayed there. Examples are known both from the Continent and from Britain, and this evidence too can display considerable variability. It seems indisputable that the skulls from near the gateway of the fort at La Cloche at Les Pennes-Mirebeau in the Bouches-du-Rhône were intended for display: when found at least one was still transfixed by the iron nail that had held it in position (Chabot 2004). A series of skulls recovered close to the apparent 'massacre deposits' at Bredon Hill, but within the gateway of that site are perhaps best interpreted as the result of collapse from a fixture at the gate. In his field project at Stanwick, North Yorkshire, Wheeler (1954) encountered a human skull and an iron sword in its wooden sheath in the wet deposits at the base of the ditch terminal adjacent to Gate B; these were surmised to have been redeposited from a trophy set within the entranceway. The east gate of the *oppidum* at Manching produced two human skulls, which certainly might originally have decorated it; contrastingly, the skeleton of a young child had been placed in a pit below the entranceway, suggesting these human remains had been intended for a very different purpose. Dating from very much earlier in the Iron Age, the excavated gate of the early, lightly defended hilltop of Harting Beacon (West Sussex) contrastingly provides interesting evidence for the sequential manipulation of a skull, but not incontrovertibly for its display: here individual teeth belonging to a skull that was recovered nearby in the ditch terminal were found in the fills of individual post-holes of the entranceway.

ANIMAL REMAINS

Probably the most extraordinary suite of animal deposits associated with the earthworks of a hill-fort in England are the skeletal remains recovered from the western entranceway of Blewburton Hill, Berkshire (Harding 1976, plates VIII and IX), a site already considered because of the apparent horse and rider recovered from the western ditch of this fort. Lying on a cobbled surface that showed signs of repair, and overlain by earth and imported limestone collapsed from the adjacent rampart terminals, were a number of complete or partial skeletons. These were related to the last phase of the entrance's use, when the passage had been narrowed to some 7.5m in overall width. In the centre of the street were the skull of a cow and of a horse, and seemingly towards the interior of the site, fragments of the skull and the forearm of a young child. Further animal remains were also encountered towards the gateway's inner margin. The articulated skeleton of a deer with only its hind quarters displaced had been buried below collapsed stonework from the southern revetment wall; whereas two complete horse skeletons were recovered in a similar position below tumble from the north revetment. One lay with its spine towards the revetment, facing west, whereas its eastern neighbour was positioned with its hoofs to the wall, facing east. The pair of horses from the western entrance, apparently small ponies since they were comparable in size to that from the ditch, were initially interpreted by Collins (1953, 57) as evidence for a disaster: he discussed, alongside charcoal considered to have originated from the burning of the gate, '…corpses of animals strewn about the street and covered by the crashed-in ramparts…'. Further excavation directed by Dennis Harding in 1967 on the inner margin of the entrance, however, produced another pair of horses, as well as a single example in a pit (Harding 1976, 143 and plate IX), and – in conjunction with the absence of evidence for fire-reddening of the rampart stonework, or of charcoal in quantity – their presence suggests that the accumulating evidence is not indicative of destruction in warfare, but rather deliberate deposition, probably at a time when this gateway was going out of use. Definitive interpretation of some of these features undoubtedly remains problematic, exacerbated by the fact that the deposits may seem to be related to the abandonment, perhaps associated with the partial deliberate destruction, of this gateway.

At Crickley Hill, Gloucestershire, contrastingly, the partial remains of animals were intimately linked to the construction of the first of the Iron Age gates. Here, four of the post-holes associated with the gate within the entrance passage contained

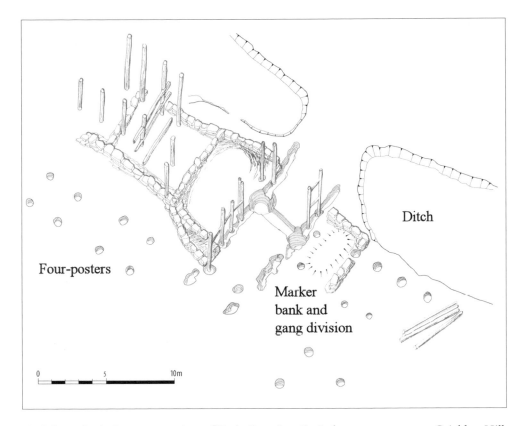

61 A hypothetical reconstruction of Early Iron Age Period 2 entranceway at Crickley Hill, Gloucestershire, in course of construction. This had dry-stone faces and upright timberwork braced by transversals, with much heavier use of timber in the lining of the gateway itself. Traces of cross-walls and marking-out banks suggest divisions in the labour involved in the preliminary lay-out of the gate. The superficial stone from the ditch was used eventually for hearting, but at the outset some was pressed into service as facing material. More substantial stone was recovered at greater depth. The four-post arrangements are envisaged as free-standing towers, set just inside the wall. It was from the main gate post-holes of this entrance that animal skulls and jaws were recovered. *Drawn by Karen Clarke after Dixon 1994*

animal bone: on the left on the way in were the lower jaws of boars, whereas on the other side two post-holes contained goat skulls. 'Presumably some purpose such as the conferring on the gates of the vitality of the animals was here intended,' remarked the excavator Philip Dixon (1994) (*61*).

In other instances the nature of the deposits encountered in association with the fortification strongly point to a ritual or symbolic intent. Thus the discovery of the partially-burnt remains of an adult horse in a pit below the outer rampart at the early hill-fort on Eildon Hill North, Scottish Borders (Owen 1992, 50), seems redolent of a special activity for a definite purpose, even if its nature now wholly eludes us.

THE SOUTH-WEST GATE AT SOUTH CADBURY, SOMERSET

Since the original interim publication in the early 1970s (Alcock 1972), the interpretation of the extraordinary series of deposits inside the south-west, Sutton Montis, gate, of this long-lived site have attracted attention, not least as a result of the description of the unearthing of the final Iron Age deposits within the gateway contained in the interim publication. The excavator recounts finds of brooches and weapons and then remarks:

> Fragments of human skull…a human leg, complete from the toes to the head of the femur, but with no body attached…the richest and most macabre archaeological deposit I have ever excavated.

In all, fragments of some 30 men, women and children were located 'in every imaginable state of dismemberment strewn along the entrance passage' (Alcock 1972, 105). So gruesome was the scene, that some of the volunteers refused to work there; in all a picture very different from the orderly scene of excavation conveyed by the author's colour plate VI. But, while Leslie Alcock was immediately prepared to recognise in these deposits, with their quantities of brooches and of spearheads too, signs of a battle between native defenders and Roman assailants, it was also clear that the deposit could not be interpreted simply in these terms. A battle and massacre had taken place, it was suggested, but one which produced few skeletal injuries, and after which the human remains were left unburied subsequently to be disturbed and pulled apart by wolves. Only some time thereafter did Roman troops, Alcock argued, return to burn down the gate and witness its collapse over the human and material debris remaining from the earlier conflict.

Subsequent detailed work on these deposits and the finds from them has allowed a rather more elaborate sequence of events and processes to be teased out of these extraordinary deposits (Woodward and Hill in Barrett 2000, 114-5), and which certainly extends the time frame involved. In sum, the revised interpretation certainly allows for some of the deposits dug, and finds made, by Alcock's team to be related to a battle close in date to the Roman conquest, and this extends both to the destruction of the gate and some of the human remains. At least six other types of activities could also be recognised from the immediately overlying deposits and the objects they held. These include items – of both material culture and human skeletal origin – displaced from funerary pyres placed upslope; burnt skull fragments considered to have been redeposited from a trophy or similar display originally sited within the entranceway; personal possessions lost in flight through the gate; human remains and bent weapons showing signs of calculated manipulation; and ultimately, after some natural inwashing and silting had occurred, the sealing over of the deposits during the creation of a new road surface for the later entrance.

Although far from exactly analogous with the evidence from sanctuary sites such as Ribemont-sur-Ancre across the Channel, above a tributary of the Somme (Brunaux 2004), what the deposits suggest is a much-extended treatment of the human remains derived from the conflict, altogether in line with the indications from Ribemont of exposure, special treatments, and reordering extending over protracted periods, during which the remains were accorded a particular respect. In the case of South Cadbury, though, these activities do not occur in the countryside, but in the immediate environs of a set of fortifications.

MATERIAL CULTURE

Finds of metalwork in close association with ramparts have been made on a number of sites, and Richard Hingley (1990) in particular has critically reviewed the remarkable associations between currency bars and hill-fort enclosures in southern Britain. In this instance, the fact that some of these finds were made long since, in the nineteenth century, means that the precision with which the original findspot is known can be less than wholly satisfactory. For example, at Salmonsbury, Gloucestershire, one of the biggest hoards of currency bars from England – comprising nearly 150 examples – was found whilst extracting gravel from the rear slope of the earthwork. Unfortunately, both the exact context of the find, and an apparent association with human remains, signalled by Sir Cyril Fox (Fox 1940: 433), are not wholly secure. Despite such uncertainties, associations between some kinds of metalwork and fortifications, and occasionally between hoards of metalwork and fortifications, certainly suggest deliberate intentions which need to be interpreted.

An excellent example of this is offered by recent excavations of the wall of the hill-fort on the Gründberg near Linz in Upper Austria. Here, Otto Urban (2000, 350) found in close proximity (less than 2m apart) three hoards of ironwork, each amounting to over 10kg in weight, in the body of the rampart just behind its outer wall-face. These cannot be written off as equipment carelessly lost during the construction process.

It is, however, currency bars from southern England that continue to provide some of the most telling evidence. Trow's (1988) examination of The Ditches at North Cerney (Gloucestershire), for example, located a hoard of 10 such bars beneath a layer of limestone slabs at the bottom of the ditch near one of its terminals. The classic relationship between currency bars and ramparts explored by Richard Hingley is for them to be in a secondary position. At Madmarston (Oxfordshire) for example, Peter Fowler (1960) recovered a hoard of currency bars and other iron objects from a pit dug into the tail of the internal slope of the rampart. At Nadbury, Warwickshire, excavation in 1983 (McArthur 1990) similarly led to the identification of a single currency bar and the mandible of a cow from a pit cut into the slumping bank of this 7ha univallate enclosure.

Another association between material culture and lines of enclosure has been remarked in Scotland and elsewhere, where it has been noted that quern-stones

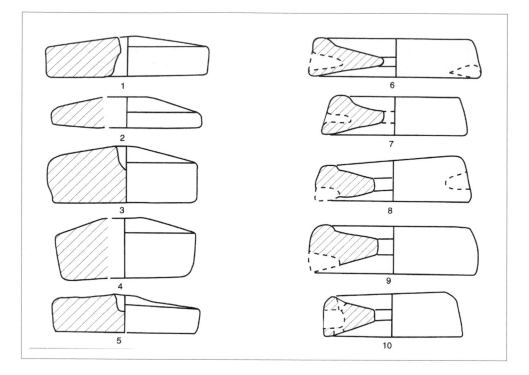

62 Rotary quern-stones from the surviving fragment of the primary *murus gallicus* at the Porte du Rebout, Mont Beuvray. *After Buchsenschutz* et al. *1999. Courtesy: CAE Mont Beuvray*

are perhaps too frequently incorporated into ramparts, at sites such as Castle Law, Midlothian, and Hownam Rings, Roxburghshire, to indicate an early recycling project to reuse broken or worn items of this kind. Such evidence also occurs on the Continent at Mont Beuvray for example, where, at the Porte du Rebout, the surviving fragment of the external wall-face of the earliest and slightest *murus gallicus* (62, Buchsenschutz *et al.* 1999) contained several broken rotary quern-stones.

If this chapter reads as a rather eclectic selection of evidence and propositions, that is probably a relatively fair reflection of the fact that the emergence of such non-prosaic explanations for the content and context of at least some Iron Age ramparts is a relatively recent one. As, too, with much of the evidence considered under other headings, what is presently known underscores the diversity of the indications that these fortifications conveyed a range of symbolic meanings to those who built them, maintained them, and came across them during their daily routines.

7

VITRIFIED FORTS:
A BURNING QUESTION

In the village of Bègues, just outside Gannat in the Départment of the Allier in central France, stands a church containing a statue of the Virgin in a domed, stone-built grotto (*colour plate 19*). In itself, this icon is fairly unremarkable, were it not that in this instance the stones mortared into the grotto were collected at the local promontory fort, less than a kilometre away towards the northern margin of the Massif central, just at its contact with the southern fringe of the Paris Basin. These stones include limestones and harder, crystalline rocks, and both sets include many examples which show unmistakable signs of exposure to great heat. Local archaeologist Janick Vernioles took me to the fort site. Set beyond a gentle valley containing arable fields, with an open outlook to the north, little of its interior is now cultivated. The position of the rampart – including a small clandestine excavation – is still readily distinguished by a marked talus slope (*63*), and at a number of points, some close to the fortification line, others slightly more distant from it, are piles of stone. Produced by clearing the land but undoubtedly derived from the fortification, many show the same admixture of rock types as in the grotto. An accident of geology attributable to its location at the junction between limestone and surface hard rocks has meant that the remarkable site at Bègues, also important because it has produced a few sherds of Greek pottery of First Iron Age date, is the only 'vitrified' *and* 'calcined' fortification known to me (*64*).

What this evidence suggests is that, even if 'vitrified' and 'calcined' forts are not always the outcome of equivalent processes, there must be a considerable overlap between the two, for at Bègues diligent searches through the stone heaps can even produce heat-altered blocks in which rocks of these distinctive formations are found which have, as a result of this exposure, effectively been soldered together. In this chapter, then, the writer is going to consider these two phenomena as essentially the product of the same processes in different geological conditions.

The overall distribution across Europe of sites displaying evidence of either vitrification or calcination is quite widespread. There are marked concentrations in Scotland (MacKie 1976) and in France (*65*), but over a dozen examples with some evidence of vitrification occur in Sweden, and other cases are known in, for

63 The promontory fort at Bègues near Gannat occupies the raised zone at the end of this spur

64 A variety of rocks at Bègues show evidence of alteration through heating

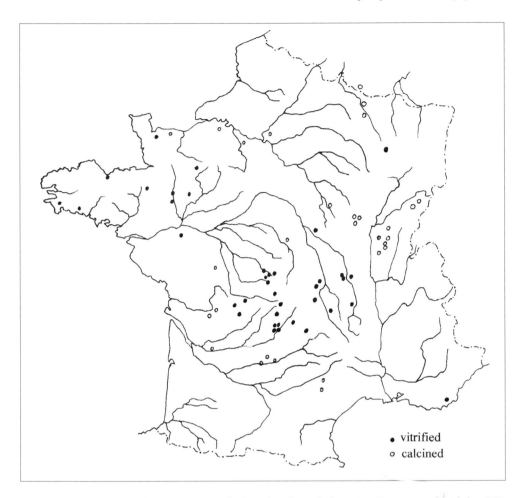

65 The distribution of over 80 vitrified and calcined forts in France, updated by J.D. Vernioles. *Drawn by Samantha Dennis from Gruat* et al. *2003*

example, Germany, the Czech Republic and elsewhere in the British Isles. Relatively recently, an extreme outlier of the distribution has been recognised far to the south-west, in the hinterland of Évora, Portugal, and further research in Iberia shows it is not wholly isolated there (*66*).

Vitrified forts in particular have attracted attention since at least the eighteenth century, initially as the kind of curiosity to be visited on tours through the landscape in search of the sublime and the curious. Over the intervening years, explanations have been sought for the phenomena that are recognised in them, sometimes according to principles close to scientific ones of conjecture, hypothesis construction, and refutation, in others rather more speculatively or haphazardly. The diagnostic characteristic of a vitrified fort is the presence in its enclosure wall not simply of heat-shattered stone, but of stones that have been more thoroughly changed by their exposure to great heat. Shattered stone is certainly a characteristic of some of these

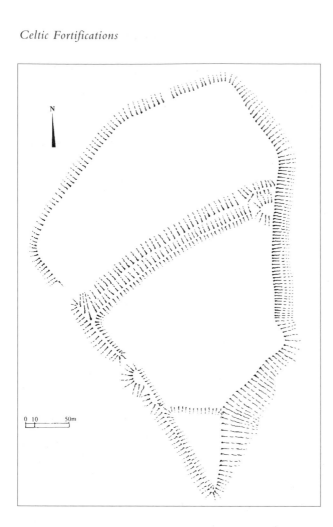

66 Castelos de Monte Novo, near Évora, Portugal. This major site, occupying a steep-sided spur above a tributary of the River Guadiana, was noted to display extensive evidence of vitrification at its northern end. Note, too, the likely presence of a tower bordering the western entrance to the central enclosure. Artificial defences are largely absent on the steepest, east side. *From Burgess* et al. *1999. Courtesy: Colin Burgess*

sites, but material of this kind also occurs of course on other settlement classes, not least the uninspiringly-named 'burnt mounds', found in various areas of Britain and Ireland at different periods of prehistory, and interpretable in a number of ways – as the by-products of saunas or sweat lodges on the one hand, and on the other as cooking places dedicated to prehistoric applications of 'boil-in-the-bag' technology, most likely based on animal intestine containers. Such heat-shattered material is thus on its own insufficient for a wall to be included in the category.

The distinctive characteristic of vitrified forts is rather that their stonework exhibits a variety of more substantial alterations attributable to the application of heat, often changes that laboratory analyses confirm to have necessitated temperatures in excess of 1,000 degrees Celsius. Individual stones have cracked; others show vesicular bubbling on their surfaces; there are resolidified runs of glassy material, including what are in effect fossilised drops of what was once molten material; and, on cooling, individual stones may have fused together to form craggy, irregular masses of stonework (*67*). Casts in the stones provide rough indications of the former presence of timber elements (*68*) in the wall-cores: these wooden elements have eventually burned away but have achieved this without disrupting the imprint they had made in the formerly molten stonework.

Vitrified forts attracted attention early: for example the conspicuous hilltop site of Craig Phadrig on the outskirts of Inverness was planned, as a diversion from his duties examining the potential of the estates forfeited by Prince Charlie's supporters, by the mineral engineer John Williams in 1777. Given the characteristics of the stonework noted on these sites, it is perhaps not surprising that pioneer visitors, like Thomas Pennant on his late eighteenth-century tour of Scotland, first considered the stonework masses as having been produced by volcanoes (*colour plate 20*). This initial interpretation was all the more feasible since some of the first sites to be examined were in northern Scotland, and belonged to the class of gateless, oblong forts located on conspicuous summits and which thus appeared at first sight not wholly dissimilar from some forms of volcanic craters.

Since then, a whole raft of explanations as to how the changes noted in their examination may have come about has been proposed, either to be discarded or

67 A mass of vitrified stonework on the circuit of the main wall at Carradale Point, Saddell and Skipness, Argyll and Bute

68 Cast of former timber in vitrified stone work at Knockfarrel, Fodderty, Highland

countered. It has, for instance, been suggested that the visible evidence is the product of lighting strikes, or the by-product of an industrial process (and high temperature working of e.g. metals can admittedly produce similar debris). Alternatively, albeit perhaps less likely, vitrification has been considered as the result of placing beacon fires – or 'great fires for religious or other purposes' (McHardy 1906, 139) – on the tops of walls. Views of the last kind were quite favoured, especially in the nineteenth century when ideas about the importance of the inter-visibility of hill-forts were periodically in vogue. By the end of the eighteenth century, however, the key competing hypotheses had been put forward. In the red corner, the favoured view was that the vitrified forts were deliberate constructions, in which the molten and resolidified rocks served to cement the constructions in which they occurred, a view put forward by Williams and supported by famous engineers then working in the north of Scotland, notably Thomas Telford and James Watt. Advocates drew attention to Caesar's passage in which he remarked on the resistance of the *murus gallicus* style of wall to battering rams (*de Bello gallico*, VII, 23), and noted how much stronger the solidified masses produced by the process of vitrification would have been. In the blue corner stood the advocates of the theory that the phenomena were the result of the destruction by fire of a wall containing, or in some versions enclosed by, quantities of timber. This view seems first to have been put forward in a paper to the Royal Society of Edinburgh in 1790 by James Tytler, later Lord Woodhouselee, but it did not then find much favour. In more recent times, it has garnered increasing amounts of archaeological support.

During the later nineteenth century, too, a much greater range of field observations became available, in France (e.g. de la Noë 1892) and Germany as in Britain. To these could increasingly be added the results of scientific tests and the experimental reproduction in the laboratory of the distinctive phenomena noted above. By this time it had become patently clear that vitrified ramparts were not a natural phenomenon, but a product of the firing of man-made structures. The tenor of the argument therefore moved on to the central question that has dominated discussion ever since: were the recognisably vitrified features of these forts the outcome of a constructional process or rather a by-product, more-or-less accidental, of the destruction by fire of redundant or conquered sites? In either case, given the elevated temperatures required to melt rock, had an extra ingredient been deliberately added, a flux that would have served to lower the temperatures required to produce the physical and chemical alterations that could be observed?

In essence, that central question is one which has, in some students' eyes at least, not yet been satisfactorily resolved. A consideration of some of the available evidence therefore seems justified, since vitrified forts are – potentially at least – distinctly different from all the other forms of fortification considered in these chapters. Up to now, all the sites considered in this book have been classified on the basis of what archaeologists have been able to surmise about what their original builders set out to achieve; contrastingly, if the vitrified (and calcined) forts are the product not of constructional intent but an outcome of destruction, their classification as a coherent group of sites rests on an altogether different basis. Even if the latter hypothesis is correct, it is none the less reasonable to assume that the original form and components of the wall were also important to the process, in that they made the outcome that was achieved possible. A related problem is whether the vitrification of forts is a phenomenon so extraordinary as to have been practiced only for a restricted period in a given cultural setting or whether its use was more widespread. Traditionally, it has been seen almost as an event horizon: Gordon Childe for example, in due course to be followed by Sir Mortimer Wheeler, was tempted to see the north and western British examples as the product of a particular historical episode, and preferred the campaigns of Agricola in the later first century AD as the likely occasion of the firings. For Wheeler a slighting on the scale indicated by the distribution of these forts was not to be matched until Cromwellian times (1952, 78).

The problems posed by the evidence from these sites have been tackled in three ways: in the laboratory; by excavation; and by outdoor experiments on more-or-less full-scale models. A series of laboratory-based analytical approaches, starting in the nineteenth century, has probed the nature of the vitrified materials. In the twentieth century, scientific techniques have also been used to obtain absolute dates with regard to when the ramparts were vitrified. In the case of thermoluminescence, results will potentially be at a considerable remove from when the walls were built if the 'destruction hypothesis' holds good, since it is assumed that it is the impact of the temperature regime at the time of destruction that will be recoverable. Other experimental work, underpinned by detailed geological analyses on the composition of the walls, has investigated the temperatures that were necessary to produce the alterations that have been noted in the stonework. Numerous figures have been put forward, generally in excess of 1,000 degrees Celsius depending on rock type, although in reality these temperatures would also have varied somewhat depending on the duration of the adjacent fires.

A second approach is provided by detailed archaeological observation, especially during excavation when the walls of vitrified forts are sectioned. This enables the characteristics of the wall concerned to be examined in three dimensions, and thus provides insights that examination of the surface characteristics of the wall cannot achieve on its own. Thirdly, there have been a number of more-or-less full-scale replicas constructed, with a view to reproducing the phenomena noted on fortifications of this kind. In general, the dictates of research programmes or other constraints have required that such attempts at firing walls have had to be conducted with replicas that were newly-built when they were ignited, and ones that may have had to use substitutes for particular materials, such as supplies of oak, that were too costly to use.

ANALYTICAL WORK

If, in cultural terms, vitrified forts were a narrowly circumscribed phenomenon, it would be reasonable to assume that they would produce coherent dating evidence attributing them to a period of relatively restricted duration. In some areas, this is far from holding true, a fact that is especially noticeable in the case of the extensive series from Scotland, where various approaches to obtaining absolute dating have been employed. These include radiocarbon, thermoluminescence and archaeo-magnetism.

It has already been noted that there is reason to suspect that in at least some of the fortifications discussed above, pieces of wood recovered from earlier structures were reused in their construction. This is perhaps especially likely when such walls included one or other of the varieties of internal timber frameworks, for in such cases appearance would be unimportant and old, but serviceable, wood would in all likelihood have made an acceptable building material. It therefore follows that radiocarbon determinations produced by such timbers may point to dates distinctly earlier than the fortifications in which they were eventually incorporated. In contrast, another interest of the vitrified forts – given the temperatures that they imply – is that other dating techniques may be particularly appropriate to them, whether or not the high temperatures were obtained during construction or destruction. Here, both archaeomagnetism and thermoluminescence are of relevance.

Thermoluminescence dates (TL) for Scottish sites, first published during the 1980s, have always been problematic in that sites which archaeologists would regard as likely to have been built in a particular, limited cultural context, so similar in form are they, produced apparent ages that were radically – that is to say millennia – different. This was the case with the closed oblong-shaped forts characteristic of Scotland north of the Forth–Clyde isthmus: Tap o' Noth (*colour plate 20*) was attributed to the beginning of the Bronze Age, whereas the physically-similar Finavon (Angus) produced a Pictish, Early Historic, date. Doug Gentles' consideration of these vitrified sites (1993), again focused principally in north-east Scotland, provided a series of archaeomagnetic dates for six sites that have the merit of relative coherence, and which accord more readily with conventional archaeological expectations. These suggest the last centuries of the first millennium BC as the prime period for the vitrification of the oblong vitrified sites, and would be broadly consistent with the view that, whereas radiocarbon dates often furnish a *terminus post quem* for the erection of fortifications, absolute dates for vitrification generate a *terminus ante quem*.

Thermoluminescence dating techniques have been applied more widely to the vitrified ramparts at numerous sites, more particularly in Continental Europe and especially by Peter Kresten and his associates, but not without some apparent problems emerging, including dates that continue to be radically different from archaeological predictions based on other factors. In some instances, these dates have been rather younger than the results anticipated on other grounds (for example, the availability of radiocarbon dates for the same structure, or indeed, in the case of a Scottish site like Finavon, Angus, from the material culture recovered from it by excavation); in others the opposite effect has been noted, with thermoluminescence determinations proposing a calendrical date distinctly older than the likely result put forward on alternative bases. Whilst a number of people have been disquieted by this without being able to put forward a solution to the dilemma, work by Peter Kresten and collaborators in Sweden and Germany (2003) has resulted in a likely identification of the solution to the problem. This seems to relate to the temperature range of TL-dating. On the one hand, as has been recognised for some considerable time, it is likely that insufficient heating causes TL-dates which are erroneous, being far too old: the date obtained is explicable by the inclusion of remnant geological luminescence. But what of the contrary case, if the temperatures attained are more substantial? Kresten's examination of samples taken from a section through the inner wall of a Swedish hill-fort called the Broborg (a site discussed further below) show a strong correlation (for temperatures above 900 degrees Celsius) between increasing firing temperatures and apparently younger thermoluminescence ages. It is thus apparent that the use of this technique for dating vitrified walls needs to be rethought, as others have already suggested (Alexander 2002).

The broad tenor of other analytical work has been to suggest that most vitrified forts are built of local rocks, so that deliberate selection of constructional materials on geological grounds is not supported. Scientific analyses to date also suggest that there is no convincing evidence that materials other than the basic constructional elements that would be anticipated in such fortification walls, i.e. stone and timber, were involved in the process. In other words, there is no evidence for the use of any flux material which might have served, for example, to lower the temperature at which the rocks in the construction would begin to melt and flow. Some analytical work does indicate a slightly raised phosphorous content in the samples from a proportion of wall-cores and, whilst this would not be inconsistent with the incorporation of bone as a minor component in the hearting materials, it could simply be attributable to the composition of the particular fused rock that was analysed.

Some analysts, notably Youngblood and collaborators (1978; 1983) seem to have been particularly exercised by the temperature range (in excess of 900 through to around 1,100 degrees Celsius) necessary to produce the visible changes to the rocks, and therefore considered that simply burning a wall of *murus gallicus* type (the usual shorthand in the literature on vitrified forts for any wall with internal horizontal timber-lacing) could not have produced the observed outcomes. In an ingenious, if ultimately unconvincing, variant of the usual hypotheses, these researchers sidestepped the question as to whether the vitrification of these walls was deliberate, by suggesting that in the original wall build, the constructors had planned that the wall would remain *in situ* were it to be fired; this was achieved, it was argued, by such factors as controlling the ventilation arrangements within the wall to provoke reducing conditions. The present writer would argue that changes consistent with the natural ageing of walls through time would produce such effects – for example by the settling and consolidation of core materials, and by the colonisation of the wall-faces by vegetation over time, thereby little by little blocking air-holes in the dry-stone built external faces and thereby reducing overall the flow of air (and thus oxygen) into the core of the wall.

FIELD OBSERVATIONS

Examination of the field record at the international level highlights a number of points. First, taking the known set of vitrified forts as a whole, all the bigger national datasets seem to suggest the same key features. If, in some cases, the extent of vitrification relative to the overall length of the fortifications is considerable, in other cases it is very localised, sometimes only occurring over a few linear metres in circuits that may be many times that in length. This has long been acknowledged as a significant observation: and generally is not one easy to reconcile with the constructional hypothesis. Lieutenant-Colonel McHardy, latterly a Vice-President of the Society of Antiquaries of Scotland, pointed out 100 years ago that in some of the Scottish examples their vitrified portions were those where this characteristic – had it been a device to increase their defensive capabilities – would have been least beneficial, being along the top of cliffs or at the seaward end of promontories only readily approached overland. Equally McHardy noted that the solidified slaggy masses in the walls of numerous sites could overlie loose, unconsolidated stonework, again an observation detrimental to vitrification envisaged as a structural procedure. Very generally, the geological study of the fort walls indicates that the stonework of vitrified walls is essentially local, whether gathered on the surface or quarried. There seems to be no evidence to suggest deliberate selection of particular geological types that would facilitate vitrification. Overall, a recurrent theme is the variability of the data. In cases where it is possible to distinguish this from the examination of the position and extent of the vitrification relative to the overall dimensions of the wall, for example, there are instances where the fire seems to have spread from the outer face inwards; in other forts, the opposite applies. In some cases, vitrified stonework extends all the way to the bottom of the wall (*69*), and the lowest stonework may even have become soldered to the subjacent bedrock; in other examples the altered rock is at some height within the surviving wall materials. At Dun Lagaidh in Wester Ross, Scotland, Euan MacKie's trench through an outwork (1969, plate 1) produced good evidence for the framework of timber in the form of beam-holes in a wall-face, surviving below the vitrified stonework in that site beside Loch Broom (*70*).

In general it is possible to conclude that vitrification, whether one considers that the intended outcome was construction or destruction, was not always very successfully achieved. For every successfully vitrified fort, there is, so to say, a Monday morning or Friday afternoon model. It has to be allowed, none the less, that this variability may not be entirely the result of the same process being carried out with varied success, but rather of the application of different processes – in effect that a single explanation may not satisfactorily account for all the variation recovered in the examination of geographically-widespread sites of different dates.

The suggestion that vitrification is the product of firing a wall-and-fill rampart with internal timber-lacing, with the intention of destroying it, is further underpinned by a number of pieces of evidence. Firstly, as has been noted above, on numerous sites it is possible in the field to observe on the surviving vitrified blocks, negative casts with traces indicative of where pieces of wood have burnt out. Other Scottish examples show variations on the theme of traces of wood surviving in walls at levels below that at which vitrification occurs: at Castle Point, Troup, on the north Aberdeenshire

69 In excavations directed by Guy Lintz, vitrified stonework was found fused to bedrock at the Puy de Sermus, Saint-Geniez-ô-Merle, Corrèze, France

70 The positions of surviving beam-holes below vitrified material are marked in this image by Euan MacKie of a wall at Dun Lagaidh, beside Loch Broom in Wester Ross. *Courtesy: Euan MacKie*

coast, for example, Colvin Greig was able to identify a raft of carbonised oak timbers, laid transversely, below the vitrified stonework of the inner line of fortification on the promontory fort at Cullykhan, whereas, along the same Moray Firth seaboard, my excavations at Green Castle, Portknockie, Moray, produced a Pictish wall with elaborate carbonised timber-lacing, fire-reddened core materials, but only the very occasional stone that had been characteristically altered to a vitrified state by the heat. At a general European scale, too, there is a broad geographical correlation between those areas that produce vitrified forts with those that have other evidence for timber-laced wall-and-fill rampart structures (e.g. Ralston in Guilbert 1981).

Other field observations, particularly on supposedly calcined ramparts, do sometimes point the other way. It has to be acknowledged that walls in such geological settings do require that a note of caution be struck, since limestones or chalks behave very differently from crystalline hard rocks when substantial heat is applied to them. The evidence from Bègues with which I opened this chapter suggests that in some cases Occam's razor can be wielded and the proposition advanced that vitrified and calcined forts are essentially the same phenomenon, as de la Noë did over a century ago, but counter-arguments have been put forward for at least some examples of the latter series. Thus the cores of a set of walls of forts located in Val-Suzon, near Dijon in Burgundy, excavated by Jean-Paul Nicolardot, are now considered not to be the product of deliberate burning, but rather a natural environmental change occurring in the buried sediments. These include sites such as the Châtelet d'Etaules. In these instances, the chemical changes that have occurred and have led to the production of a compact solidified lime core have been argued not to be due to heat, but this explication does not necessarily fit the evidence from other members of the series.

If much of the field evidence tends to accord reasonably well with the 'destruction hypothesis', or to be explicable in other ways as in the Val-Suzon examples, it needs to be said that some evidence continues to be interpreted by archaeologists and scientists working on these sites as an indication of constructional intent. Two examples, one calcined, one vitrified, may be described.

THE CAMP D'AFFRIQUE AT MESSEIN, MEURTHE-ET-MOSELLE, FRANCE

This is a major bivallate plateau-edge fort of some 7ha, accompanied by outworks on its eastern side, built on limestone and overlooking the valley of the Moselle in Lorraine, France. Including its annexes, the site occupies some 14ha. It was examined about a hundred years ago by Beaupré, and has been most recently dug during the 1980s (Lagadec, Duval and collaborators 1993). At their most imposing, the enveloping works now consist of two substantial banks each fronted by a ditch, providing a defensive zone over 50m wide, and some 12m from rampart top to ditch bottom. Excavation of a 4m-wide cutting through the inner bank near the north-east corner of the main enclosure revealed a complicated stratigraphic sequence, which included two separate solidified masses of lime. The existence of two such features in a single bank seems to be very rare. Of these, the larger, overlying deposits interpreted as the remains of a timber-laced bank, consisted of an enormous and solid mass of lime over 7m wide and a maximum of nearly 2m high. This contained some vitrified stones, essentially pebbles most likely imported from a nearby river valley. The absence of any carbonised wood in this mass and the regularity of its limits suggested to the excavators that this calcined mound could not be the product of the destruction of a timber-laced wall. Supported by analytical work, they proposed that the mass of lime was produced as a deliberate outcome of a constructional process, essentially as a variant of a lime-kiln used on a single occasion within each sector of the wall, with underlying timber providing the heat required. If the interpretation is correct, some 150–200 separate firings, each resulting in the deliberate calcinations of some 60 tons of material, may have been required along the length of the wall. Both radiocarbon and artefactual evidence – in particular late Hallstatt varieties of brooch – suggests that this rampart was in use towards the end of the First Iron Age (Lagadec *et al.* 1993; Ploquin *et al.* 1993). In a more recent summary (1997, 6) the authors maintain the position that the process was a deliberate one intended to enhance the solidity of the structure, but propose that the motivation for doing this may have had more to do with a desire for prestige than defensive aims.

THE BROBORG, NEAR UPPSALA, SWEDEN

Peter Kresten, the Swedish geologist who has worked tirelessly on these sites for a considerable number of years, has examined an Early Historic vitrified fort at Broborg, some 20km from Uppsala, Sweden. Broborg is one of the three most fully vitrified forts so far identified in that country. With his collaborators Leif Kero and Jan Chyssler, Kresten interpreted the results of excavation and analyses to suggest that the vitrified material encountered here was produced as the result of a deliberate constructional process.

Broborg consists of a D-shaped enclosure, with a substantial dry-stone wall supplemented on the south-east side, where the single entrance is found, by a crescentic outwork, also constructed of dry-stone. The inner wall, parts surviving to *c.*2m high, shows evidence of vitrification around much of its perimeter. None of the wall-faces displays beam-holes for transversal timbers, such as are found in some sites elsewhere. Counts of the composition of the walls against the background rock types of the vicinity suggests that amphibolite, a rock present in the local drift, is disproportionately represented only in the vitrified portions of the inner wall, a construction in which it is otherwise relatively rare. Gneissic granite, also present, has reacted entirely differently to heat. On excavation the vitrified layer, which can be demonstrated to exist around the bulk of the inner circuit, forms a superficial layer some 40–70cm thick, and up to 1.5m wide, which is described as lying along the inner face of the inner wall; it includes abundant negatives marked by 'wood casts'. Under this the wall, primarily consisting of granitic gneisses, showed signs of fire-cracking; hollows may indicate places at which individual stones have entirely disaggregated. The basal layers of the wall are reported as being unaffected by heat. Detailed analyses suggest that some of the glasses have a higher phosphorus content than could arise naturally simply from melting amphibolite, allowing the proposition that phosphorus-rich material, such as animal bone, may have been included in the make-up of the wall (such material of course also sometimes occurs in wall-cores elsewhere, and is assumed to have been scraped up and redeposited from middens or similar locales). Alternatively it is suggested here that this material may have been added deliberately to act as a flux, lowering melting temperatures; the evidence here is uncertain. The Swedish team also suggest that the wood casts are the product of burning out charcoal, rather than wood itself. They noted too that that the vitrified part of the wall appeared to have been built in 'boxes' *c.*2 x 1.5m, dimensions coincidentally not too different from the kinds of timber frameworks found in some timber-framed walls, notably in the *Kastenbau* tradition.

They conclude that the wall had to be vitrified in sections. They suggest this was achieved by igniting the top layer of the wall, comprising a deliberate selection of *c.*50 per cent amphibolite amongst its stonework, surrounded by beds of prepared charcoal. The inner wall-face and the summit of the wall would have to be covered with soil to provide the confined space for vitrification to occur and, rather than relying on the wind, a draught would have been forced in through the outer wall-face using bellows. This would imply constructive vitrification.

Ingenious as this hypothesis is, I consider that much of the evidence could equally have been produced by the destruction by fire of a wall: I have, however, never inspected any of the Swedish evidence at first hand. The observation they make relating to the use of bellows is a useful one, and of course these could have been used too in the other circumstances outlined.

It thus remains questionable whether a single hypothesis – what might be called the calculated destruction scenario – is adequate to explain all the circumstances in which vitrified and calcined material is recovered from defensive works. Whilst the focus above has been on two individual cases, it should be noted that the constructional hypothesis has re-emerged in other contexts, for example to explain the presence of vitrified material within some medieval castle mounds – mottes – on the north-western margins of the Massif central of France, in Limousin.

TRIAL BY FIRE

Addressing the fellowship of the Society of Antiquaries of Scotland in February 1906, Lieutenant-Colonel McHardy noted that the vitrification of the larger masses encountered in some of the forts must have been 'a troublesome business' (1906, 140) and so it has proved to be in modern experimentation. McHardy, attracted initially to the 'beacon theory' for vitrification, carried out a number of experiments outside Edinburgh and latterly on the west Highland coast of Scotland at Arisaig, first using sizeable open fires, one of which was kept ablaze for a day and a half without producing more than some cracking and roasting of the stones. He rightly reached the conclusion that '...the burning was too rapid, and that the supply of air had to be reduced' (1906, 144) if vitrification was to be achieved. A second series of fires – McHardy is undoubtedly responsible for more attempts experimentally to produce vitrified material than anyone before or since in modern times – therefore saw more combustible material added to a succession of experimental fires set in a square stone-built enclosure, and latterly to one built on the Arisaig shore. A key observation he made on vitrified stones showing wood casts from a number of hill-fort sites was that – to judge from the orientation of the glassy runs and droplets – the wooden fuel had been under, rather than above, the stonework, and it was this possibility that McHardy pursued in his last, but ultimately successful, experiment. This produced a small quantity of vitrified material, in a fire that was progressively built up by adding alternate layers of combustible material and then stones. That said, the relationship between this construction and any of the fortification walls actually known might reasonably be described as distant.

The next Scottish experiments to be written up were those conducted by Gordon Childe and Wallace Thorneycroft following Childe's excavations of vitrified walls at Finavon in Angus and Rahoy in Morvern, Argyll. Childe's sections at Finavon demonstrated the vitrified masses to be situated within the collapse of a wall which elsewhere was largely unvitrified; at Rahoy the presence of quantities of charcoal (in a wall section that had to be dynamited!) and the recovery of an Early La Tène brooch brought to mind the site of Castle Law at Abernethy in Perthshire and Kinross (which had produced a similar fibula), dug in the late 1890s and famously photographed illustrating a line of unambiguous beam-sockets for the former transversal timbers (*21*) showing clearly in the masonry of its external wall-face. In their experimental work, then, the idea of vitrification as the product of firing a timber-laced wall was always central.

The Childe-Thorneycroft experiments in essence consisted of attempting to produce vitrified rock by igniting a ready-built timber-laced wall, modelled – at least loosely – on examples from Scotland. A detached length of experimental wall was first built in the colliery at West Plean, Stirlingshire; this was some 3.5m long by under 2m high and the same wide. Transversal timbers, consisting of pit props some 15cm in diameter, formed a basal layer, overlaid by a longitudinal layer of timbers. Further layers of dry timber were added, and the core of the wall was infilled with basalt rubble, while the facing was made of old fireclay bricks; the inclusion of arched bricks at the bottom of the wall-face simulated the air-holes found in real wall-faces.

The West Plean wall was successfully ignited in a March snowstorm accompanied by an east wind by firing timber set against the wall-face. The external conflagration burnt well and the fire was carried back along the horizontal timbers into the wall-core. The fire continued to smoulder the next morning, the outer wall-face having collapsed after the blaze had been alight for some three hours. A contributory factor in the rapidity of this falling away may have been that few of the beam-holes for the transversals were lintelled over, as is apparent from a photograph of the experiment (Childe and Thorneycroft 1937, fig. 3). The result was that, as the wood burnt back into the wall-core, the stonework overlying the beam-ends in the wall-face would have been unsupported. The surviving fragments of wall were in due course demolished, and the product of the experiment examined. Substantial quantities of vitrified material were recovered, amounting to almost 10 per cent by weight of the stonework in the wall; and these lumps of vitrified basalt, the heaviest weighing almost 200kg, displayed many of the characteristics – including drops of glassy material and timber casts – noted in the real constituents of vitrified walls.

The experiment was subsequently repeated, by building a wall using local materials in the excavation cutting through the original wall at the Rahoy site. Although there were problems with the draught and the external fire was rekindled some hours after it was first ignited, there were clear signs of the internal timberwork turning to charcoal, a necessary stage in the process before vitrified stonework was again produced.

On April Fool's Day 1980, I had the opportunity to set fire to another experimental sector of wall, built on the City of Aberdeen's rubbish tip at East Tullos, overlooking the grey North Sea (Ralston 1986). This was expertly built by my friends Robin Callendar and George Blackhall and their assistants, using a variety of materials (*colour plate 21*) obtained by the television company that commissioned it for a programme in the series *Arthur C. Clarke's Mysterious World*. The day before the experimental firing, the wall had been soaked in a downpour. This may not have been the massive disadvantage it initially seemed: Professor David Smith tells me that wood smouldering within the thickness of the wall and with limited access to air – and thus in reducing circumstances – and with water percolating through the wall could create certain hydrocarbon gases which would burn at temperatures significantly higher than ordinary wood fires. This experiment was broadly successful, in so far as the fire was satisfactorily transferred from the external wall-face into the core of the wall along the transversal timbers – in this case of fast-burning pine, rather than oak (*71, 72*). There were, it has to be said, major problems along the way: a change in wind direction meant that the air being carried into the wall-core was cold, having not had to traverse the external flames. The temperature of the hearting material (measured using thermocouples) which had began to climb, plunged. During the course of the day, various changes had to be made to the placing of the external fires, and all did not go smoothly.

This wall was still alight the following morning, some 21 hours after it had been ignited. The external wall-face had collapsed, although much of the internal (*73*) timberwork was still uncharred and still in place. Had the wall not had to be demolished at this stage to see whether vitrified material had been produced, it is likely that it would have continued to burn for a considerable time. That said, examination of the core materials in the wall as it was demolished by bulldozer produced only small pieces of altered rock, with only some 3kg of vitrified material being recovered in total (*74*).

71 The first fire built against the wall-face begins to die down, as smoke and steam emerge from the other side of the wall

72 The transversal timbers – the main element of the internal timber-lacing – carry fire back into the core of the wall, the face of which is fire-cracked and distorted

73 The morning after: the wall, still alight some 21 hours after it was initially ignited

74 Some of the small pieces of vitrified material produced at East Tullos

75 The wall at Torsburgen, scene of the Swedish experimental work. *Courtesy: Ian Keillar*

About the same time, experimental work in Sweden, this time on a limestone wall at Torsburgen (75), also managed to replicate the changes noted in the wall in a destructive fire (Engström 1984). The writer remains convinced that the really successful replication of the phenomena noted in vitrified walls will require a wall that is built of suitable rock types and with its core materials of a sufficient size and sufficiently compacted, so that they will not settle too readily; and hardwood timbers – preferably oak – in sufficient quantity for the timber lattice-work. Furthermore, it would be a good idea if the wall were allowed to settle and age, and be colonised by vegetation, for some time before it was ignited. In such circumstances, I believe a destructive fire, lit in the right wind conditions, could produce the slaggy, solidified lumps of stonework of the kind that have attracted attention for well over two hundred years.

CONCLUSION

One of the points noted in the original publication of the Aberdeen experiment and worth renewed emphasis here is that the destruction of the isolated length of wall built on the City's waste disposal site was spectacular, even seen against the orange glow of the night-time light pollution produced by a modern city (*colour plate 22*). How much more awesome must the burning and vitrification of these walls have seemed in a world where, aside from the light of the moon and the stars, the nights would have been inky black? In Scotland, the highest vitrified wall is that represented by the major upstanding line of Tap o' Noth, at a little under 600m a conspicuous landmark over wide tracts of the north-east of the country (see also Chapter 9). Tap o' Noth's circuit is amongst the more fully vitrified fort walls in Scotland, and it can be suggested from the experimental evidence that – given the important of wind direction in fanning the fire in the right direction, contributing to the raising of temperatures in the wall-core, and so on – the systematic destruction of the wall over its entire length may have been quite a lengthy process, certainly taking days and nights, and perhaps weeks, to achieve.

This is a landscape where, many centuries earlier, archaeologists know that people were regarding the night sky from within the numerous recumbent stone circles that are characteristic of the area, sometimes, it is suggested, watching the moon, low in the sky, appear to roll along the tops of the recumbent slabs. We can only guess what may then have been on their minds, whether optimistic anticipation or trepidation, watching the works of nature unfold. Their successors, perhaps some two millennia later, would have witnessed something entirely different. The intense glow from the burning fort on the summit above them was not natural, but a spectacular display of calculated destruction. In other examples, that glow would have been reflected across the neighbouring water, as at Dun Lagaidh on Loch Broom, mentioned above, the small vitrified dun on the Burnt Isles in the Kyles of Bute, or the innermost wall of the promontory fort at Trudernish Point, between Claggan and Aros Bays on the east coast of Islay.

Those who knew how to achieve the effects may have had the *braggadocio* of later expert setters of fireworks; the nightly spectacle – like fireworks displays, also affected by wind and undoubtedly curtailed by rain – must have been a clear intimation of the power of those who commanded the process. It is perhaps as near as the European Iron Age got to Las Vegas lit against the Nevada desert or, more sinisterly, the destruction of Coventry or Dresden.

8

CONCLUDING REMARKS

Some 50 years ago (1955), W.H. Auden had *The Old Man's Road* run:

> Near hill-top rings that were so safe then,
> Now stormed easily by small children.

It is abundantly clear that the earthworks considered above have lost their original purposes, and a few of them are well on their way to becoming, to paraphrase Ludovic Kennedy, '…stations of the cross in the great new theme park…' that is our new Europe, with its sometimes shaky assumptions of a common inheritance. Of course, in some measure, the shared architectural traditions and other practices associated with these sites do point to currents flowing at least vaguely in that direction, as I hope this book has shown. That said, the sites considered above were also on occasion the refuges of militarised and bombastic elites and their retinues, both equally fearful of their neighbours' intentions. That aspect of these places should not be airbrushed out of the picture. And while I have focused here on hill-forts of the pre-Roman Iron Age, it is reasonable to insist that in many areas they re-emerged in later centuries, in some areas in the later Roman period, and in others in Early Historic times, from Scotland across the Continent to the Slavic areas of north-central Europe.

Once their enclosing works were no longer maintained, many of these sites enjoyed an afterlife as venues for fairs, markets or pilgrimages, but others did not entirely escape the military sphere. Numbers of examples are occupied or overlain by later *mottes*, like Huelgoat in Finistère, Brittany, their enclosures forming sizeable ready-made *basse-cours*. Others have medieval castles erected within them, including, at Dunnideer in Aberdeenshire, an example largely built of the vitrified stonework of the fort that long preceded it on the summit. And sites could continue to be used, perhaps largely incidentally, in war: Sir Mortimer Wheeler (1957, 126, no.76) almost laconically concludes his description of the Camp de César at Mareuil Caudert, across the lower River Somme from Abbeville, in northern France, by remarking: 'The camp was a battlefield in 1940 and is scarred by "fox-holes" and other modern military works'. Around the same date, far to the north, at Burray on South Ronaldsay, Orkney (*colour plate 23*), the remains of a miniature Atlantic stronghold – a broch – with an open view over Holm Sound at the entrance to Scapa Flow were substantially modified by the addition of the concrete required for a gun emplacement, an observation tower and associated structures, which was in service until 1943, when the twin six-pounders were removed for use elsewhere. What now survives on this site is an incongruous but telling structural admixture of the ancient and the modern.

The record of the types of site considered here continues to evolve, as further research is undertaken, including excavation, survey both ground and remote, geophysical prospection and reconstruction. It may be anticipated that new examples of later prehistoric fortifications will continue to be found, perhaps particularly as cropmarks or, in some areas of the Continent, in denser woodland or at higher altitudes than archaeologists have traditionally looked. Elsewhere, it will be work within present-day towns that will produce new evidence. In some instances, this will be at sites such as Bourges or Geneva, where the stratigraphic accumulations associated with long-term settlement have meant that it has been difficult without the impetus derived from rescue archaeology, environmental assessment, and other modern pressures and procedures, to reach the archaeological correlates of their protohistoric occupation, although the locations have been long established as the sites of early forts from textual sources. In places, it may even be the creation of visitor facilities for monuments of other periods that throws new light on their protohistoric occupations, as in the case of Edinburgh Castle. In other cases, less predictable, the nature of the new evidence can be astonishing: mention has already been made of the skeletal finds within Aylesbury, but another British case where a major site has been defined piece by piece is Oram's Arbour at Winchester. Small-scale excavation within the city of Metz in north-east France produced evidence of its rebuilt timber-laced rampart and suites of dendrochronological dates that corresponded almost too uncannily well with historically-known dates of conflict in the area from the late second century BC onward (Faye *et al.* 1990). It would be reasonable to imagine that most new discoveries will be in a relatively degraded condition, although there will always be exceptions.

Just occasionally, too, an entirely new strand of evidence may come to light. Is it utterly unreasonable to hope that on a rock surface somewhere – Val Camonica, Portugal, Scandinavia – there is a recognisable depiction of a hill-fort or the incised trace of its rampart scratched into the living rock? Might some Celtic mercenary, recovered from his terror at facing elephants or military machinery in the hinterland of the eastern Mediterranean, have decided to emulate the carved scenes of warfare displayed on public monuments there? Such a find would complement the possible representation of a length of walling cut into a recently-found stone from Provence (*76*).

If it is reasonable to assume additions to the record of hill-forts in years to come, the future cannot always be seen in such a benign light. Like many components of the archaeological record, later prehistoric fortifications are prone to attrition from both natural and human causes. Coastal erosion is wearing away at promontories and severe or exceptional weather can cause problems, from tree-falls to the collapse

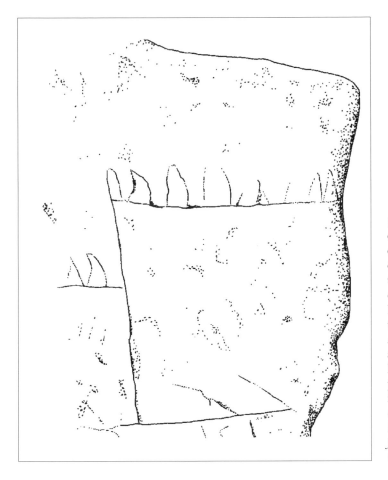

76 New types of
evidence? This
carving on a block
of stone from
the fortified site
of Verduron in
Provence, belonging
to the Second Iron
Age, appears to show
a crenellated wall-
head. May further
pieces of hill-fort
iconography be
expected? *Drawn
by Samantha Dennis
from a photograph in
Chausserie-Laprée 2000*

of stonework. The gamut of man-made pressures, from routine agricultural activities
to the catch-all of development, is certainly significant; to Auden's small children we
should add usually unwitting damage by their bigger brethren on foot and in sundry
vehicles from mountain bikes to 4x4 Chelsea tractors.

Like other earthworks, some of these fortifications are also targets for burrowing
or other fauna. In some upland areas, they can provide depths of soil and other
deposits not matched in nature and thus a particular attraction to such creatures. The
earthworks around the multivallate Brown Caterthun in Angus, for example, show
wide-scale evidence of collapse brought about by an invasion of rabbits. Andrew
Dunwell's project on this site examined both damaged and undamaged portions of
the earthworks, and made plain the serious information loss and radical change to
the character of the works that are caused by warrening. Much further north, John
Hunter's excavations at the Landberg promontory fort on Fair Isle demonstrated
that burrowing puffins could be as much of a problem. On a more localised scale,
other animals, notably badgers, can provoke catastrophic local damage, as is shown
by a sett in the rampart at the low-lying Oxfordshire fort at Cherbury (*77*).

77 A badger sett in the rampart at Cherbury, Oxfordshire

Overall, the point to be made is a simple one. Centuries after they have lost their primary uses, the evidence for these earthworks – both the academic evidence and, more prosaically, their external appearance – continues to evolve. If the earthworks of hill-forts were once essentially about making places in the ancient world, many are now about marking them in the contemporary one.

9

TWENTY HILL-FORTS TO SEE

When I originally thought of creating this list, I proposed to put together a relatively comprehensive gazetteer of hill-forts to visit, but clearly any such exercise at the temperate European scale – if it were to be of use to the reader – would have required considerable resources to check that matters such as ownership, car-parking arrangements, availability of toilet facilities, and access, were up-to-date. Rather, I list below a selection of sites I have visited over the years, alone or in the company of colleagues, and to which public access for the reasonably fit is possible. Some, but not all, are guardianship monuments or their equivalents; but others are in private ownership. No-one should, of course, try to get to any of these sites without taking into account local trespass laws, countryside codes and the like when arranging a visit.

What follows is thus a kind of personal 'Top Twenty', in which I have concentrated on prioritising variety. I also bias the choice towards cases where the visibility of the defences is significant; but that does not necessarily imply that they are particularly imposing. Some of these sites also have partial reconstructions of their defences on site. Sites are ordered alphabetically. Large numbers of very famous, and numbers of very well-laid out, sites are thus excluded, many for no better reason than the fact that I have not yet got to them. These include places with extensive series of reconstructions like Castell Henllys in Pembrokeshire, and ones with iconic settings, such as the Ipf-bei-Bopfingen or England's highest fort, Ingleborough. *Mea culpa.* I hope that this selection is none the less not hopelessly eclectic and dilettante in flavour. Website information was verified in December 2005.

1 CASTRO DE BAROÑA, LA CORUÑA, GALICIA, SPAIN

This site, located on a low, rocky boss on the coastal edge south of Porto de Son and overlooking the Ria de Muros, an inlet of the sea west of Santiago de Compostela, is included on account of the particularity of its location (*colour plate 24*). It is approached across a sandy spit. The site, including rocky outcrops, is over 2ha in area and has been known since the 1930s. It has been substantially excavated and consolidated. Its externally-tiered triple defences consist of dry-stone walls, sheltering both round and rectilinear buildings; the gate exhibits a bar-hole. An internal wall subdivides the site. Baroña's *floruit* lay in the last part of the local Iron Age, but other *castros*, such as that now displayed at Viladonga (north-east of Lugo, Galicia, and with a good site museum), had major occupations in the late Roman period. Baroña is open at all times and there is a small interpretation centre in Porto de Son itself. (http://www.agalicia.com/portodoson/castrodebarona/)

2 BEN GRIAM BEG, KINBRACE, SUTHERLAND, SCOTLAND

At 620m, this is the highest hill-fort in Scotland and one of the furthest from a public road. It is included here as it throws literally into high relief all kinds of questions to do with the inhabitability of, let alone the need to defend, such sites. This mountain top has been described by Mercer (1991, 141; plan at fig. 8.1) as '…today a terribly hostile environment'. Ben Griam Beg, with its partner Ben Griam Mor, form an isolated block of upland near the conjunction of the Strath of Kildonan and Strath Halladale, with the smaller summit (Beg) lying some 6km south-west of Forsinard. Recent commentators have stressed the likely early date of the site, postulating that its use predated the climatic decline during the first millennium BC; but it is formally undated.

The visitor is rewarded for the long hike in by an elaborate series of dry-stone built enclosures (*colour plate 25*; cf. *11*), looping downslope from the summit, itself

78 Ben Griam Beg: walling distorted by soil creep; lichen and bare rock; and the prospect towards Strath Naver to the north-west

only intermittently walled as much of it is edged by crags. These take in over 1ha. The summit enclosures are complemented at lower altitude by a series of dry-stone built settlement sites, primarily on the sandstone slopes with a more favourable aspect for cultivation. It seems likely that it is the more fertile soils derived from sandstone that attracted settlement here. But now the summit where, not bare of vegetation, is covered with lichen and moss and many of the walls are actively slipping downslope in the sub-arctic conditions which prevail there (*78*).

3 THE BROWN CATERTHUN, NEAR BRECHIN, ANGUS, SCOTLAND

The Brown Caterthun is physically the less imposing of a pair of hill-forts set on detached hills covered by moor and rough grazing close to the Highland Boundary in inland Angus. They are separated by a slight saddle now occupied by a minor road which provides the most convenient access to them. Both were amongst the sites protected under the first Ancient Monuments Act of 1882. Excavations in the mid-1990s, focused on the fortifications, were a response to signs of burgeoning rabbit damage (Dunwell and Strachan forthcoming). Whilst the innermost of the White Caterthun's principal defences consists of a very substantial wall (*79*), even if several of its outer lines resemble those found on its neighbour, all eight lines of enclosure around the Brown Caterthun are relatively slight, and most are punctuated by several gates. It is these characteristics that prompt its inclusion here.

From the summit downslope, these lines consist of an incomplete slight grooved arc, seemingly overlain by the first clear line, a stony bank with five entrance gaps defining an area a little under half a hectare in extent. Running on a different alignment below this is a wall (with surviving stonework intermittently visible) and upslope quarry scoops. Irregularities in its circuit suggest gang work and it displays nine entrances. It encloses over 2ha, which are in turn enveloped by two slight earthworks, sometimes accompanied by a medial ditch, further downslope. These show 10 entrance gaps, nine of which are aligned with those of their upslope neighbour. The following bank downslope is distinctly different in character: it is more substantial, doubled for much of its circuit by quarry scoops, and displays occasional kinks and twists in its alignment. Of its nine entrance gaps, six correspond with those of the circuits upslope from it. This encloses some 6ha. The final complete circuit takes the total surface enclosed to approximately 8ha. This consists of a bank with an external ditch and accompanying counterscarp bank. At least nine entrance gaps are recognisable; some of these are edged inside the enclosed area, by embanked passages leading upslope to the entrances in the next circuit in. A further incomplete feature, perhaps an unfinished bank, or a marker line for a circuit that was never to be constructed, completes the series.

These earthworks have been described in some detail since their character would be exceptional if this were a conventional hill-fort. In particular, the numbers of

79 The Caterthuns, Angus: the Brown Caterthun, discussed here, occupies the rounded summit in the background, with its neighbour, the White Caterthun in the foreground. The large boat-shaped stone enclosure of the White Caterthun is arguably the best-preserved hill-fort wall in Scotland and displays very slight evidence of vitrification

entrances through many of the enclosures – points of weakness in any defensive system – have given rise to the suggestion that the Brown Caterthun is a northern exemplar of the causewayed camps of southern England. The CFA work allows that proposition firmly to be rejected. Radiocarbon dates for all the circuits that could be dated fall firmly within the Iron Age, and broadly indicate that the site expanded outwards from some 2ha during the course of the pre-Roman Iron Age, subsequently to contract in its final centuries.

The entrances that were examined mostly show little evidence for gate furniture, but contrastingly display accompanying features suggesting the channelling of access towards the interior. This, with the slightness of the evidence for permanent settlement within this fort, suggests it served a different function or functions. Noting that the innermost of the more significant circuits had entrances separated by a maximum of 80m, Dunwell and Strachan conclude by seeing similarities between this Caterthun and early southern British hilltop enclosures, as described by Barry Cunliffe. Brown Caterthun, too, may thus have been a communal meeting place for people drawn from the wider locality, for which ideas of defence were of relatively minimal concern. Open at all times.

4 BURGHEAD, MORAY, SCOTLAND

Although there is evidence of finds of earlier date from Burghead (*80*) and its immediate vicinity, the essentials of the defences of the promontory fort as they are known date to the first millennium AD, and in north-east Scotland this is thus a Pictish fort. As planned in the eighteenth century, the site consisted of a pair of enclosed 'courts' occupying the end of the sandstone promontory jutting into the Moray Firth, one at about 18m OD, and the other some 10m lower, combined with a triple series of ramparts drawn across the neck of the promontory, but again set lower than the 'upper court'. Two main reasons underlie its inclusion here: the character of the defensive works, parts of which are still upstanding at the seaward end; and as an example of the partial survival of the site within a much more recent settlement, although in this instance without the continuity of settlement that can be argued for elsewhere.

Several excavations since the nineteenth century in the seaward defences indicate that these were of very varied construction, albeit using the combination of dry-stone, earth and timber found in many other contexts. As in the *murus gallicus* construction, nails have sometimes been found in the wall make-up – a characteristic matched at one other Early Historic fort in Scotland, Dundurn in Perthshire. The construction of a fishing station and harbour here destroyed much of the landward portion of the site, although excavation in gardens has revealed at least one of the ditches, and other banks and ditches can be detected amongst the leaning gravestones of St Aethan's

80 The surviving portions of the enclosed 'courts' at the seaward end of Burghead. Traces of the banks that traversed the headland can be seen in St Aethan's cemetery within the later village

cemetery. Burghead has also produced many Pictish bull carvings and contains a remarkable rock-cut well. A seasonal visitor centre is located in the former look-out station within one of the ramparts. The village is also notable for its fire celebrations at the Old New Year.

(www.burghead.com)

5 CAHERCONREE, DINGLE PENINSULA, COUNTY KERRY, IRELAND

This inland promontory fort occupies a triangular, cliff-edged spur of land at high altitude (650m) in the Sliabh Mish mountains of the Dingle Peninsula, County Kerry (*colour plate 2*). It is about 1ha in extent. On the side of easiest approach it is defended by a single, now generally tumbled, dry-stone wall up to 5m wide. The site enjoys – on a clear day – wide views over the landscape, from Loop Head in County Clare to the north, west to the Blasket Islands and south to Macgillicuddy Reeks, Ireland's highest mountains. Aside from a few structures attached to the back of the wall, there seems to be no evidence for occupation, and the categorisation of the site as a refuge seems altogether justified.

There is no archaeological dating evidence either. The site is traditionally associated with Cú Roí mac Dáiri, who appears in the Ulster Cycle of Legends; and the story of how the Ulster hero, Cú Chulainn eventually got the better of Cú Roí involves a battle at the site. The key character is Bláthnait, justly taken by Cú Roí for his part in assisting the Ulstermen in battle. Her treachery encouraged him to send his people, the Clan Dedad, off in search of every standing stone in Ireland to build a new fort wall. She then signalled the Ulstermen to approach, telling her husband, whom she was busy delousing, that they are his men returning with stones and timber for the construction. Leaving all the doors of the fort open, she tied her husband to the bed by his hair. The general slaughter which followed saw the fort burned, Cú Roí beheaded and his charioteer surrendered to a leading Ulsterman, only to kill him by driving straight into a rock. In the general mayhem, Bláthnait too was killed: Cú Roí's poet grabbed her and, crushing her ribs, leapt over the cliff with her in her arms. This legend of treachery, bloodshed, arson, suicidal driving and wall construction should remind us that other approaches to these remarkable sites are possible.

6 LE CHESLÉ DE BÉRISMENIL, LA ROCHE-EN-ARDENNE, LUXEMBOURG PROVINCE, BELGIUM

This is one of several sites set largely in woodland in the Ardennes of southern Belgium which have been excavated over recent decades and had parts of the defensive circuits reconstructed. The site occupies a steep-sided promontory extending to *c.*14ha overlooking the downcut, meandering valley of the upper River Ourthe. Man-made defences are apparent both at the junction of the promontory with the neighbouring upland, and at the break-of-slope around the circuit, except where natural defences suffice. A more intermittent second line, corresponding initially to a ditch, is visible outside this alignment.

Reconstructions show three of the constructional phases of the defences as identified by J. Papeleux (1988; Papeleux and de Boe 1987). The first consists of a palisade of upright posts set 1.5m apart, with intervening panels of horizontal timbers, backed by a slight mound. A date towards the end of the First Iron Age may be proposed (*15*). The second defence, set marginally upslope and placed, unusually, on a prepared surface dug slightly into natural, consisted of the first build of a *Pfostenschlitzmauer*, with regularly-spaced upright timbers, again 1.5m apart, set into natural, and interspersed with stone panels built of local schist both front and back (*81*). Its fills were of a variety of materials, with a stone capping. Internal timberwork was encountered in the form of traces of carbonised wood, taken to be wood treated by fire to make it last better, but perhaps simply an indication of reused wood from another structure. This defence (and certainly its successor) were probably fronted by a small U-shaped rock-cut ditch.

Unusually, this wall was then enveloped in a second *Pfostenschlitzmauer*, with thicker wall-faces and a greater overall width of *c.*6m. Constructional details suggest that this fortification was more poorly built than its predecessor. In due course, an additional outer wall was constructed on the counterscarp below the ditch. This was again fronted with vertical posts interspersed with schist-built wall panels, but its

81 The reconstruction of the *Pfostenschlitzmauer* at Le Cheslé de Bérismenil

inner margin consisted only of a dry-stone ramp set within the pre-existing ditch. This approximates to the *Kelheim* style of defences seen elsewhere. Dating here was hampered by the lack of small finds, but the indications suggest reuse towards the end of the Iron Age. Interestingly, this is a rare but not unique case where partially timber-built walls are retained and modified rather than being replaced by a dump rampart.

The site is located some 2km south of Bérismenil on a recognised walking path and is open at all times. (http://www.opt.be/hr/owa/MtrAttrEven.GetAVDInfo?AVD_ID=35130&CLAN GUE=FR&RG=A)

7 DANEBURY, HAMPSHIRE, ENGLAND

Danebury, thanks to the work of Professor Barry Cunliffe and his team, is one of the most extensively excavated and published Iron Age hill-forts in Europe. With some 100,000 visitors a year, the fort can be busy at times, and in places erosion of the earthworks through visitor pressure has become a cause for concern (*82*). The site (near Stockbridge), owned by Hampshire County Council Countryside Service since 1958, is usefully complemented by the Museum of the Iron Age in nearby Andover, where many of the artefacts and a reconstruction of the box rampart are displayed. (http://www.hants.gov.uk/countryside/danebury/)

82 Walking through the main entrance at Danebury gives an impression of the elaboration of the defences here

8 ENTREMONT, NEAR AIX-EN-PROVENCE, BOUCHES-DU-RHÔNE, FRANCE

Entremont is well known for the extensive collection of stone statuary that this small *oppidum*, the likely capital of the *Saluvii*, a Celto-Ligurian tribe living in the hinterland of Marseilles, has produced. The first elements of this were added to public collections in the early nineteenth century and more were unearthed by German troops during the war. Excavations began in 1946; and the site itself has been in state care since the 1950s.

Occupying a plateau, partially edged by free faces, in the Eguilles range on the northern outskirts of the modern city of Aix-en-Provence, which it overlooks, Entremont underwent rapid growth in the second century BC. Two successive defences are known, the earlier, taking in less than a hectare, enveloped in the south-west part of its successor within a matter of a few decades. Extensive sectors of the interior have been excavated and the stone-footed structures displayed. The site suffered two

83 Roughly-shaped limestone blocks in the main wall of the second, outer enclosure at Entremont

successive Roman attacks, related to the takeover of Provence, the original 'Provincia'. The first occurred *c.*130/120 BC; the second a generation or so later.

The earlier fortification enclosed a rectangular area, and the best-preserved wall, on its northern side, was fronted by four irregularly-spaced towers. The wall itself was a thin curtain approximately 1.5m wide of roughly-shaped limestone blocks held together with clay mortar. Its successor (*83*), some 400m long, almost quadrupled the enclosed area and was altogether a more impressive construction, being 3.5m wide and fronted by a massive rectangular tower approximately every 20m (*colour plate 15*). These projected over 5m from the wall and were about 10m wide; it is suggested that they may have stood to a height of 8m. The main entrance was on the west side.

The site is open daily, except for Tuesdays; and the key finds are displayed in the Musée Granet in Aix.

(http://www.culture.gouv.fr/culture/arcnat/entremont/en/index2.html)

9 HEUNEBURG, BADEN-WURTTEMBURG, GERMANY

The inclusion of this site is a slight cheat, because I have not visited it since it has been equipped with a series of major reconstructions. Its setting above the river Danube — here a much smaller watercourse than it becomes on its lengthy Black Sea journey — is readily appreciable (*colour plate 26*). The reconstructions include a sector of the defences around the south-west gate, full-height and glistening white: these look very imposing (*84*). One of the immense late First Iron Age (Hallstatt)

84 The south-west gate at the Heuneburg, as recently reconstructed. *Courtesy: Ian Shepherd*

buildings identified during the excavations has been reconstructed inside. Further excavations in the vicinity are currently demonstrating that the site is at the core of a much more extensive settlement area in the adjacent landscape: interim accounts of this work are available on the web.

Still surviving not far away are numbers of the barrows in which the Heuneburg's elite were eventually interred with their accoutrements of drinking, driving, feasting, fighting and generally flaunting it; these include the Hohmichele, still the biggest later prehistoric barrow in Europe. Not far away and cloaked in woodland is the lesser-known Grosse Heuneburg fort. The Heuneburg is here preferred over Mont Lassois, but very marginally, as an Early Iron Age princely seat. The latter's setting above the headwaters of the Seine and the gravegoods of the 'Vix Princess' in the museum of the neighbouring town of Châtillon-sur-Seine made this a particularly close call.

(http://www.fuerstensitze.de/1062_Home.html)

10 MAIDEN CASTLE, DORSET, ENGLAND

This is the quintessential southern British multivallate hill-fort, which would have to be in anyone's list *honoris causa*. On a long, low summit south-west of Dorchester within open agricultural country, its setting and configuration remain readily appreciable and limited erosion due to foot-traffic is kept in check. The sinuous character of the banks (*colour plate 9*) and the imposing scale of the western gateway in particular especially impress. Elements of its previous existence (Neolithic) and afterlife (Roman temple) are visible. Despite its fame, I have never found it to be overrun with visitors. Maintained by English Heritage, it is open year-round without charge.

(http://www.english-heritage.org.uk/server/show/conProperty.279)

11 LA MESA DE MIRANDA, CHAMARTÍN DE LA SIERRA, PROVINCE OF AVILA, SPAIN

La Mesa de Miranda is one of the major forts and subsequently *oppida* of the *Vettones* in western Spain and is set in the Amblés Valley, located between the valleys of the Duero and the Tagus in Avila province, at an altitude of over 1100m. The site was excavated by Juan Cabré Aguiló in the 1930s, but new excavations are now under way. Its dry-stone built defences include numerous remarkable details, including an imposing entrance arrangement built of very large blocks and flanked by dual passages (*colour plate 27*) to the most recent enclosure; the site also has extensive areas of *chevaux-de-frise* ('piedras hincadas'). La Mesa de Miranda has produced at least one of the remarkable massive bull carvings of fourth–third century BC date known from this area. Just outside but also partially overlain by the latest, eastern enclosure is the important cemetery of La Osera, where some of the dry-stone cairns have also been partially reconstructed. Initial occupation may date to around the fifth century BC, with the site eventually extending to some 30ha. It seems to have been abandoned in the first century BC.

The site consists of an initial univallate enclosure at the end of a granite promontory; additional works at the southern end include a single tower adjacent to the western gate, a ditch fronting the most accessible approach from the south, and sectors of *chevaux-de-frise* outwith both entrances. Within the main Iron Age period, a second enclosure enveloped this southern part of the plateau, and took in approximately a further 4ha. The wall here was again fronted locally by 'piedras hincadas'. Later, a third, incomplete, bastioned enclosure, with the remarkable monumental entrance noted above and a further inturned entrance, was added on the east side, partially overlying the cremation cemetery of the fourth and third centuries BC (Álvarez-Sanchís 1999; plan at fig. 63). Entrance is free.
(http://www.fundacionpatrimoniocyl.es/ARQU.asp?id=7)

12 MONT BEUVRAY, NEAR SAINT-LÉGER-SOUS-BEUVRAY, SAÔNE-ET-LOIRE AND NIÈVRE, BURGUNDY, FRANCE

'*Oppido Haeduorum longe maximo et copiosissimo...*' – 'By far the biggest and richest *oppidum* of the *Aedui...*' according to Julius Caesar, le Mont Beuvray, ancient *Bibracte*, occupies a conspicuous hill (its summits are at over 800m) some 20km west of Autun in Burgundy on the north-east margin of the Massif central. The nearest town of any size is Saint-Léger-sous-Beuvray.

85 The reconstruction of the rounded corner and 46m-long inturn of the northern side of the Porte du Rebout, photographed before the rock-cut ditch accompanying it was re-excavated

Excavated from the 1860s until just before the First World War, the site has been the subject of renewed fieldwork since 1984, initially with the support of the late President of the French Republic, François Mitterand. Mont Beuvray now has the most elaborate archaeological infrastructure of any temperate European hill-fort. It is also located within a regional natural park (for the Morvan).

It is possible to walk round both the main circuits of defences (the inner, some 5.25km long, takes a leisurely hour) (*57*); and the north-east gate, the Porte du Rebout, has been reconstructed (*85, colour plate 28*). An evolving programme of excavations undertaken by international teams ensures that there is usually at least one (and often more) site open within the 135ha inner enclosure during the summer months. Displays on the hilltop itself are matched by the contents of the large modern site museum at the Croix du Rebout beside the access road, with car parking and other facilities. The site is open at all times; there is a charge for the museum. With the lowland Bavarian site of Manching, near Ingolstadt, Mont Beuvray is archaeologically the most extensively examined of the temperate European *oppida*. (http://www.bibracte.fr/indcx_uk.php)

13 MONT VULLY, BAS-VULLY, FRIBOURG CANTON, SWITZERLAND

This fort, reasonably presumed to be one of the 12 *oppida* of the *Helvetii*, occupies the eastern end of a detached upland plateau south of the lac de Neuchâtel in the Trois Lacs region of the Swiss Mittelland. It enjoys wide views over the landscape, including across formerly ill-drained lowlands towards the site of the Iron Age bridges at La Tène itself. The fort, much of its outline naturally protected by steep descents from the summit, has been the subject of a campaign of research (Kaenel *et al.* 2004; Kaenel and Curdy 1988) over the last quarter-century, during which two fortifications barring the easiest access to the site have been examined. A third set, mostly located over 1km to the west, dates from the First World War and is an indication of the continuing strategic value of the position.

The initial fortification, set across the access to a triangular area of *c.*3ha on the summit of the plateau, seems to date to an early phase of the Late Bronze Age. Badly degraded and now marked by a slight break-of-slope, it consisted of an earthen core behind a stone external face, which had largely disappeared. Vertical timbers are also postulated. In due course a second, probably Late La Tène, rampart was built over the decayed remains of the first defence and may have enclosed an area of similar extent.

Some 120m to the west and slightly downslope, a much more imposing wall was subsequently built running north–south across the entire plateau, substantially (to 50ha) increasing the enclosed area. It is this wall which has been subject to more extensive examination, and which is now partially reconstructed on site. The main fortification was an elaborate variant of the *Pfostenschlitzmauer* type, now partially reconstructed on site (*86*) with a secondary earthen ramp up to 28m wide built

86 The recent reconstruction of the elaborate version of a *Pfostenschlitzmauer*, with horizontal timbers in the wall-face, at the entrance into Mont Vully

87 Reconstruction drawing of a tower on the line of the outer wall of Mont Vully. *Drawn by Jem Heinemeier after Kaenel and others 2004*

against its inner margin. An inturned entrance passage (probably one of two) was also identified but not examined in detail. Some 12m wide, it was flanked to north and south at a distance of approximately 30m by two timber towers, accessed at ground level from the interior of the site through gaps, faced with timber, in the inner ramp (*41* and *87*). These represent the most significant discovery of the explorations at Vully. Based on a framework of nine major vertical posts, they were initially *c*.6 x 7m in extent, but were of unknown height; their size may subsequently have been increased as part of a rebuild.

The oak posts in the external wall-face were massive – up to 0.85m across – and were matched by a further row some 3–4m to the east, to which they were probably attached by horizontal beams. Superimposed horizontal timbers, set into mortises cut in the vertical posts, also ran parallel through the wall-faces, and were recognised more particularly in the entrance. The quantity of exposed timber was thus considerably increased. The wall was preceded by a berm, and a flat-bottomed ditch. At some stage during the use of the wall, when the external wall-face was becoming dilapidated, it seems to have been equipped with a new outer face, for which only the post-holes for the upright timbers have been encountered in the excavation. A detailed engineering and work effort study by Leopold Pflug (in Kaenel *et al.* 2004) suggests the construction of this wall may have taken up to 400 builders three or four months to achieve.

The wall was apparently finally destroyed by fire, which had been lit and taken hold along its inner margin. There were no broken weapons or other signs of violence in the destruction layer, and the most likely explanation is that Mont Vully was one of the sites deliberately destroyed by the *Helvetii* in 58 BC in preparation for their planned emigration, as recorded by Julius Caesar. A problem is that the associated material culture belongs largely to the end of La Tène D1b, a phase now dated to around 80 BC. This does not, however, preclude the preferred hypothesis, particularly since Mont Vully does not seem to have been intensively occupied; the objects recovered simply provide a *terminus post quem* for the fire. Although there are slight and localised signs of subsequent reoccupation, the defences were not to be rebuilt. Open at all times.
(http://www.memo.fr/LieuAVisiter.asp?ID=VIS_SUI_FRI_043)

14 NAVAN FORT/EMAIN MACHA, NEAR ARMAGH, COUNTY ARMAGH, NORTHERN IRELAND

This 6ha enclosure is a major part of an extraordinary group of sites, sometimes called the 'Navan Complex', located some 3km west of Armagh, and considered the most important series of pre- and protohistoric monuments in Northern Ireland. It is equated with *Emain Macha*, the main centre of the Ulaid in the Early Historic period, according to the Ulster Cycle literature. Important neighbouring sites include a small lake, Loughnashade, Haughey's Fort, a multivallate enclosure with significant

Late Bronze Age use, and a broadly contemporary artificial pool, the King's Stables. Armagh itself was an important early ecclesiastical centre. Remarkable finds continue to be made in this landscape, most recently a substantial collection of Late Bronze Age metalwork including Central European vessels of about the tenth century BC.

In the gently rolling landscape in which it is set, Navan enjoys wide views, although it is only at 60m OD. The most remarkable feature is that the univallate enclosure, some 250m in diameter, consists of a substantial internal ditch, up to 4m deep, and external bank, spread to 15m wide. When this was laid out is uncertain, although on analogy with henge monuments a Neolithic date is possible: a single radiocarbon date for a timber recovered from its fill indicates it had been dug before about the fourth century BC. Of the two main internal excavations led by Dudley Waterman, that at the ring ditch revealed a long sequence of constructions and use beginning in the middle of the first millennium BC and continuing into Early Historic times. The Great Mound had been heaped over a rather different sequence of activities, starting in the Neolithic, but including, for later prehistory, a remarkable, repeatedly rebuilt, series of structures with conjoined enclosures and indications that they were used by the local elite, set within a 45m-diameter ditch initially excavated in the Bronze Age. Unusual features, notably the absence of internal post rings, suggest that they may not have been dwellings: the skull of a Barbary Ape was recovered from one of them. By 94 BC all this had been replaced by a huge circular timber building over 40m in diameter, which was soon rapidly infilled with limestone blocks. Thereafter its outer timber wall was set on fire, and the whole structure interred within a turf mound. The apparently ritual focus of these processes is mirrored by finds of skulls and elaborate bronze horns from Loughnashade, and echoes the unusual characteristics of the principal enclosure. In sum, there is little to suggest that Navan was ever a fort in any conventional defensive sense.

Navan Fort, now government-owned, is managed by the Environment and Heritage Service. The Navan Centre, opened to much acclaim in 1993, is closed at the time of writing. (http://www.ehsni.gov.uk/places/monuments/navan.shtml)

15 SRÒN UAMHA, KINTYRE, ARGYLL

Nearly at the southernmost point of the Mull of Kintyre, about 8km west-south-west of Southend, and with wide views over the North Channel towards the north of Ireland, this small multivallate fort is enclosed by triple dry-stone walls (there are no ditches) on its landward side (*88*). An unknown proportion of the site has been lost through erosion of the 100m-high cliff on its seaward side, and the surviving internal areas show no signs of prehistoric structures. The walls are locally well preserved, with facings standing to *c*.1.5m, probably in part due to their remoteness – the site is some 2km across rough moorland from the nearest road. The fact that the single entrance runs through all three lines may be an intimation that they

88 Sròn Uamha perched above the North Channel

represent a single build. Sròn Uamha is relatively easy to approach from landward and is locally overlooked by higher ground close by. Unlike some of the other coastal forts of western Scotland, such as Dunagoil on Bute with its two circuits of vitrified walling and its rich collection of Iron Age artefacts, this little fort is manifestly not positioned for easy access to the western seaways (RCAHMS 1971, no.176). (http://www.rcahms.gov.uk/pls/portal/newcanmore.newcandig_details_noimgsum mary?inumlink=38308)

16 STANWICK, STANWICK ST JOHN, NEAR RICHMOND, NORTH YORKSHIRE

I have included the great site of Stanwick, which extends to some 290ha, as an example of how analytical fieldwork accompanied by targeted excavation can rapidly nuance earlier interpretations of a set of earthworks. Often considered as the largest hill-fort in Britain, the site is in fact mostly low-lying. The most readily appreciable sector extends over about a square kilometre, centred on Stanwick church. The classic sequence for the site is that expounded by Sir Mortimer Wheeler (1954) following excavations (focused almost exclusively on rampart cuttings and ditch sections) and in essence envisages explosive growth during the first century AD, when the site is considered to have been the main centre for King Venutius of the *Brigantes*. The core, for Sir Mortimer, was formed by a 7ha enclosure at The Tofts, surrounded by a dump rampart. A first extension (in fact rendering the Tofts enclosure redundant) enlarged the site to some 50ha. This had imposing defences, consisting of a limestone-slab-fronted massive bank preceded by a flat-bottomed, vertical-sided, rock-cut ditch 12m wide and 4m deep. The ditch terminal adjacent to the entrance into this enclosure produced a sword and skull which may originally have embellished the entranceway. Thereafter a massive southward expansion enveloping a further 240ha was planned but, it is argued, could not be completed by the time the Romans attacked, an event preceded by rapid modifications to these works including the cutting of the approach causeway through the unfinished southern entrance. A fourth phase of works was left undated in the Wheeler scheme. Neatly as the sequence seemed to fit with the turmoil in the Brigantian royal house, it has not gone unchallenged; in particular it is now known that the occupation sequence at the Tofts (preceding the defences) is of longer duration than Wheeler's proposed chronology allowed; and it has been suggested that the more substantial 50ha works may even post-date the 240ha expansion.

More recent survey and excavation (Welfare *et al.* 1990; Haselgrove *et al.* 1990) has tended to nuance the reading of these earthworks further, on the one hand commenting favourably about the way they are set into the local topography and on the other postulating that some adopt the lines of earlier, non-defensive landscape divisions (while other initial banks seem to have served as marking-out works). Evidence points irrefutably to access routes being established before the construction of some of the entranceways, and to occupation of the core area of the Tofts preceding the construction of any of the known defensive works. Further, the security of the sequential development proposed by Wheeler has been challenged, and the new work suggests that relationships between the various earthworks might more usefully be probed from a functional, rather than a narrowly chronological, perspective. At the same time, Colin Haselgrove and his team acknowledge the fragility of any interpretation necessarily built up from examinations which are very restricted in extent compared to the 8km of enclosing works on this substantial site. A reconstructed section of the 50ha enclosure is located close to Forcett Village and is open at all times. (http://www.english-heritage.org.uk/server/show/conProperty.384)

17 TAP O' NOTH, NEAR RHYNIE, ABERDEENSHIRE, SCOTLAND

Dominating the village of Rhynie in inland Aberdeenshire is the conspicuous conical Tap o' Noth, rising to some 564m and occupying the west end of the Hill of Noth. The easiest access is from the small car park at Brae of Scudargue. This, the second highest hill-fort in Scotland, enjoys very wide views over north-east Scotland. The corollary is that, alight and glowing red, its defences on fire must have been equally widely visible against the black night sky.

The most celebrated feature of the site is the substantial vitrified wall, over 6m thick, which defines an area some 100 x 30m on the summit (see Chapter 7).

The vitrified material includes some very substantial blocks of fused rock. This fortification is constructed primarily of native hornfels and shows no sign of an entrance. Inside are traces of a depression marking a rock-cut cistern, as well as some indications of an earlier fortification line and two hut-circles. Much further downslope is preserved a slighter stone wall, taking in some 23ha of the summit, the slopes above this being pock-marked by numerous platforms, some of which may simply be quarries, but many of which are likely to represent the former stances of houses (*colour plate 29*). These outer works are likely to pre-date the vitrified fort, but no absolute dating evidence for them is available. The vitrified wall has provided markedly different dates by the use of thermoluminescence and archaeomagnetism. (http://www.aberdeenshire.gov.uk/archaeology/sites/forts/taponorth.asp)

18 TRE'R CEIRI, LLANAELHAERN, GWYNEDD, WALES

The so-called 'City of the Giants' in the Llyn peninsula in the former county of Carnarfonshire is assuredly one of the most spectacular of British hill-forts, but choose a better day to visit it than I did; this account depends heavily on the descriptions of others. Set on the second highest of the triple Yr Eifl peaks, it is at an altitude of 485m. The main circuit of walling, up to 3m thick, surrounding a summit area nearly 300m north-east–south-west by up to 100m, is best preserved on the north and west, where the wall-walk and dry-stone parapet are visible on a wall that is still locally some 3.5m high. There is plentiful scree in the vicinity. On the north-west, there is a detached length of outer wall, which is probably secondary. Surviving details on the major circuit include stone ramps from the interior providing access to the wall-head and three, metre-wide postern gates, that at the north with covering lintels still in place, providing supplementary exits from the site. (The collapse of such posterns could account for the apparently gateless forts of Scotland, already discussed.) There are also two more conventional gates. That at the north-west seems to have been the main route into the site, being matched by a gap with flanking out-turns in the outer wall and that on the west was modified in the second century AD to judge by associated finds.

The interior contains an admixture of round and rectilinear stone-footed buildings, some of the latter being modifications of earlier circular buildings. There have been a number of excavations, generally producing evidence of occupation of the site in the Roman period through to the fourth century AD. An apparent absence of quern-stones may be an indication that the site was only occupied seasonally. Initial construction of the site has not been dated, but may lie within the pre-Roman Iron Age.

The easiest approach is up a track from the south, passing by external garden plots. A programme to stabilise the remains, which have been suffering from considerable visitor pressure, has been underway since the late 1980s. Open at all times. (http://www.coflein.gov.uk/pls/portal/coflein.w_details?inumlink=6001663)

19 UFFINGTON CASTLE, WHITE HORSE HILL, BERKSHIRE

Adjacent to the modern alignment of the long distance route, the Ridgeway, and close to the splendid equine hill-figure of the White Horse, Uffington Castle is a well-preserved univallate fort of about 3ha. It sits towards the northern margin of the Lambourn Downs overlooking the Vale of the White Horse. The single rampart is fronted by a substantial ditch and a counterscarp bank (*89*), representing a Middle Iron Age (fourth century BC) remodelling of an earlier work. This dump rampart, which also blocked the eastern entrance, was placed over the decaying remains of an earlier box rampart, itself constructed towards the beginning of the Iron Age and equipped with opposed, east and west, entrances as frequently encountered in southern Britain. The other gaps in the circuit appear to have been made in Roman times and give access to the Ridgeway and to the White Horse.

The defensive sequence, wall followed by dump, is thus classic. The relationship between the defences and the White Horse has to be founded on the assumed date of the latter. If stylistic comparisons between the Horse and Late Iron Age coinage are upheld, the Horse would have been initially created at a time when the hill-fort seems to have been out of use. Optically stimulated luminescence dates with large error terms, contrastingly, would place the Horse contemporary with either period of the defences, or indeed with the major Late Bronze Age boundary at the end of which the fort was subsequently positioned.

Geophysics and trial excavations in the interior suggest that Uffington Castle was never densely settled (in contrast to nearby Segsbury, for example) and give rise to

89 The bank-and-ditch at Uffington Castle are still imposing features

the idea that the rampart may have served to delimit the meeting place of people drawn from the surrounding area for ceremonial or other purposes. In Victorian times, thousands came for a week-end's amusement while the Horse was scoured. The site is now in the care of English Heritage (neighbouring parts of White Horse Hill are owned by the National Trust) and is open at all times. (http://www.english-heritage.org.uk/server/show/conProperty.224)

20 WETHER HILL, NEAR WOOLER, NORTHUMBERLAND, ENGLAND

Wether Hill (or Corbie Clough) is one of a series of hill-forts to be found near Ingram in the Breamish valley of north Northumberland. It has been investigated over recent years as part of a wider archaeological project in the southern Cheviots and is included here as an example of the extraordinarily high degree of detail that can be detected on the surface in numerous sites in the Northumberland National Park and in nearby areas of the central Southern Uplands of Scotland. A combination of thin soils failing to mask slight slots and other indentations of archaeological origin, and the grazing of flocks of sheep effectively trimming the grass to a kind of sheepscape, mean that here, and on many other sites, it is possible to identify the former presence of palisades, the positions of the walls of timber roundhouses and the like without resorting to digging.

At Wether Hill itself, fieldwork by English Heritage followed up by the Northumberland Archaeological Group indicates a complicated sequence, beginning with an unenclosed phase consisting of timber roundhouses, still visible by the ring-grooves of their outer wall-lines. The initial defence consisted of a wooden stockade, which surrounded most, but not all, of these buildings. A bivallate earth-and-stone walled fort succeeded this, indicating a much more impressive defence than previously. Stone-walled houses in the interior may post-date this. Elements of the wider context and related fieldwork are explained at the National Park's visitor centre outside Ingram (McOmish 1999 with plan at fig. 1; Frodsham and Hedley 2005). (http://www.northumberland-national-park.org.uk/AboutUs/Community/Projects/HillfortHeritage/BreamishValley.htm?)

SELECTIVE GLOSSARY

Annexe – term applied to an outer enclosure around part of the circuit of a hill-fort, normally equipped with its own entrance.

Bastion – projection attached to, but standing forward of, a wall-line and which is – unlike a tower – of the same height as the wall.

Batter – the inward taper of a wall from base to top.

Berm – a generally narrow, generally horizontal platform located between wall/rampart and external ditch.

Bivallate – equipped with two lines of fortification.

Box rampart – wall fortification equipped with timber framing to front and rear; in English usage normally implying vertical posts with intervening panels of timber or stone, and not to be confused with the horizontal timber frameworks implied by German term *Kastenbau*.

Breastwork – protective work to shelter defenders placed on or near the summit of a fortification; little evidence of these survives in Iron Age Europe, and it is not known whether they were crenellated as in the contemporary Aegean and western Asiatic worlds.

Calcination – process by which limestone in a fortification has been altered, generally by the application of heat, and thus broadly comparable as a process to vitrification.

Chevaux-de-frise – placed outwith the main lines of defence, or sometimes on the berm between fortification and ditch, these are irregular but earthfast arrangements of angular stones or, rarely, pointed stakes (cf. Roman *lilia*), designed to break up a charge, albeit generally not of horsemen but of infantry.

Cliff castle – promontory fort, generally small, on sea-girt hard rock headland.

Cistern – artificial rock-cut depression not attaining the local water table for storing surface run-off.

Contour fort – hill-fort with its line or lines of enclosure conforming to the contours of its topographic setting.

Counterscarp bank – upcast bank placed on the downslope, outer margin of a ditch.

Cross-ridge dyke – a linear earthwork set across a spur of land generally in the vicinity of a hill-fort, but without any direct link to its fortifications.

Dead ground – land in the immediate vicinity of a fortification but invisible from it owing to the nature of the intervening topography such as the curvature of a slope.

Fécamp rampart – massive rampart of heaped-up materials which can be of the order of 10m high, fronted by a broad, flat-bottomed ditch, and originally considered by Sir Mortimer Wheeler as the response of the Belgae to Roman styles of warfare. Named after a site near this port in lower Normandy.

Glacis rampart – a generally substantial dump bank presenting a sloping face to the exterior.

Guard chamber – a cell or cells in the side wall of an entrance passage assumed to have held a sentry.

Hallstatt – main First Iron Age culture of western Continental Europe lasting from the eighth to the fifth century BC. Named after a cemetery, mine complex and settlement in Austria.

Hearting – smaller stone used as fill in the core of a wall.

Hornwork – external projection from a rampart or wall-line designed to provide additional defence at an entrance.

Inturned entrance – gateway in which the fortification on either side is turned inwards to flank a passage, particularly developed at the end of the Second Iron Age. German = ***Zangentor***.

Kastenbau – constructional style based on the juxtaposition of a series of conjoined casements defined by horizontal timberwork, variously infilled.

Marker bank/ditch – slighter features identified on the same alignment as a more significant feature of the same type, and considered to represent a preliminary constructional stage and thus an unfinished site.

Military crest – the line around a slope from which there is no invisible dead ground below on the lower slopes.

Multivallate – enclosed by multiple walls or ramparts.

Murus duplex – the addition of internal built stone facings within the overall thickness of dry-stone built walls.

Murus gallicus – second to first century BC style of timber-laced wall found in temperate Continental Europe, with beam-holes in its vertical wall-face. Decribed initially by Julius Caesar in his account of the siege of *Avaricum* in 52 BC, hence the 'Gallic war'. Sometimes now defined by the long iron spikes at the intersections of the internal timberwork, although these were not a detail noted by Caesar.

Oppidum – large (generally over 25ha) enclosed site of Late Iron Age date, sometimes with evidence of elaborate, even proto-urban, occupation.

Palisade – free-standing timber fence, generally set in a prepared slot or a slight upcast bank. Examples in more defensive situations are sometimes referred to as stockades.

Pfostenschlitzmauer – German generic term for wall fortifications with upright posts separated by panels of stonework in their façades, the upright posts being tied back into the wall-cores.

Quarry scoop – relatively informal depression, generally upslope from a rampart or wall, from which materials have been extracted for construction.

Revetment – generally used of the external retaining wall-face or faces in a wall-and-fill rampart that fronts or surrounds hearting.

Stockade – a wooden palisade, more surely defensive in character, by extension stockaded camp.

La Tène – main Second Iron Age culture of western Continental Europe lasting from the fifth century BC to the Roman conquest. Named after a collapsed bridge, with much associated metalwork, in Switzerland.

Timber-framed – generic term for walls with vertical timberwork in their front, or their front and rear faces, normally including additional horizontal ties.

Timber-laced – internal timberwork, generally laid solely horizontally, within a wall.

Tower – stone- or timber-built feature that projected above, as well as normally in front of, the general height of a defensive wall.

Unfinished fort – a term used to describe any defensive scheme which seems incomplete; much favoured by previous generations of archaeologists, more recent commentators consider that, in some instances, such schemes represent different defensive objectives in cases where uniformity was not essential.

Univallate – enclosed by a single wall or rampart.

Vitrification – process whereby the character of hard rocks have been substantially deformed through the application of considerable heat, and have subsequently resolidified.

Zangentor – see inturned entrance.

A GUIDE TO THE LITERATURE

The following guide attempts to provide an introduction to the literature of hill-fort defences of temperate Europe in a wider context. It makes no pretence at offering a complete survey, and privileges well-illustrated and/or relatively recent and accessible and/or English-language literature. It provides some sources on the architecture of defence in the Mediterranean, Aegean and western Asiatic worlds, as well as on defensive architecture in other times and places (including earlier examples in Europe), domains in which the temperate European protohistorian may feel well out of his or her depth, but which they ignore entirely at their peril. The inclusion of particular site reports is biased in favour of those sites selected for discussion or illustration here. A number of English-language sources on the European Iron Age are provided, for those who wish to pursue the cultural milieux in which many of hill-forts considered occurred.

GENERAL REVIEWS OF FORTIFICATION

de la Croix, H. 1972 *Military considerations in city planning: fortifications*. New York: George Braziller.
This slim volume in the series 'Planning and cities' packs much good sense into its introductory pages.

Moxham, R. 2001 *The great hedge of India*. London: Constable.
Not all boundaries are inorganic: the hedge as customs barrier.

Nicholson, H. 2004 *Medieval warfare. Theory and practice of war in Europe 300-1500 AD*. Basingstoke: Palgrave Macmillan.
This recent survey, although not primarily focused on fortifications, provides an excellent introduction to the literature on medieval European warfare.

Toy, S. 1955 *A history of fortification from 3000 BC to AD 1700*. London: Heinemann. Although predominantly focused on castles and other medieval fortifications, this general introduction includes salient points.

NEOLITHIC, CHALCOLITHIC/COPPER AGE AND BRONZE AGE ENCLOSURE

Enclosed and defended sites were not an invention of the Iron Age. The following deal with Neolithic and Bronze Age sites.

Andersen, N. H. 1997 *The Sarup enclosures.* Moesland, Denmark: Jutland Archaeological Society Publications 33.
The second half of this volume (p.133 ff.) provides a well-illustrated and wide-ranging review of Neolithic and Earlier Bronze Age enclosed sites, from the Aegean to the NW of the Continent, including the British Isles.

Harding, A. 2000 *European societies in the Bronze Age.* Cambridge: Cambridge University Press.
Chapter 8 provides a succinct overview of warfare and the forts of the Bronze Age.

Harding, J. 2003 *The Henge Monuments of the British Isles.* Stroud: Tempus.

Mazar, A. 1995 'The fortification of cities in the Ancient Near East', in (ed.) Sasson, J. M. Civilizations of the Ancient Near East, vol. 3, 1523-1537. New York: Charles Scribner's Sons.

Mordant, C. & Richard, A. (eds.) 1992 *L'habitat et l'occupation du sol à l'âge de bronze en Europe.* Paris: Editions du Comité des travaux historiques et scientifiques.

Primas, M. 2002 'Taking the high ground: continental Hill-forts in Bronze Age contexts', *Proceedings of the Prehistoric Society* 68, 41-59.
Includes a review of recent work largely originally published in German.

Varndell, G. & Topping, P. (eds.) 2002 *Enclosures in Neolithic Europe.* Oxford: Oxbow Books.
Collected papers from a 1999 conference reviewing causewayed enclosures and their equivalents in Neolithic Europe, but considered more widely.

THE MEDITERRANEAN CIVILISATIONS: MILITARY ARCHITECTURE AND WARFARE

Adam, J.-P. 1982 *L'architecture militaire grècque.* Paris: Picard.
Copiously illustrated with both photographs and measured plans and illustrations, this survey introduces the architectural elements in Greek military architecture through to Hellenistic times, but also provides brief introductions to a range of sites on mainland Greece as well as in Asia Minor and west to Sicily.

Edwards, R.W. 1987 *The fortifications of Armenian Cilicia.* Washington: Dumbarton Oaks Studies XXIII.
Somewhat remote from our interests, but offers concise and insightful explanations for a variety of features, not all of which are pertinent to Celtic Europe.

Hackett, (Sir) John (ed.) 1989 *Warfare in the Ancient World.* London: Guild Publishing.
Well illustrated by Peter Connolly, this is a good start point for the archaeologist of the European barbarian world to get to grips with southern and eastern developments.

Lawrence, A.W. 1979 *Greek aims in fortification.* Oxford: Clarendon Press.
This is a comprehensive guide ranging from a consideration of the built elements through the types of site on which they were deployed to the assault techniques employed.

Marsden, E.W. 1971 *Greek and Roman artillery. Technical treatises.* Oxford: Clarendon.
One of the main drivers of development in fortifications in the last millennium BC was the development of artillery pieces, capable of dealing death from a distance. These impacted later on Celtic fortifications, than on those further south. Marsden provides translations of key classical texts, and illustrations of the main machines.

Winter, F.E. 1971 *Greek fortifications.* Toronto: University of Toronto Press.

EUROPEAN LATER PREHISTORY

Key texts on the European Iron Age, largely in English, include:

Audouze, F. & Buchsenschutz, O. 1992 *Towns, villages and countryside in Celtic Europe.* London: Batsford.
An excellent overview, largely from the perspective of the settlement evidence.

Collis, J. R. 1984/1995 *The European Iron Age.* Batsford: London, reissued (1995) by Routledge: London.
Twenty years on, still the best basic introduction to the subject in English.

Cunliffe, B.W. 1997 *The ancient Celts.* Oxford: Oxford University Press.

Cunliffe, B.W. (ed.) 1994 *The Oxford Illustrated Prehistory of Europe.* Oxford: Oxford University Press.
A briefer treatment than Cunliffe 1997, but includes important statements e.g. by Dr Tim Taylor on Thracians, Dacians and Scythians.

Green, M. (ed.) 1995 *The Celtic world*. London: Routledge.
A massive compendium, but with brief authoritative chapters in English that are worth dipping into on just about anything and everything. Easier to read in general than Moscati (ed. 1991), although the latter is more profusely illustrated.

James, S. 1993 *Exploring the world of the Celts*. London: Thames and Hudson.
Double-page illustrated spreads on lots of topics provide concise and authoritative start points.

Kristiansen, K. 1998 *Europe before history*. Cambridge: Cambridge University Press.
A thought-provoking overview from Bronze Age to Iron Age.

Kruta, V. 2001 *Les Celtes: histoire et dictionnaire*. Paris: Laffont.
A fairly traditional text, juxtaposed with a hugely useful gazetteer, bibliography, and list of museums.

Moscati, S. 1991 *The Celts*. Milan: Bompiani, republished by Thames and Hudson.
Profusely illustrated catalogue of a blockbuster exhibition held in Venice.

Wells, P. S. 1984 *Farms, Villages and Cities*. Ithaca: Cornell University Press
Especially Chapters 3-6. The same author's Chapter 2 'Europe before the Roman conquest' in *idem* 1999 *The barbarians speak*. Princeton: University Press, provides a more up-to-date summary of the final development of prehistoric Europe. Little has been written in English on the 'princely seats' of the First/Hallstatt Iron Age, so that *idem* 1980 *Culture contact, culture change*. Cambridge: University Press, is still of considerable use.

Wells, P.S. 2001 *Beyond Celts, Germans and Scythians*. London: Duckworth.
With Chapter 3 of Simon James 1999 *The Atlantic Celts*. London: British Museum Press, provides a challenging views on the idea of the Celts in prehistoric later times.

TOOLS AND RELATED EQUIPMENT

Some sources on tools and working practices, to indicate what would have been available in Iron Age Europe.

de los Angeles, M. & Mayor, M. 1980 *Instrumentos de hierro de Numancia*. Madrid: Ministry of Culture.

Guillaumet, J.-P. 1996 *L'artisanat chez les gaulois*. Paris: Errance.

Jacobi, G. 1974 *Werkzeug und Gerät aus dem Oppidum von Manching*. Stuttgart: Franz Steiner (= Die Ausgrabungen in Manching 5)

Rees, S.E. 1979 *Agricultural implements in prehistoric and Roman Britain*. Oxford: Brit Archaeol Rep 69.

APPROACHES TO HILL-FORTS

Bowden, M. and McOmish, D. 1987 'The required barrier', *Scottish Archaeological Review* 4, 76-84.

Bowden, M. and McOmish, D. 1989 'Little boxes: more on hill-forts', *Scottish Archaeological Review* 6, 12-16.

Graham, A. 1951 'Archaeological gleanings from Dark-Age records', *Proc Soc Antiq Scot* **85**, 64-91.
Includes a useful discussion on literary evidence for forts and their uses, and the deployment of fire in attacking them.

Collis, J.R. 1996 'Hill-forts, enclosures and boundaries', in (eds.) Champion, T.C. and Collis, J.R. *The Iron Age in Britain and Ireland: recent trends*, 87-94. Sheffield: J.R. Collis (= Recent Trends 4).

Hawkes, C.F.C. 1931 'Hill-forts', *Antiquity* 5, 60-97.

Hill, J.D. and Cumberpatch, C.G. (eds.) 1995 *Different Iron Ages*. Oxford: British Archaeol Rep Internat Ser 602.

Ralston, I. 1995 'Fortifications and defence', in (ed.) Green, 59-81.

Trigger, B.G. 1990 'Monumental architecture: a thermodynamic explanation of symbolic behaviour', *World Archaeology* 22, 119-132.

Wheeler, R.E.M. 1952 'Earthwork since Hadrian Allcroft', *Archaeological Journal* **106,** (supplementary volume) 62-82.

HILL-FORTS IN GENERAL

Brun, P. and Chaume, B. (eds.) 1997 *Vix et les éphémères principautés celtiques*. Paris: Errance.
Vade mecum to the key sites of the end of the Hallstatt Iron Age.

Collis, J.R. 1984 *Oppida: earliest towns north of the Alps*. Sheffield: J.R. Collis Publications.
Still the best and fullest English-language introduction to Continental *oppida*. For a more recent and well-illustrated treatment of the subject see Fichtl, S. 2000 *La ville celtique*. Paris: Errance. Both volumes have useful gazetteers.

Collis, J.R. and Ralston, I.B.M. 1976 'Late la Tène defences', *Germania* 54, 135-46.

Glodariu, I. 1983 *Architectura Dacilor – civilă și militară*. Cluj: Editura Dacia.
Dacian architecture of second century BC to first century AD usefully illustrated. Also see Stefan, A. 1986 'Archéologie aérienne en Roumanie', *Photo interpretation* 25, 1-8.

SPAIN AND PORTUGAL

A copious literature is emerging on numerous aspects of the protohistoric fortifications of the Iberian peninsula. I found Moret 1996 and various volumes in the *Complutum* series from Universidad Complutense, Madrid, of particular value. The catalogue of the major exhibition held at Ávila (Almagro-Gorbea *et al.* 2001) provides a well-illustrated overview.

Almagro-Gorbea, M., Mariné, M. and Álvarez Sanchís, J.R. 2001 *Celtas y Vettones*. Ávila: Diputacíon provincial de Ávila.

Almagro-Gorbea, M. and Martín, A. 1994 *Castros y oppida en Extremadura*. Madrid: Complutum Extra 4.

Harbison, P. 1968 'Castros with *chevaux-de-frise* in Spain and Portugal', *Madrider Mitteilungen* 9, 116-147.
Incomplete now, but still a useful English-language source.

Lorrio, A.J. 1997 *Los Celtíberos*. Alicante: Univ Alicante/Univ Complutense, Madrid. Complutum 7.
Chapter 3 on settlement is very usefully illustrated.

Moret, P. 1996 *Les fortifications ibériques de la fin de l'âge du Bronze à la conquête romaine*. Madrid: Collection de la Casa de Velázquez 56.
A *tour de force*: dealing with Levantine (Iberian) Spain, this is one of the best regional surveys of the evidence of hill-fort fortifications known to me. Extends into southern France.

Queiroga, F. M.V. R. 2003 *War and castros: new approaches to the northwestern Portuguese Iron Age*. Oxford: Brit Archaeol Rep Internat Series 1198.

A useful English-language introduction to the increasing evidence for *castros* from north Portugal, even if it suggests that data on the architecture of their defences remains scant. Palisades, walls and ramparts and ditches are all represented.

FRANCE/GALLIA

This really embraces two literatures: one for the temperate areas, the other from the Mediterranean coastlands and their immediate hinterland.

Delétang, H. 1999 *L'archéologie aérienne en France*. Paris: Errance.

South
Bretaudeau, G. 1996 *Les enceintes des Alpes-Maritimes*. Nice: Institut de Préhistoire et d'Archéologie des Alpes Mediterranée.

Brun, J.-P., Congès, G. and Pasqualini, M. 1993 *Les fouilles de Taradeau*. Paris: CNRS Editions (= Rev Archéol Narbonnaise Suppl 28).
Main report of the site of Le Fort.

Chausserie-Laprée, J. (ed.) 2000 *Le temps des Gaulois en Provence*. Martigues: Musée Ziem.
Many sites wonderfully illustrated.

Dedet, B. and Py, M. (eds.) 1985 *Les enceintes protohistoriques de Gaule méridionale*. Caveirac: Assoc Recherche Archéologique de Gaule méridionale Cahier 14.
Excellent, if ageing, brief outline of the key sites.

Garcia, D. 2004 *La Celtique méditerrannéenne*. Paris: Errance.

Gruat, P., Marty, G. and Marchand, G. 2003 'Systèmes de fortification de l'habitat de hauteur du Peuch de Mus à Sainte-Eulalie-de-Cernon (Aveyron) au Ve s. av. J.-C.', *Documents d'Archéologie méridionale* 26, 63-157.
Describes a rapid evolution of fortification styles making heavy use of wood but apparently very different from those normally encountered further north.

Py, M. 1993 *Les Gaulois du Midi*. Paris: Hachette.

Saumade, H. 1996 *Les sites protohistoriques de l'Ardèche dans leur contexte mediterranéen*. Aubenas: chez l'auteur.

North
Buchsenschutz, O. 1984 *Structures d'habitats et fortifications de l'Age du fer en France*

septentrionale. Paris: Mémoires de la Société préhistorique française, 18.

Cahen-Delhaye, A., Duval, A., Leman-Delerive, G. and Leman, P. (eds.) 1984 *Les Celtes en Belgique et dans le nord de la France. Les fortifications de l'Age du Fer.* Lille: Revue du Nord numéro spécial. (= Actes VI Col Assoc française Etude Ages Fer). Conference considering the hill-forts of northern France and Belgium.

Chaume, B. 2001 *Vix et son territoire à l'Age du Fer.* Montagnac: Editions Monique Mergoil (= Protohistoire européenne 6).
Dominated by the artefacts, but summarises the fortification evidence for Mont Lassois before the current campaigns.

Faye, O., Georges, M. and Thion, P. 1990 'Des fortifications de la Tène à Metz, Moselle', *Trierer Zeitschrift* 53, 55-126.
Dendrochronological dates point to later second, and mid-first century builds of a *murus gallicus.*

Metzler, J. 1995 *Das treverische Oppidum auf dem Titelberg.* Luxembourg: Dossiers d'Archéologie du Musée national d'histoire et d'art, 3. 2 vols.

Papeleux, J. and Boe, G. de (eds.) 1988 *Fortresses celtiques en Wallonie.* Brussels: Archaeological Belgii Speculum 14.
Well-illustrated guide to selected south Belgian (Wallonian) sites.

Ralston. I. 1992 *Les enceintes fortifiées du Limousin.* Paris: Editions Maison des Sciences de l'Homme. (= Documents d'Archéologie française 36).

Musée départmental des antiquités Rouen 2001 *Au temps des Gaulois: découvertes récentes en haute-Normandie.* Rouen: Musée départmental des antiquités.
New work across the Channel at Braquemont, Quièvrecourt, Vernon etc.

Wheeler, R.E.M. and Richardson, K.M. 1957 *Hill-forts of northern France.* London: Res Rep Soc Antiq Lond 19.

Beuvray

Almagro-Gorbea, M. and Gran-Aymerich, J. 1991 *El estanque monumental de Bibracte.* Madrid: Complutum Extra 1.

Buchsenschutz, O., Guillaumet, J.-P. and Ralston, I. 1999 *Les ramparts de Bibracte: recherches sur la porte du Rebout et le tracé des fortifications.* Glux-en-Glenne: Centre archéologique européen du mont Beuvray. (= Collection Bibracte 3).

Goudineau, C. and Peyre, C. 1993 *Bibracte et les Eduens.* Paris: Errance.

Gruel, K. and Vitali, D. 1999 'L'oppidum de Bibracte: un bilan de 11 ans de recherches', *Gallia* 55, 1–140.

Guillaumet, J.-P. 1996 *Bibracte: bibliographie et plans anciens*. Paris: Editions Maison des Sciences de l'Homme. (= Documents d'Archéologie française 57).

SWITZERLAND

Kaenel, G., Curdy, P. and Carrard, F. 2004 *L'oppidum de mont Vully; un bilan de recherches*. Fribourg: Academic Press (= Archéologie fribourgeoise 20).

Müller, F., Kaenel, G. and Lüscher, G. (eds.) 1999 *La Suisse du Paléolithique à l'aube du Moyen-Age. IV: Age du Fer*. Basel: Verlag Schweizerische Gesellschaft für Ur- und Frühgeschichte.
Settlement evidence is reviewed in Chapter 5 by Peter Jud and Philippe Curdy.

Müller, F. and Lüscher, G. 2004 *Die Kelten in der Schweiz*. Stuttgart: Theiss.
General survey, but with gazetteer entries for some key sites.

GERMANY AND AUSTRIA

A new overview of the Celts in Germany (Rieckhoff & Pauli) provides excellent brief introductions to numerous sites. Also particularly helpful are other well-illustrated publications from Theiss Verlag, including an excellent introduction to some of the sites of the old German Democratic Republic (Herrmann 1989) and to the Iron Age of Baden-Wurttemburg. (Bittel *et al.* 1981). There are also numerous regional surveys (e.g. Biel 1987), some of considerable merit, as well as detailed excavation reports on individual sites. Of the latter, those dealing with the Heuneburg (particularly for the Hallstatt period) and Manching (for Late la Tène) are the most extensive. The most accessible English-language sources on German fortifications are those by Heinrich Härke (e.g. 1979).

Biel, J. 1987 *Vorgeschichtliche Höhensiedlungen in Südwürttemburg-Hohenzollern*. Stuttgart: Konrad Theiss (= Forschungen und Berichte zur Vor und Frühgeschichte in Baden-Württemburg, 24).

Bittel, K., Kimmig, W. & Schiek, S. 1981 *Die Kelten in Baden-Wurttemburg*. Stuttgart: Konrad Theiss.

Härke, H. 1979 *Settlement types and settlement patterns in the West Hallstatt province*. Oxford: Brit Archaeol Rep Internat Ser 57.

Herrmann, J. (herausgeben von) 1989 *Archäologie in der Deutschen Demokratischen Republik*. Stuttgart: Konrad Theiss. 2 vols.
Multiperiod survey and illustrated gazetteer of former East Germany, with numerous later prehistoric and Migration Period hill-forts discussed and illustrated.

Koch, K.-H. & Schindler, R. 1994 *Vor- und frühgeschichtliche Burgwälle des Regierungsbezirkes Trier und der Kreises Birkenfeld*. Mainz: Trierer Grabungen und Forschungen 13.

Rieckhoff, S. & Biel, J. 2001 *Die Kelten in Deutschland*. Stuttgart: Konrad Theiss.
Up-to-date text and extensive, well-illustrated, well-referenced gazetteer.

Schindler, R. 1977 *Die Altburg bei Bundenbach*. Mainz am Rhein: von Zabern (= *Trierer Grabungen und Forschungen* 10).
The first complete excavation of a hill-fort.

Urban, O. 2000 *Der lange Weg zur Geschichte: die Urgeschichte Österreichs bis 15 v C.* Vienna: Ueberreuter.
General overview by Austria's premier rampart excavator.

Manching
Sievers, S. 2003 *Manching: die Keltenstadt*. Stuttgart: Theiss (= Führer zu archäologischen Denkmälern in Bayern. Oberbayern 3).
Overview of this key site, with a guide to the earlier literature.

Van Endert, D. 1987 *Das Osttor des Oppidums von Manching*. Stuttgart: Franz Steiner (= Die Ausgrabungen in Manching 10).
The evidence for the elaborate Torhaus.

CENTRAL EUROPE

Drda, P. and Rybová, A. 1994 'Bohemia in the Iron Age: a recent view', in *25 Years of Archaeological Research in Bohemia*, 82-92. Prague: Památky Archeologické Supplementum 1.

Rybová, A and Drda, P. 1995 *Les Celtes de Bohême*. Paris: Errance.
Overview of evidence from the Czech Republic.

Szabo, M. 1992 *Les Celtes de l'Est*. Paris: Errance.

UNITED KINGDOM

Allcroft 1908 is a classic, and is a characteristic product arising from the surveys and inventories that were prevalent in the later nineteenth century and the years before the Great War. In terms of fortifications, Avery (1993) is the most detailed consideration of the southern British evidence.

Allcroft, H. 1908 *Earthwork of England*.

Alcock, L. 1995 *Cadbury Castle, Somerset: the early medieval archaeology*. Cardiff: University of Wales Press.

Alcock, L. 2003 *Kings and warriors, craftsmen and priests*. Edinburgh: Society of Antiquaries of Scotland Monogr Ser
Last overview, including much on early historic fortifications in northern Britain, by the doyen of the subject.

Armit, I. 2003 *Towers in the North*. Stroud: Tempus.
The major suites of small, heavily-walled structures of the Atlantic Iron Age of Scotland are not considered here, but Armit furnishes a useful overview of these types of architecture and the competing interpretations that currently surround them.

Avery, M. 1993 *Hillfort defences of southern Britain*. Oxford: Brit Archaeol Rep 231.
Full publication of Dr Avery's Oxford doctoral thesis of 1979 on the topic, providing him with a much more extensive canvas than his excellent introduction to hill-forts in general in (ed.) Harding 1976.

Barrett, J.C., Freeman, P.W.M. & Woodward, A. 2000 *Cadbury Castle, Somerset: the later prehistoric and historic archaeology*. London: English Heritage Archaeological Report 20.
A conscious effort to write a new style of excavation report, and offering a marked difference of emphasis from the interim synthesis put out by the original excavator:
Alcock, L. 1972 *'By South Cadbury is that Camelot...'*. London: Thames and Hudson.

Bradley, R. 1975 *Rams Hill*. Oxford: Brit Archaeol Rep 19.
For reassessment of dating of the early phase, see Needham, S. and Amber, J. 1994 'Redating Rams Hill and reconsidering Bronze Age enclosure', *Proc Prehist Soc* 60, 225-44.

Cunliffe, B.W. 1995 *Danebury: an Iron Age hillfort in Hampshire. Vol. 6 A hillfort community in perspective*. York: Counc Brit Archaeol Res Rep 102.
The defensive sequence at this key site summarised.

Cunliffe, B.W. 2005 *Iron Age communities in Britain*. London: Routledge fourth ed.
Thirty years on from the first edition, still the best overview of the British Iron Age
and its hill-forts, albeit distinctly more at home in the south of the country.

Dixon, P. 1994 *Crickley Hill: the hillfort defences*. Nottingham: Crickley Hill Trust/
University of Nottingham.
The later prehistoric defences of this site (also with Neolithic and first millennium AD
use) comprehensively considered. A classic excavation, producing a comprehensive
and well-illustrated report.

Dyer, J. 1992 *Hillforts of England and Wales*. Princes Risborough, Bucks: Shire.
As ever, the Shire product is a good, brief, well-illustrated introduction.

Forde-Johnston, J. 1976 *Hillforts of the Iron Age in England and Wales*. Liverpool:
Liverpool University Press.
Well-organised and well-illustrated consideration of the surface evidence.

Gregory, T. 1992 *Excavations in Thetford 1980-1982: Fison Way*. Dereham: East Anglian
Archaeol Rep 53.

Guilbert, G. 1981 (ed.) *Hill-fort studies*. Leicester: Leicester University Press.
A useful collection of essays in homage to the former doyen of hill-fort studies, Dr
A.H.A. Hogg.

Hamilton, S. & Manley, J. 2001 'Hillforts, monumentality and place: a chronological
and topographic review of first millennium BC hill-forts of south-east England',
European Journal of Archaeology 4, 7-42.
New approaches thoughtfully presented.

Harding, D.W. 1976 (ed.) *Hillforts: later prehistoric earthworks in Britain and Ireland*.
London: Academic Press.
A useful collection of essays, including the classic introductory statement drafted by
Harding's colleague, Michael Avery.

Hill, D. & Jesson, M. (eds.) 1971 *The Iron Age and its hill-forts*. Southampton:
Southampton University Archaeological Society.
The Wheeler Festschrift contains a number of studies still of considerable use, such
as Hawkes' overview of fortification styles, Feachem's review of 'unfinished forts' in
Britain, and Rivet's consideration of the mentions of individual sites in Caesar's text.

Hill, P.H. 1982 'Broxmouth hillfort excavations 1977-1978: an interim report', in (ed.)
Harding, D.W., *Later prehistoric settlement in south-east Scotland*, 141-88. Edinburgh:
Univ Edin Dept Archaeol Occas Pap 8.

Hogg, A. H. A. 1975 *A guide to the hill-forts of Britain*. London: Hart-Davis, MacGibbon; subsequently issued by Granada as a Paladin paperback.
A hundred-page introductory essay packed with concise thoughts and good writing, and an excellent bibliography coupled with an alphabetic gazetteer of sites worthy of a visit the length and breadth of the country.

Hogg, A.H.A. 1979 *British Hill-Forts: an index*. Oxford: Brit Archaeol Rep 62.

Jobey, G. 1978 'Burnswark Hill, Dumfriesshire', *Trans Dumfries Galloway Natural Hist Antiq Soc* 53, 57-104.
The classic statement by the excavator of Burnswark, but its relations to the Roman works around it are reassessed in Campbell, D. 2003 'The Roman siege of Burnswark', *Britannia* **34**, 19-33 and in RCAHMS (= Royal Commission on the Ancient and Historical Monuments of Scotland) 1997 *Eastern Dumfriesshire: an archaeological landscape*. Edinburgh: HMSO.

Lane, A. and Campbell, E. 2000 *Dunadd: an early Dalriadic capital*. Oxford: Oxbow.

Miles, D., Palmer, S., Lock, G., Gosden, C. and Cromarty, A. M. 2003 *Uffington White Horse and its Landscape. Investigations at White Horse Hill Uffington, 1989-95 and Tower Hill Ashbury, 1993*. Oxford: Oxford Archaeology Thames Valley Landscapes Monogr 18.

Musson, C.R. 1991 *The Breiddin hillfort*. London: Counc Brit Archaeol Res Rep 76.
Univallate enclosure with both LBA and IA phases.

Piggott, S. 1931 'Ladle Hill – an unfinished hillfort', *Antiquity* 5, 474-85.
The classic unfinished fort.

Ralston, I. 2004 *The hill-forts of Pictland since 'The Problem of the Picts'*. Rosemarkie Groam House Museum Papers.

Richmond, I.A. 1968 *Hod Hill Volume 2*. London: Trustees of the British Museum.

Rickett, R. 1992 'The other forts of Norfolk', *East Anglian Archaeologist* 54, 59-74.
Forts in a lowland landscape.

Wheeler, R.E.M. 1943 *Maiden Castle, Dorset*. London Research Reports of the Society of Antiquaries of London 12.
The classic report of the classic southern British hill-fort, written up with an ebullience not since matched. For newer excavation work, and a sanguine reappraisal of the site, two publications (both 1991) by Niall M. Sharples are essential: *Maiden*

Castle: excavations and field survey 1985-6 (London: English Heritage Archaeological Report **19**); and (more accessibly) *English Heritage Book of Maiden Castle* London: Batsford/English Heritage).

Wheeler, R.E.M. 1953 'An Early Iron Age Beach-Head at Lulworth, Dorset', *Antiquaries Journal* 33, 1-13.

Whimster, R. 1981 *Burial practices in Iron Age Britain*. Oxford: Brit Archaeol Rep 90. 2 vols.
Includes a review of burial evidence in and near the earthworks of hill-forts.

IRELAND

Raftery, B. 1994 *The enigma of the Irish Iron Age*. London: Thames and Hudson.
Overview, with pertinent discussions of hill-forts.

Stout, M. 1997 *The Irish ringfort*. Dublin: Four Courts Press (= Irish Settlement Studies 5).
An excellent introduction to these numerous sites, now known to be Early Historic in date.

Waterman, D.M. 1997 *Excavations at Navan Fort 1961-71*. Belfast: Stationery Office.

HILL-FORTS, WARFARE AND CLASSICAL SOURCES

Anon 2002 *Sur les traces de César: enquête archéologique sur les sites de la guerre des Gaules*. Glux-en-Glenne: Musée Bibracte Guide.

Avery, M. 1986 '"Stoning and firing" at hillfort entrances of southern Britain', *World Archaeology* 18, 216-230.

Brunaux, J.-L. 2004 *Guerre et religion en Gaule*. Paris: Errance.
Impressive anthropologically-informed perspective, introducing key evidence from the Ribemont sanctuary.

Brunaux, J.-L. and Lambot, B. 1987 *Guerre et armement chez les Gaulois*. Paris: Errance.

Brunaux, J. L., Fichtl, S. and Marchand, C. 1990 'Die Ausgrabungen am Haupttor des "Camp César" bei la Chaussée Tirancourt (Dept Somme, Frankreich)', *Saalburg Jahrbuch* 45, 5-22.
A key site used by auxiliaries, and argued to be part of an early *limes*.

Carman, J. and Harding, A. (eds.) 1999 *Ancient warfare*. Stroud: Alan Sutton.
Useful review, from archaeological perspective, includes K. Randsborg on the Iron Age.

Deyber, A. 1987 'La guérilla gauloise pendant la Guerre des Gaules', *Études celtiques* 24, 145-83.
Archaeologist and former soldier analyses the defensive strategies employed.

Fichtl, S. 1998 'La présence militaire romaine sur les oppida dans la Gaule du Nord et de l'Est', in (ed.) Müller-Karpe, A. *Studien zur Archäologie der Kelten, Römer und Germanen in Mittel- und Westeuropa. Alfred Haffner gewidmet*, 153-68. Rahden: Marie Leidorf (= Internationale Archäologie Studia honoraria, 4).

Gresham, C.A. 1939 'Spettisbury Rings, Dorset', *Archaeological Journal* 96, 114-131.

Harding, D.W. 1977 *Celts in conflict*. Edinburgh: Univ Edinburgh Dept Archaeology Occas Pap 3.

Hencken, T.C. 1938 'The excavation of an Iron Age camp on Bredon Hill, Gloucestershire', *Archaeological Journal* 95, 1-111.

Leblanc, S.A. with Register, K.E. 2004 *Constant battles; why we fight*. New York: St Martin's Press.
A re-assessment of the role and significance of warfare in earlier societies, including complex ones, which explicitly considers hill-forts in this perspective. Part of a fresh consideration of warfare, stemming from e.g. Keeley, L. H. 1996 *War before civilization*. Oxford: Oxford University Press.

Kenyon, K. 1953 'Excavations at Sutton Walls, Herefordshire 1948-51', *Archaeological Journal* 110, 1-87.

Rivet, A.L.F. 1971 'Hill-forts in action', in (eds.) Hill & Jesson, 189-201.

Wiseman, A. & Wiseman, P. (translators) 1980 *Julius Caesar: the battle for Gaul*. London: Chatto & Windus.
This good modern translation of a key text is helpfully and extensively illustrated.

Bianchini, C. (ed.) 1994 *Vercingétorix et Alésia*. Paris: Editions de la Réunion des Musées nationaux.
The end of the Gallic War in wider context.

Alésia (Alise-Sainte-Reine, Côte d'Or)
The definitive publication of the recent work at the site is Reddé, M. & von

Schnurbein, S. 2001 *Alésia: fouilles et recherches franco-allemandes sur les travaux militaires romaines autour de Mont-Auxois*. Paris: Mémoires de l'Académie des Inscriptions et Belles-Lettres 22. 3 vols. A briefer and more accessible interim statement is in *Bericht der Römisch-Germanischen Kommission* 76, 1995.

Puy d'Issolu, Lot.
A number of interim accounts of the current project are available: that used most here by J.-P. Girault is in Musée Saint-Raymond (Toulouse) 2004 *Gaulois des pays de Garonne*. Toulouse: Musée Saint-Raymond.

SIGNS AND SYMBOLS

Olivier Buchsenschutz and I have considered aspects of this topic in a paper entitled 'Dépôts et fortifications' forthcoming in the proceedings of the Association française pour l'Etude de l'Age du Fer conference held in Bienne, Switzerland (2005). Full references are cited there. References here are to sites not otherwise mentioned in this listing.

Applebaum E.S. 1949 'Excavations at Wilbury Hill, an Iron-Age Hill-Fort near Letchworth, Hertfordshire 1933', *Archaeological Journal* 106, 12-45.

Bedwin, O. 1979 'Excavations at Harting Beacon, West Sussex, second season 1977', *Sussex Archaeological Collections* 117, 22-33.

Bedwin, O. 1983 'Miss P. A. M. Keef's excavations at Harting Beacon and nearby sites 1948-52', *Sussex Archaeological Collections* 121, 199-202.

Chabot, L. 2004 *L'oppidum de La Cloche, Les Pennes-Mirabeau, Bouches-du-Rhône*, Montagnac: Monique Mergoil.

Collins, A.E.P. 1953 'Excavations on Blewburton Hill, 1948 and 1949', *Berkshire Archaeological Journal* 53, 21-64.

Farley, M. 1986 'Aylesbury', *Current Archaeology* 101, 187-189.

Fowler, P.J. 1960 'Excavations at Madmarston Camp, Swalcliffe 1957-8', *Oxoniensia*, 25, 3-48.

Fox, C.F. 1940 'The distribution of currency bars', *Antiquity* 14, 427-433.

Hingley, R. 1990 'Iron Age "currency bars": the archaeological and social context', *Archaeological Journal* 147, 91-117.

Malim, T. 1992 *Stonea Camp, Wimbleton: an Iron Age fort in the Fens*. Cambridge: Cambridgeshire Archaeology Report 71.

McArthur, C. 1990 'Excavations at Nadbury Camp, Warwickshire', *Transactions Birmingham and Warwickshire Archaeological Society* 95, 1987-8 (1990), 1-16.

Owen, O.A. 1992 'Eildon Hill North', in (eds.) Rideout, J.S., Owen, O.A. and Halpin, E. *Hillforts of southern Scotland,* 21-71. Edinburgh: Archaeological Operations and Conservation Monograph 1.

Trow, S.D. 1988 'Excavations at Ditches hillfort, North Cerney, Gloucestershire, 1982-3', Trans Bristol Gloucestershire Archaeol Soc, 106, 19-85.

Wheeler, R.E.M. 1954 *Stanwick*. London: Res Rep Soc Antiq Lond 17.

VITRIFIED AND CALCINED HILL-FORTS

These have generated a considerable literature, although many key items have appeared in specialist periodicals. My 1986 paper summarises much of the English-language discussion up to that point as well as reporting experimental results. The contentious thermoluminescence dates from Scotland were originally published in Tables 2 and 3 of Sanderson *et al.* 1988. Kresten *et al.* 2003 have recently put forward an explanation of the rather problematically wide date range for vitrified forts that has arisen from thermoluminescence dating. Kresten *et al.* 1993 also mount the case for constructive vitrification on the basis of the Broborg evidence considered in Chapter 7 here; the Cité d'Affrique evidence is presented by Lagadec *et al.* 1993 and Ploquin *et al.* 1993.

Alexander, D. 2002 'An oblong fort at Finavon, Angus: an example on the over-reliance on the appliance of science', in (eds.) Ballin Smith, B. and Banks, I. *In the shadow of the brochs,* 45-54. Stroud: Tempus.

Burgess, C., Gibson, C. and Correia, V. 1999 'Hillforts, oppida and vitrification in the Évora area, central Portugal', *Northern Archaeology* 17/18, 1999, 129-47.
Vitrified material from Iberia.

Childe, V.G. & Thorneycroft, W. 1937 'The experimental production of the phenomena distinctive of vitrified forts', *Proc Soc Antiq Scot* **72**, 44-55.
The West Plean Colliery and Rahoy experiments, with the first photographs of the burning of experimental walls.

Engström, J. 1984 *Torsburgen*. = Uppsala: *Archaeological Studies Uppsala University Institute of North European Archaeology* **6**.

This examination of the largest hill-fort (112ha) in Scandinavia was accompanied by experiments to replicate the calcination recovered from its wall. Well-illustrated and with an English summary.

Gentles, D. 1993 'Vitrified forts', *Current Archaeology* **133**, 18-20.
Discusses archaeomagnetic dates for Scottish sites, which point generally to vitrification of the examined examples in the late first millennium BC.

Kresten, P., Goedicke, C. & Manzano, A. 2003 'TL-dating of vitrified material', *Geochronometria* **22**, 9-14.

Kresten, P., Kero, L. & Chyssler, J. 1993 'Geology of the vitrified hill-fort Broborg in Uppland, Sweden', *Geologiska Föreningens I Stockholm Förhandlingar* **115**, 13-24.

Lagadec, J.-P., Duval, P., Eveillard, J., Leroy, M. & Ploquin, A. 1993 'La Cité d'Affrique, habitat fortifié du premier Age du Fer: l'apport des nouvelles fouilles', *Actes XI Colloque Assoc Française Etude Ages du Fer* (Sarreguimines 1987) = *Archaeologia Mosellana* **2**, 149-173.
The rationale behind deliberate *calcination* is explained in Lagadec, J.-P. *1997 Les habitats fortifies celtiques autour de Nancy*. Nancy: Itinéraires du Patrimoine **146**.

MacKie, E.W. 1976 'The vitrified forts of Scotland', in (cd.) Harding, 205-35.
A generation old, but still the best overview of the Scottish evidence. Shorter, harder to find, but packed with good sense, too, on things Scottish is Nisbet, H. 1982 'Vitrification phenomena in hillforts', *Readings in Glass History* **15/16**, 21-30.

McHardy, A. 1906 'On vitrified forts, with results of experiments as to the probable manner in which their vitrification may have been produced', *Proc Soc Antiq Scot* **40**, 1905-06, 136-50.
Key military observations against deliberate construction, and a major series of early experiments.

de la Noë, G.-O. 1893 *Les enceintes vitrifiés et les enceintes calcinées.* Paris: reprinted from *Bulletin geographique, historique et descriptive* 1892.
Summarises the Continental evidence as it had accumulated by the late nineteenth century and outlines contemporary debates.

Ploquin, A., Duval, P., Eveillard, J., Lagadec, J.-P. & Leroy, M. 1993 'Les noyaux calcinés du rempart hallstattien de la Cité d'Affrique (Messein, 54): données archéométriques et interprétation', *Actes XI Colloque Assoc Française Etude Ages du Fer* (Sarreguimines 1987) = *Archaeologia Mosellana* **2**, 175-199.

Ralston, I. 1986 'The Yorkshire Television vitrified wall experiment at East Tullos, City of Aberdeen District', *Proc Soc Antiq Scot* **116**, 17 -40.

Sanderson, D.C.W., Placido, F. and Tate, J. O. 1988 'Scottish vitrified forts: TL results from six study sites', *Nuclear Tracks and Radiation Measurements* **14**, 307-316.
TL dates suggest a wide range of dates for the destruction of Scottish vitrified forts.

Youngblood, E., Fredriksson, B. J., Kraut, F. & Fredriksson, K. 1978 'Celtic vitrified forts: implications of a chemical-petrological study of glasses and source rocks', *Journal of Archaeological Science* 5, 99-121; also see Fredriksson, K. *et al.* 1983 'The Celtic vitrified forts' in (eds.) Kempe, D.R.C. & Harvey, A.P. *The petrology of archaeological artefacts*, 154-70. Oxford: Clarendon.
The outcome of a range of analytical procedures applied to a selection of Scottish and Continental vitrified forts is the suggestion that the build of the walls may have been a special variant of a timber-laced wall that could sustain either deliberate or accidental firing.

CONCLUDING REMARKS

The quotations are from W.H. Auden's *Collected Poems* edited by Edward Mendelson and published by Faber and Faber in 1976; and Ludovic Kennedy's *In bed with an elephant,* Bantam Press, 1995. I have changed the scale of his theme park: Scotland has become Europe.

TWENTY SITES

Supplementary references only.

Álvarez-Sanchís, J.R. 1999 *Los Vettones*. Madrid: Real Academia de la Historia (= Bibliotheca Archaeologica Hispana 1).

Dunwell, A.J. and Strachan, R. forthcoming *Excavations at the Brown and White Caterthuns, Angus 1995-1997*. Perth: Tayside and Fife Archaeol Monogr Ser.

Frodsham, P. and Hedley, I. 2005 *People of the Breamish Valley*. Hexham: Northumberland National Park Authority/Discover our hillfort heritage.

Haselgrove, C.C., Lowther, P.C. and Turnbull, P. 1990 'Stanwick, North Yorkshire part 3: excavation on earthwork sites 1981-86', *Archaeol Journ* 147, 37-90.

Lynn, C. J. 2003 *Navan fort: archaeology and myth*. Dublin: Wordwell.

Kaenel, G. and Curdy, P. 1988 *L'oppidum du mont Vully*. Vully: Guides archéologiques de la Suisse 22.
Guide book to complement Kaenel *et al.* 2004.

McOmish, D. 1999 'Wether Hill and Cheviot hillforts', *Northern Archaeology* 17/18, 113-21 (= Papers presented to Keith Blood).

Mercer, R. J. 1991 'The survey of a hilltop enclosure on Ben Griam Beg, ...Highland Region', in (eds.) Hanson, W.S. & Salter, E.A. *Scottish archaeology: new perceptions*, 140-152. Aberdeen: Aberdeen University Press.

Papeleux, J. 1987 'Le rempart du Cheslé à Bérismenil, commune de La Roche', *Archaeologia Belgica* 3, 83-95.

RCAHMS (= Royal Commission on the Ancient and Historical Monuments of Scotland) 1971 *Argyll 1: Kintyre*. Edinburgh: HMSO.

Waterman, D.W. and Lynn, C.J. 1997 *Excavations at Navan Fort 1961-71*. Belfast: Northern Ireland Archaeol Monogr 3.

Welfare, H., Topping, P., Blood, K. and Ramm, H. 1990 'Stanwick, North Yorkshire part 2: a summary description of the earthworks', *Archaeol Journ* 147, 16-36.

INDEX

Bold = colour plate; ***bold italics*** = illustration
British Isles including Eire by counties; abroad by countries